WARD-PERKINS, John Bryan. Pompeii A.D. 79, by John Bryan Ward-Perkins and Amanda Claridge. Knopf (dist. by Random House), 1978 (c1976). 215p ill map 78-13870. 25.00 ISBN 0-394-50491-7. C.I.P.

Written as an accompaniment to the international exhibition of Pompeian art organized by the British Museum and circulated in America, the book comprises a first part presenting, in an attractively written manner, an introduction to the cultural and artistic history of Pompeii, and the catalog of the exhibition in the second part. The authors are authorities on Roman architecture and the Roman figural arts respectively. This well-produced and abundantly illustrated volume supersedes all previous general books on Pompeii in English. Two criticisms: although numerous, the illustrations are not all well reproduced; and there is no discussion and documentation of the effect of Pompeian art on 18th- and 19th-century Western art following the excavations. The text is accompanied by an ample bibliography with a special section on recent books in English.

The text is by two scholars who made the original selections for the exhibition, John Ward-Perkins, Director Emeritus of the British School at Rome, who is currently involved in archaeological research in the Mediterranean world, and Amanda Claridge, a graduate of the Institute of Archaeology, London University, who is now Assistant Professor of Classical Archaeology at Princeton. Additional selections were made by the Museum of Fine Arts, Boston. Their words and the 450 pictures provide an unprecedented view of the day that time stopped for Pompeii, and of the Roman world of 1900 years ago.

POMPEII A.D. 79

Treasures from the
National Archaeological Museum, Naples,
and
the Pompeii Antiquarium

Essay and catalogue by
John Ward-Perkins and Amanda Claridge
with additions by the
Department of Classical Art,
Museum of Fine Arts, Boston

Alfred A. Knopf, New York

in association with the
Museum of Fine Arts, Boston
1978

Treasures from the
National Archaeological Museum, Naples,

Essay and catalogue by
John Ward-Perkins and Amanda Claridge
with additions by the
Department of Classical Art,
Museum of Fine Arts, Boston

Alfred A. Knopf, New York

in association with the
Museum of Fine Arts, Boston
1978

POMPEII A·D 79

The original catalogue and
exhibition were made possible by grants
from The National Endowment for the
Humanities and Xerox Corporation

THIS IS A BORZOI BOOK
PUBLISHED BY ALFRED A. KNOPF, INC.

Copyright © 1978
by Museum of Fine Arts,
Boston, Massachusetts

Text copyright © 1976
by John Ward-Perkins and
Amanda Claridge

Published in the United States
by Alfred A. Knopf, Inc., New York, and
simultaneously in Canada by Random House
of Canada Limited, Toronto.
Distributed by Random House, Inc., New York.

First Trade Edition

Library of Congress Cataloging in Publication Data

Ward-Perkins, John Bryan [date]
    Pompeii A.D. 79.
    1. Pompeii–Exhibitions. 2. Italy–Antiquities–
Exhibitions. I. Claridge, Amanda, joint author.
II. Title.
DG70.P7W34   937'.7   78-13870
ISBN 0-394-50491-7

Manufactured in the United States of America

Typeset by Wrightson Typographers,
Newton, Massachusetts, and
Dumar Typesetting, Dayton, Ohio

Printed by Case-Hoyt, Rochester, New York

Layout and typography by Carl Zahn

Jacket and binding designed by the publisher

Title page:

1

Pair of villa landscapes
Width 53 cm, height 22 cm
From Pompeii

Two separate views of villa façades probably
from the lateral panels of a Third Style scheme
(see illustration, p. 27), now mounted as a pair.
The left-hand view shows a straight porticoed
façade upraised on a platform with a tall columnar central porch; in front of the portico is a garden with a large axial enclosure and at either end,
rising from a lower level, is a double portico, of
two orders, facing outward. Above and beyond
the right-hand portico is the façade of a temple-
like building facing inward; there may have been
other buildings or trees in the damaged upper
left-hand part. The right-hand view shows a central gabled porch at the junction of two gable-
ended, inward-facing porticoes, enclosing on
three sides a trapezoidal space concentric to
which is an enclosure with posts at the angles.
Above and behind rise a number of other buildings including a circular *tempietto (tholos)* and
another colonnade. The perspective of these
scenes is syntactic, and some of the detail (e.g.,
the half-gables of the flanking porticoes on the
left-hand panel) is without parallel in surviving
contemporary architecture, but it is generally
accepted that such façades were a feature of the
wealthy *villae marittimae*.

*All objects shown in color plates are from the
National Archaeological Museum, Naples*

Photograph Credits:

Photographs for nos. 30, 31, 34–36, 42, 43, 45,
46, 48, 49, 51, 53, 54, 73, 93, 95, 96, 112a,b,
132, 134, 142, 157, 158, 160, 163, 169, 172,
181, 203, 205, 212, 228, 237, 258, 259, 263,
269, 271–274, 287a, 298, 324, 326 were supplied by Giuseppe Musco on behalf of the Soprintendenza Archeologica delle Province di Napoli
e Caserta.

Photographs of the objects owned by the Metropolitan Museum of Art and the Museum of Fine
Arts, Boston, were supplied by the museum
concerned.

All other photographs by Eric de Maré, maps
and diagrams by Michael Robinson except those
listed below.

Pages 33 (both), 39 (below), Nos. 185, 243,
260–262, 264, 265, 267, 268, Amanda Claridge

Pages 96 (center row), 100 (top left, bottom
right), 103 (bottom), Nos. 115, 116, Deutsches
Archäologisches Institut, Rome

Map of Pompeii pages 46 and 47, Hans Eschebac

Pages 36, 39 (top), 82 (top), 96 (bottom row),
100 (far right, top, and left center), No. 20, Foto
Alinari, Rome

Plan for No. 90, Sheila Gibson

Pages 96 (center row), 100 (middle of top row),
Nos. 27, 108, 193, 236, 277, 279, 280, 282–287,
327, Edgar Hyman and Peter Chorley

No. 38 (profile), Alan Irvine

Sources of plans for page 53, Dr. Ann Laidlaw

Nos. 11, 12, Museo della Civiltà Romana

Pages 60, 63, 82, 90, 105–108, Nos. 3–5,
7–10, 29, 33, 39, 55, 58, 68, 80–84, 86, 89, 92,
106, 109, 114, 129, 137, 147, 152, 154, 162,
177, 178, 180, 190–192, 196, 197, 199, 200,
206, 219, 241, 244–247, 253, 276, 293–295,
311, 312, 325, Museo Nazionale Archeologico,
Naples

Page 51, Pubbli Aerfoto, Milan

Cover, title page, pages 6, 7, 14, 15, 17, 18, 19,
20, 21, 22, 23, 25, 26 (left), 27, 65, 66, 67, 68,
69, 70, 71, 72–73, 74, 75, 76, 77, 80, Strüwing
Reklamefoto, Birkerod, Denmark

Reconstruction drawing for No. 87, Florence
Wolsky

ACKNOWLEDGMENTS

The introductory essays and the majority of the entries in this catalogue were reprinted from the British edition of *Pompeii* A.D. 79. The authors, John Ward-Perkins and Amanda Claridge, kindly consented to the "conversion" in their text from British to American usage in spelling and punctuation. References to objects shown in London but not in this exhibition have been omitted. The Soprintendenza Archeologica delle Province di Napoli e Caserta has granted the loan of several objects almost identical to the pieces withdrawn, and for these substitutions the entries of Mr. Ward-Perkins and Miss Claridge have been modified as necessary. We thank Peter Saabor, of Carlton Cleve Limited, London, for facilitating contact between authors and editors and for arranging the loans of the exhibition material belonging to Imperial Tobacco Limited.

Since the London exhibition, the Soprintendenza Archeologica has generously granted a number of important new loans for the showings of "Pompeii A.D. 79" in Denmark and the United States. Entries for new objects, Nos. 30, 31, 33–36, 42, 43, 45, 46, 48, 49, 51, 53–55, 58, 73, 87, 89, 95, 96, 112a,b, 117–128, 132, 134, 142, 157, 158, 169, 172, 181, 203, 206, 212, 228, 237, 253, 258, 259, 263, 271–274, 287a, 293–295, 298, 311, 312, 324–326, were written by members of the Department of Classical Art, Ariel Herrmann, John Herrmann, Cornelius Vermeule, and Florence Wolsky. Mary Comstock had a vital role as organizer of our efforts and as editor and researcher. In preparing the entries, we were greatly aided by Hans Eric Wallin of the Louisiana Museum, Humlebaek, Denmark, who placed at our disposal the photographs and descriptions provided him by the Soprintendenza Archeologica. We are grateful to Mr. Wallin and to Margaret MacLeod of the WGBH Educational Foundation, Boston, for arranging for several new color photographs. We also wish to thank Dr. Maria Giuseppina Cerulli-Irelli, Director of Excavations, Pompeii, Dr. Mariarosaria Borriello d'Ambrosio, and Giuseppe Tucci of the Naples Museum for advice and for research on provenances. Catherine Springer kindly provided information for the cataloguing of the frescoes from the Metropolitan Museum of Art.

A special word of appreciation should go to the conservators and handlers responsible for the condition and safety of the objects: the laboratory of the Soprintendenza Archeologica, directed by Dr. Ciro Piccioli, and Dr. Ermanno de Marinis, responsible for packing and for shipping the objects to the United States; and the Research Laboratory of the Museum of Fine Arts, Boston, which not only supervised the handling of the American material but also undertook conservation of the Boston frescoes to prepare them for display. Thanks are also due to the designers of the exhibition, Tom Wong and Judith Downes, whose mountings will travel to the participating museums. The advice and skills of these technicians were necessary preconditions for the new loans as well as for the continuance of the exhibition.

Finally, we acknowledge with gratitude the collaboration of the many museum colleagues who gave their time and talents to this project; we are especially indebted to Linda Thomas, registrar, Lisa Simon, grants coordinator, and the staff of the Design Department.

JOHN HERRMANN
Exhibition Coordinator
Department of Classical Art
Museum of Fine Arts, Boston

April, 1978

Authors' note

We could not have written this catalogue had it not been for the unstinted help we have received from many friends, among them Simon Bendall, Joanna Bird, John Callaghan, Maria Giuseppina Cerulli-Irelli, Anna Fazzari, Martin Frederiksen, Antonio Giuliano, Wilhelmina Jashemski, Anne Laidlaw, Demetrios Michaelides, Massimo Pallottino, Toby Parker, Enrica Pozzi Paolini, Dale Trendall, Luciana Valentini, Angela Wardle, Helen Whitehouse, and Fausto Zevi. But there have been many others as well, too numerous to name individually. To all of them we offer our sincere thanks.

We would also like to take this opportunity of expressing our deep sense of personal gratitude to our Italian friends, both in Naples and in Rome, who gave us so much of their time and trouble in resolving the thousand and one difficulties, great and small, that inevitably arise in the preparation of an enterprise of this sort and size. But for their patience, understanding, and unfailing kindness, it would have been a very different story. We are very conscious of our debt.

This is not the first time, and it will surely not be the last, that the authors of an exhibition catalogue have had to do their work far more hurriedly than they would have wished, often without any possibility of reference back to the objects themselves to resolve doubtful points. We have aimed at accuracy, but we are all too aware that we have not always achieved it.

JOHN WARD-PERKINS
AMANDA CLARIDGE

November, 1976

2
Painting of a villa beside the sea
Diameter 25 cm
From Stabiae

Roundel portraying the two-storied columnar
façade of a *villa marittima*. The center of the
façade curves inward, toward a tower-like circular feature. In front is a platform with two projecting jetties, human figures, and statues.

Painting of a sanctuary beside the sea
Width 62 cm, height 52 cm
From Pompeii

This fragment portrays a sanctuary, set on a
rocky island or promontory, and in the foreground two boats. The details of the sanctuary
are conventional: a central, circular shrine, or
tholos, flanked by porticoes and a re-entrant
façade wall; in front of this, facing onto the
water, is an open platform, on which are several
groups of figures, including a woman and a dog.

7

PREFACE

The catastrophic events of August 24, A.D. 79, that submerged Herculaneum and Pompeii in an avalanche of ashes, pumice, and volcanic mud brought life in these prosperous Roman towns to a sudden and total stop. Through the ages the volcanic debris that so tragically cut short the life of the inhabitants acted as a protective layer shielding the towns with all that was inside from the ravages of time. Unearthed by archaeologists in the course of excavations that extend over more than two centuries, the objects are preserved very much as they were 1,900 years ago.

As we walk along the streets and enter the villas of the rich and the taverns of the poor, it is as if the occupants had gone a moment ago to one of the many shops, to the theater, or to one of the temples in which they paid homage to their many different gods. The colorful story of their life unfolds before our eyes as we see the paintings that adorned the walls of their houses, the inexhaustible variety of paraphernalia that surrounded them, the utensils they used, and the games they played until the moment of the catastrophe. The exhibition "Pompeii A.D. 79" consists of many rare and beautiful works of art that can be viewed and admired for their own intrinsic artistic merit. But above and beyond that the exhibited pieces together evoke the spirit of the people of Pompeii and make us understand how they lived, what their aspirations were, and what they believed in.

Now that "Pompeii A.D. 79," after its unprecedented success in the capitals of Europe, begins its triumphal tour of the United States, I consider it a privilege to acknowledge our deep indebtedness to all of those who have made this unique cultural manifestation possible.

First and foremost we wish to express our gratitude to the government of the Republic of Italy, the Ministry of Foreign Affairs, and the Ministry of Cultural Heritage for graciously permitting this exhibition of great cultural treasures to travel to the United States. We especially thank His Excellency Dr. Vittorio Cordero de Montezemolo, formerly Director General for Cultural, Scientific, and Technological Cooperation, Ministry of Foreign Affairs; his successor in that office, His Excellency Sergio Romano; and His Excellency Raniero Paolucci di Calboli, Vice-Director, Directorate General for Cultural, Scientific,

and Technological Cooperation, Ministry of Foreign Affairs, for their help and advice during the negotiations; we also thank Dr. Guglielmo Triches, Director General for Antiquities and Fine Arts, Ministry of Cultural Heritage, for his generous help in the decisions on sites and schedules.

Many demanding tasks connected with preparing the exhibition were patiently and efficiently discharged by the staffs of the Naples Museum and the Pompeii Antiquarium, and we gratefully acknowledge the cooperation of Professor Fausto Zevi, Superintendent of Antiquities, Naples and Caserta; Dr. Enrica Pozzi-Paolini, Director of the National Archaeological Museum, Naples; and Dr. Maria Giuseppina Cerulli-Irelli, Director of Excavations, Pompeii. Dr. Marco Miele, Director of the Italian Cultural Institute, New York, acted as an invaluable intermediary with the Italian authorities. His constant interest and encouragement have been highly appreciated. We also wish to express our thanks to Alitalia for the special care with which they handled the shipments from Naples to Boston.

On the United States side we would like to thank first of all The Honorable John Volpe, formerly United States Ambassador to Italy, whose enthusiastic response when first approached with our proposal created the first impetus toward the realization of this project. His successor, The Honorable Richard N. Gardner, assisted by Richard T. Arndt, Cultural Affairs Officer, and Mrs. Susan Lowe Modi, Assistant Cultural Attaché, provided the indispensable liaison with the Italian authorities. They were most helpful and generous with their experienced advice.

The exhibition is made possible by grants from the National Endowment for the Humanities and Xerox Corporation; it is supported by a Federal Indemnity from the Federal Council on the Arts and Humanities. The liaison with our corporate sponsor was provided by Ruder & Finn.

A project of this scope and importance involves many people and leaves hardly any department of a museum unaffected. It was logical, however, that the primary responsibility for "Pompeii A.D. 79" should rest with the Department of Classical Art, which has responded with an enthusiasm that permeated the entire organization. John Herrmann, assistant curator of classical art, was involved in the project from its

very inception and followed it through to completion. The other members of the Department of Classical Art, Kristin Anderson, Miriam Braverman, Mary Comstock, Ariel Herrmann, Emily Vermeule, Cornelius Vermeule, and Florence Wolsky, each made their own contribution to the exhibition and its catalogue. The catalogue was edited by Margaret Jupe and Judy Spear.

To name all of those in the four participating museums who have contributed to this unique cultural manifestation is impossible. May all enjoy the exhibition with a sense of gratitude and pride.

JAN FONTEIN, *Director*
Museum of Fine Arts, Boston

April, 1978

CONTENTS

The Forum at Pompeii,
Vesuvius in background

House of Neptune and Amphitrite
at Herculaneum

INTRODUCTION

On the morning of the twenty-fourth of August, A.D. 79, the long-dormant volcano of Vesuvius blew up, and by the evening of that day the two flourishing towns of Pompeii and Herculaneum and the nearby coastal resort of Stabiae were dead, already half-buried by the rain of ash, pumice, and volcanic mud beneath which they were to lie entombed for more than sixteen centuries. Before long their very locations were lost. It was not until 1709 that well-diggers hit upon the theater of Herculaneum, and it was another thirty years before, in 1738, the Bourbons put in hand the program of organized treasure hunting (*zufälliges raüberisches Nachwühlen*, "haphazard, predatory grubbing," is how Goethe described it) that furnished the first nucleus of the royal collections that were eventually to come to rest in the National Museum of Naples. Then in 1748 attention was diverted to another Vesuvian site, where peasants had recently made promising finds and where digging was easier. This proved to be the lost Pompeii. Here too exploration was at first haphazard and destructive, and it was really only with the appointment of Giuseppe Fiorelli (1860-1875) that systematic excavation may be said to have started. It was he who hit upon the idea of making casts of the victims of the eruption, and who introduced the system of nomenclature, still in use today, whereby any building in the town can be located in terms of its region, its city block, and the serial numbers of its street entrances. It was again he and his successor, Michele Ruggiero, who first adopted the modern principle of restoring buildings and of conserving finds in place, instead of ripping out the more spectacular and leaving the rest to disintegrate.

The first and overwhelming impression these sites leave on the modern visitor today is the immediacy of this ancient tragedy. As one gazes on the table set for breakfast, on the posters for the next municipal elections, on the pathetic huddle of bodies clustered in a cellar, the intervening centuries fall away. It is just as if yesterday some sudden and dreadful natural catastrophe had overwhelmed all the familiar things of one's hometown, preserving every intimate detail of the houses and the supermarket for the archaeologists of future millennia. This sense of yesterday, this powerfully enduring presence of all the little everyday things that constitute the externals of a way of life, this is something unique to Pompeii and Herculaneum.

But it is not the tragedy of 24 August A.D. 79 as such that is the subject of this exhibition. We are concerned with one particular aspect of the event, namely to present, so far as is possible in terms of objects that can be transported, a cross-section of the art and craftsmanship of the buried cities, as it stood at the moment when the clock of history was so dramatically stopped: that of Pompeii in the first instance, because the setting is there more complete and the range of available material wider, but supplemented where necessary from Herculaneum, from Stabiae, and from material now in the National Museum of Naples of which the precise Vesuvian source is no longer known.

Art and craftsmanship: one uses the double term advisedly because the modern distinction between artist and craftsman would have had very little meaning, at any rate with reference to contemporary artists. Throughout most of classical antiquity, and very much so in Roman times, the artist was by definition a craftsman, working to supply the specific needs of a patron or, more generally, the demands of public taste. This fact is bound to influence any modern attempt to present his work. Certain categories and certain individual products of ancient art may be timeless, transcending all accidents of time and place. It does not really matter that a fifth-century Athenian viewed the Parthenon frieze under very different conditions from ourselves, and with very different eyes: the quality still shines through. Even so, there can be very few products of ancient art that do not gain an added dimension from being viewed within their historical and social context. This is emphatically true when the objects in question are the products of a society as complex and many-sided as that of Rome, and doubly true when they represent not some single, homogeneous masterpiece, nor the accumulated artistic treasure of some single great patron, but a selection of the objects that just happened to be assembled on the walls and in the streets of a town of provincial Italy on that fateful August day when, without warning, history stood still.

One has therefore to present the art of Pompeii in its context. In the case of the paintings this is quite literally true, physically as well as metaphorically. The Romans did possess panel paintings, as we do, but very few of these have survived, and the paintings that now adorn the walls of museums and galleries were all once parts of much larger decorative complexes, detached from which they have much the same artistic significance as a panel cut from a Tiepolo ceiling. We can still enjoy many of their qualities, but viewed in isolation they have certainly lost something of their original artistic intention. One has to remember too that the artists who painted them, most of them simple craftsmen, both slaves and freedmen, were operating within a context of ideas very different from our own. Many of the presuppositions of the society for which Tiepolo and his assistants worked are still common currency, making it relatively easy for us to enter into the spirit of their work. Roman society is a very different matter. It is true that certain aspects of the daily life of Pompeii do strike a startling note of modernity. Water supply and sanitation; paving and street drainage, and the organization of such public services as markets and the disposal of refuse; the mechanisms of commerce and banking; the life of the tavern and bar; the addiction to spectator sport; all of these are still quite near enough to our own recent past (and indeed in some cases to our present) to strike an immediate response of comfortable recognition. But the moment one scratches a little deeper, one is aware also of a number of profound, underlying differences. The position of the family within the social structure, religious beliefs and ethics, the status of the professions, the accepted functions and duties of patronage, these are some only of the aspects of Pompeian life without some awareness of which it is very hard to arrive at any true evaluation of the material remains. The art of Pompeii was an integral part of this wider culture.

An exhibition can and should concentrate on allowing the objects displayed to speak for themselves. We hope that by our selection and our presentation we may have conveyed something also of the wider message that, unbeknown to itself, Roman Pompeii was busy compiling for us to read.

CAMPANIA

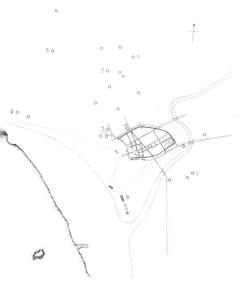

Sketch map to show the possible position of the port, the mouth, and ancient course of the river Sarno in relation to Pompeii. Country villas in the neighborhood are indicated by an open circle.

1. *Villa Rustica, Boscoreale*
2. *Villa of P. Fannius Synistor, Boscoreale*
3. *Villa of Agrippa Postumus, Boscotrecase*
4. *Oplontis*
5. *Villa of the Mysteries*
6. *Villa of Diomedes*
7. *Temple of Dionysus, S. Abbondio*
8. *Large storerooms, shops, and other buildings belonging to the port*

Today, a century after the unification of modern Italy, it is not always easy to recall that what was achieved in 1870 was not the restoration of a natural, self-evident state of affairs that had been briefly disrupted by external forces; it was the re-creation of a national entity that had been laboriously built up by classical Rome, only to disintegrate into its component parts as soon as the authority of the Western Roman Empire collapsed. One of the geographical units that make up Italy is Campania, the region of which Naples is today the capital. Long before it was a part of Roman Italy Pompeii had been a city of Campania, and for two of the three thousand-odd years since central Italy first emerges into history Campania has been independent of, and frequently in conflict with, Rome. Somewhere between Rome and Naples the South begins. This is still one of the salient facts of Italian political and economic life and it is a truth rooted in history.

The heart of Campania has always been the Bay of Naples, together with the fertile coastal plain that is bounded on the north by the river Volturno and on the east and south by the western slopes of the Apennines and the mountains of the Sorrento peninsula. Both geographically and historically it constitutes a remarkably well-defined unit. Except for the mountains to the south and east, this is all very fertile country of recent volcanic origin, and it first took historical shape when in the eighth century B.C. the Greeks, finding themselves debarred from further progress up the western coast by the Etruscans, and later by the Romans, established here a number of thriving settlements. During the course of the fifth century B.C. these Greek colonies and trading stations, together with the Etruscan outpost of Capua, lost their independence, passing under the control of Italic tribesmen who had moved down from the mountains of the interior. The latter were quick to learn the lessons of civilization and the union was a fruitful one, resulting in a culture that in varying proportions was both Greek and Italic. Campania never lost its Greek cultural roots or its Greek commercial contacts and aptitudes; but at the same time the Italic component remained strong enough to enable this mixed society to adapt without too much difficulty to the consequences of the inexorable southward advance of Rome. Whereas over much of southern Italy the Roman conquest was a sorry story of pillage, disruption, and catastrophic economic decline, Campania was the exception. Power and authority had moved to Rome, but in terms of commerce, culture, and the arts Campania enjoyed a prosperity fully equal to, and in certain respects in advance of, that of Rome itself.

The history of Pompeii, summarized in the following section, is in most respects that of Campania in miniature, but we may single out two aspects of the broader scene that were especially important for the cultural and artistic life of the Campanian cities. One was the fact that until the emperor Claudius created his new, artificial harbor at the mouth of the Tiber, the chief seagoing port of Rome was Puteoli, the modern Pozzuoli. With the establishment of Rome as a world power in the second century B.C. came, inevitably, great material prosperity, one facet of which was the settlement at Puteoli of a large and prosperous commercial community, derived very largely from the Hellenistic East. It is symptomatic that as early as 105 B.C. Puteoli should already have had a temple of the Egyptian divinities Isis and Serapis, and there are many traces of other oriental cults. Puteoli was where St. Paul landed on his journey to Rome.

13

Facing page:
217
Wall painting: sacro-idyllic landscape with shepherd and goats (detail)
Height 50 cm, width 49 cm
From Pompeii, exact location unknown

Landscape from the center of a wall panel, probably of the Fourth Style. It portrays an idealized rustic shrine, set within a rocky landscape with trees. In the foreground a man is pushing a goat toward the shrine, perhaps for sacrifice.

153
Wall painting: the Three Graces
Width 53 cm, height 56 cm
From the *tablinum* of the House of Titus Dentatus Panthera (IX, 2, 16)

Panel cut from the middle of a Fourth Style wall. The Three Graces, or *Charites,* daughters of Zeus by various mothers, personified beauty, grace, and intellectual and moral wisdom. There are innumerable examples of this group both in painting and in sculpture, all obviously copied from the same original, presumably a well-known Hellenistic sculpture. The Graces are commonly portrayed, as here, holding or wreathed with spring flowers. This explains the presence of flowers in the landscape setting, a feature not represented elsewhere in Pompeian mythological scenes.

Roman Campania

Another aspect of the Campanian scene very closely related to Rome's new-found position as a world power was that of the changes that the sudden access of wealth inevitably brought about in Roman upper class customs. Among these was one that calls for no comment today, namely the determination of every well-to-do Roman to acquire a seaside property. Gaius Marius had a villa at Misenum, Sulla the Dictator one near Cumae. Among the many prominent Romans known to have possessed such seaside retreats during the last half-century of the Republic were Julius Caesar, Pompey, Lucullus, the notorious Clodia, Varro the historian, many distinguished ex-consuls, and several of Cicero's clients; Cicero himself had no less than three Campanian properties, at Cumae, at Puteoli, and at Pompeii. By the time the emperor Augustus established himself on Capri, the Bay of Naples was ringed around with the playgrounds of the rich. As we shall see, these *villae marittimae* constituted a natural field for imaginative architectural experiment, while at the same time they ensured that the decorative tastes and fashions of Roman society found an almost immediate expression in Campania, and vice versa. They were also a bountiful source of artistic patronage. Each year there is fresh evidence to show that the Bay of Naples, and especially the area around Puteoli, was busy with the workshops of sculptors, potters, stuccoists, and painters. Late Republican Campania was one of the most active creative centers of the late Hellenistic world.

The area to the south and east of Vesuvius lay somewhat on the fringes of all this creative activity. It contributed to and profited from the general prosperity, and the latest contemporary artistic fashions were reflected on its walls. But its own interests were predominantly agricultural and its population, as the family names of Pompeii clearly show, was very largely Italic, many of the families being of Samnite origin but with a generous admixture of newcomers from other parts of Italy, reinforced in 80 B.C. by the establishment of colonies of Sullan veterans at Nola and Pompeii. Compared with Puteoli or Baiae Pompeii was perhaps a trifle provincial, and it lacked the Hellenic sophistication of Naples. Nevertheless, it was a prosperous and lively member of the Campanian community, at a moment when Campania was itself in the forefront of contemporary architectural and artistic progress.

Facing page:
23
Head of a young man, perhaps a member of the Popidius family
Fine-grained white marble, probably from Phrygia in Asia Minor
Height 36.5 cm
From the House of the Citharist (1, 4, 5), found together with No. 21 on 19 October 1868 in the stable block, having perhaps fallen from an upper room.

Rough surfaces on the shoulders mark the lines of drapery folds that have been dressed off, indicating that this was probably retrieved from a statue and adapted to a bust after the earthquake of A.D. 62. When found, the nose and ears were damaged and have been restored in plaster, but the repair to the lower lip was made in antiquity in Italian marble. The hair was probably painted a reddish brown, and the slightly roughened surfaces of the eyeballs may have had the iris and pupil rendered in red and black in the manner usual at this period. The unusually smooth, transparent quality of the flesh surfaces is due to the fine marble, which also permitted the sculptor a greater subtlety and sensitivity of modeling than usual.

17

Painted portrait of a man and his wife
Height 65 cm, width 58 cm
From House VII, 2, 6, on the back wall of a small
exedra opening off the atrium

The man wears a toga and carries a papyrus scroll with a red seal. His wife wears a tunic and mantle, and her hair is dressed in a fashion popular about the middle of the first century A.D. In her right hand she holds to her lips a *stylus* for writing on the two-leaved wooden tablet spread with wax which she holds in her left. Both in style and in treatment there is a striking resemblance to the Egyptian mummy portraits of the Roman period.

Facing page:
19

Wall painting: figure of a girl
Height 56 cm, width 38.5 cm
From Pompeii

The girl is probably intended to represent a figure sacrificing or in attendance upon some religious occasion.

18
Wall painting: portrait of a woman in profile
Height 52 cm, width 39 cm
From Herculaneum or Stabiae

Framed portrait from the center of the left-hand lateral panel of a Third Style wall. Old drawings of it show bands of ribbons hanging loosely down from the hair over the shoulders, and the loss of this overpainting accounts for the seeming disproportion of the neck. The same drawings indicate that the hair-band was shown as being made of some precious metal, and that from it sprang delicate sprays of flowers probably executed in pearls and emeralds on gold wire stems. The portrait itself is obviously imitating a cameo, and it has been suggested that it represents Cleopatra.

Facing page:
129
Wall painting: Europa riding the bull
Width 99 cm, height 125 cm
From the back wall of a *cubiculum* in the House of Jason (IX, 5, 18)

Third Style central panel portraying Europa, daughter of the King of Phoenicia, who, while playing on the seashore with her handmaidens, was approached by Zeus in the form of a white bull, which lured her into seating herself on its back and thereupon carried her off, across the sea to Crete. There, after bearing Zeus three sons, she married the King of Crete, who adopted her sons, one of whom, Minos, became his heir. The landscape, with its central oak tree (the tree sacred to Zeus), echoes the central scene.

On the left-hand wall of the same bedroom (*cubiculum*), by the same hand, was the painting of Pan and the Nymphs (No. 114) and on the right-hand wall a painting of Hercules, Deianira, and the centaur Nessus. Common to all three paintings was the symbolic use of trees within the landscape.

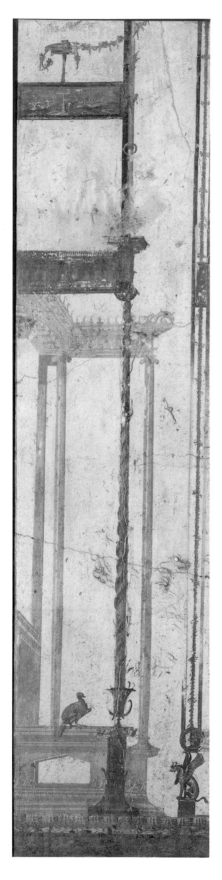

144, 145
**Wall paintings: fantasy architecture from a
Fourth Style wall**
Height 1.88 m, width 52 cm
From Pompeii, May 1760

Narrow vertical panels depicting slender fantasy
architecture in receding perspective are commonly used to frame the central panel in one
type of Fourth Style wall. On the broad plane
surface of the central panel in the scheme from
which these elements came was painted a small
framed picture of Perseus and Andromeda
(Naples Museum, inv. 8995), and in the middle
of each lateral panel were roundels (see also
Nos. 2, 141). One of these was the famous
"Sappho" (Naples Museum, inv. 9084).

Facing page:
114
Wall painting: Pan and the Nymphs
Height 1.22 m, width 93 cm
From the left-hand wall of the same *cubiculum*
in the House of Jason as No. 129

Third Style panel showing Pan, pipes in hand,
seated on a rock with a goat at his feet. To the
left are seated two Nymphs, one of them holding
two reed pipes in her hand, while to the right
another stands playing a lyre *(cithara)*. Beyond
the left-hand Nymphs is a building set in a rocky
landscape, central to which is a pine tree,
sacred to Pan.

111
Landscape panel of a rustic sanctuary
Height 34 cm, length 61 cm
From Herculaneum

150
Wall painting: woman giving water to a traveler
Width 44 cm, height 38 cm
From the *tablinum* of the House of the
Dioscuri (VI, 9, 6)

The picture formed part of a longer landscape
frieze, with painted moldings top and bottom,
over the side panels of a Fourth Style wall.

Facing page:
146
Wall painting: Theseus, slayer of the Minotaur
Width 88 cm, height 97 cm
From the *exedra* off the peristyle in the House
of Gavius Rufus (VII, 2, 16)

The central panel of the left-hand wall of a
Fourth Style scheme. It shows Theseus victorious
from his battle with the Minotaur, the bull-
headed monster of Crete to whom the Athenians
had each year to send a tribute of youths and
maidens. The Minotaur lies dead in the entrance
to his lair, the Labyrinth, and his destined
victims press round Theseus in gratitude.

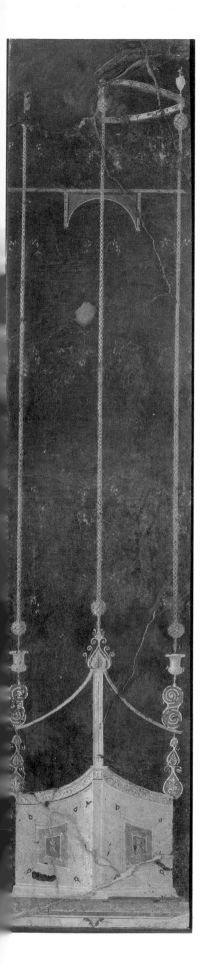

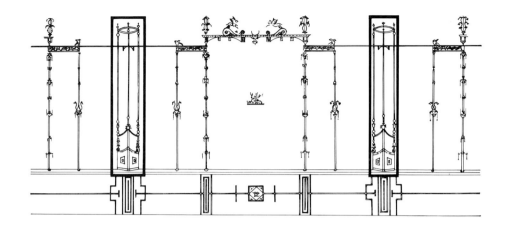

115, 116
**Wall paintings: pair of decorative details
from a Third Style wall**
Height 2.00 m, width 44 cm
From Room 15 *(cubiculum)* in the Villa of
Agrippa Postumus at Boscotrecase, excavated
1903–1905

These are two of the vertical components of
the architectonic framework of the side walls
(see reconstruction) of which the dado was a
dark red and the rest of the background uni-
formly black. Though reminiscent of the
candelabra and tripod stands from which much
Third Style ornament was derived, they are here
reduced to a purely schematic, decorative form.
The detail is extremely delicate and includes small
sprays of foliage, now largely effaced, sprouting
from the vertical stems.

Facing page:
135
Fragment of Fourth Style wall painting
Width 98 cm, height 90 cm
From Pompeii

Fragment from the upper zone of an early
Fourth Style wall, including the upper border
and an *aedicula* set in a formal quasi-architectural scheme of delicate garlands and slender
rods entwined with tendrils, reminiscent of fine
late Third Style work (as in the White Triclinium
in the House of M. Lucretius, IX, 3, 5). Within
the *aedicula* is the figure of a woman with flowing
draperies, poised as if flying.

80
Wall painting of a garden (detail)
Length 137 cm, height 32 cm
From Herculaneum

This scene, probably from the dado of a wall
of the late Third or Fourth Style, shows one
side of a garden enclosure, the trellised fence of
which is laid out symmetrically around three
semi-circular *exedrae*.

Most of the elements of this sort of fenced
garden are already present in the Garden
Room paintings from the Villa of Livia at Prima
Porta, and they recur in varying combinations
in many Pompeian paintings (see No. 79).

85
**Garden painting: a white stork and lizard and
a pet dog**
Length 1.30 m, height 55 cm
From the House of the Epigrams (v, 1, 18)

The painting stood in the southeast corner of
the peristyle, where it occupied a position closely
resembling that of the very similar paintings in
the peristyle of the House of the Menander.

260-262
Three red pottery (terra sigillata) bowls
Found in the *tablinum* of House VIII, 5, 9 on 4 October 1881, together with eighty-seven others of the same forms and thirty-seven pottery lamps, all packed in a wooden crate. The bowls were made by several different Gaulish potters.

260
Diameter 20.5 cm

Stamped in the center of the inside by the maker Vitalis, who was active about A.D. 60–85.

261
Diameter 16 cm

Stamped as No. 260 but by Mommo, one of the most prolific of South Gaulish potters.

262
Diameter 16.8 cm

The letters "MOM" were incised in the mold in large cursive letters under the decoration, probably by the potter Mommo (see No. 261).

100
Small blue glass jug (askos)
Height 11 cm, length 21.1 cm
From Pompeii, House IX, 2, 26

The glass-blower has imitated a shape long familiar in Greek pottery and in Campanian bronze ware.

101
Small jug (askos) in black and white marbled glass
Height 9.5 cm, length 13.4 cm
From Pompeii, in IX, 7, 6

Like No. 100 this is free-blown, but it is squatter in shape and made in thicker, opaque glass.

99
Ribbed blue glass bowl
Height 8.9 cm, diameter 18.9 cm
From Pompeii

These bowls were made by pressing soft glass
into a mold; the interior was polished on a whee
the exterior by a second, brief exposure to fire.
Bowls of this form, in multi-colored as well as
in monochrome glass, were popular in the first
century A.D.

104
Dark blue glass jug
Height 18 cm
From Pompeii

Fine-quality work, free-blown with a drawn-ou
spout and an applied handle. The form clearly
imitates that of a bronze vessel.

98
Stemmed goblet in cobalt blue glass
Height 14 cm, diameter of rim 15.4 cm
From one of the sites in the Vesuvius area

The body was blown into a mold; two horizon
wheel-cut lines decorate the outside. The stem i
formed from two large beads of glass and the f
added separately. Such drinking cups were use
at table; for a silver version see No. 246.

162
Gold lamp with two nozzles
Height 15.1 cm, length 23.2 cm
From Pompeii

The design of lotus leaves was worked in relief
from the outside with a punch, after filling the
interior with pitch. The plain spouts and base
were cast separately and soldered into place. The
lid, now missing, would normally have been the
most highly decorated part.

Gold bulla
Length 6.5 cm, weight 14.08 grams
From the House of the Menander (1, 10, 4)

The *bulla*, a small bag-shaped amulet, was
worn around the neck, a practice the Romans
derived from the Etruscans, among whom it
seems to have been worn as an ornament by
both sexes. Among the Romans the gold *bulla*
(sometimes known as *Etruscum aureum*) took
on a more restricted significance, being worn
from infancy by the sons of citizens as a visible
token of free birth. On coming of age and formally assuming the dress of manhood (the *toga
virilis*), it was customary to lay the *bulla* ceremoniously aside in the household *lararium* (see
no. 210). At a later date its use was permitted
also to the sons of freedmen.

47
Gold armband in the form of a snake
Diameter 8 cm, length 11 cm

One of a pair of armbands, each shaped from a
flat ribbon of gold on which the scales were
indicated with a V-shaped punch; the head was
cast separately, and the eyes were originally set
with green vitreous paste.

50
Gold bracelet
Diameter 8.3 cm
From House 1, 2, 3

Two lengths of thick gold wire loosely intertwined to form eight large loops, soldered
together at the crossings; over one of these is an
applied gold ornament.

52
Part of a necklace of gold ivy leaves
Length 53 cm
From Pompeii, 9 June 1877

The necklace consisted originally of two
concentric bands of ivy leaves stamped out of
sheet gold and linked to each other by tiny loops
of gold wire; the loops are masked by small gold
bosses. The 48 leaves of this piece converge
symmetrically upon a large convex gold disc. The
clasp that joined the two bands behind the neck
is missing.

HISTORY OF POMPEII

The town walls of Pompeii, originally built in the fifth century B.C. but repaired and heightened during successive crises (top: the Nola Gate; below: stretch of early masonry on the north wall)

Oscan inscription recording the building of the Samnite Palaestra (see page 87) in the later second century B.C. "Vibius Adiranus, son of Vibius, left money in his will to the men of Pompeii; with this money the quaestor of Pompeii, Vibius Vinicius, son of Maras, with the consent of the council had charge of the construction of this building and approved it"

The earliest history of Pompeii must remain a matter of conjecture until the relevant archaeological levels have been more systematically explored. Finds made in the city's two Archaic sanctuaries, that of Apollo beside the Forum and of Hercules (the Doric Temple), show that by the sixth century B.C. Greek influence was very strong, and it may very well be that the site was actually first colonized by Greeks from Cumae, who recognized its advantages as a river-mouth station for trading with the native Italic agricultural communities of the Sarno valley. Pottery characteristic of the latter has been found in the same contexts, suggesting close association if not intermarriage with the local peoples; and Etruscan wares indicate commerce also with Etruscan Capua. From the outset the geographical position of Pompeii made it a meeting place of cultures.

The middle years of the fifth century, after the decisive defeat of the Etruscans in 474 by Cumae in alliance with Syracuse, were a period of Greek prosperity. The original 24-acre settlement of Pompeii on the spur overlooking the river mouth was at this time greatly enlarged, to include the whole area of some 160 acres enclosed by the surviving city walls. But the period of undisputed Greek authority was short-lived. The walls themselves were symptomatic of the threat from the hardy Italic tribesmen of the interior, who were already spilling down across the coastal plain. By the end of the century the entire Greek coastland, from Cumae in the north to Poseidonia (Paestum) in the south, had succumbed to the invaders: only Neapolis (Naples) managed to retain its independence.

The newcomers were part of a loose confederation of peoples, the Sabellians, who shared a common language called Oscan, a member of the same Indo-European group of languages as Latin. These peoples appear in the literature variously as Sabellians and as Samnites, from the name of the particular tribe around which resistance to Rome's southward advance was soon to crystallize; in the Sarno valley they merged with the Oscans, a closely related Italic tribe already settled in the coastal area. At the time intertribal disputes and alliances bulked large—it was one of these Sabellic tribes, the Campani of the area around Capua, who first called in the Romans in 343 B.C.; but seen in historical retrospect, the most important thing about them was the broad common heritage of Italic peasant culture and language they shared with each other and, at one remove, with the Romans. Without this common element the story of the union of central Italy under Roman rule would have been very different. Another gift these peoples shared with the Romans was that of taking on the externals of the more advanced peoples whom they conquered. The Greek component in the resulting mixed culture was to be a very important factor in the success story of Republican Campania.

During the Samnite wars, which ended in 290 B.C. with the establishment of Roman authority over the whole of central Italy, Pompeii was still a small country town. Its economy was predominantly agricultural, based on wine and oil, with some local industry, and supplemented by a flourishing commerce in wool and woolen goods. Such other importance as it had at this stage was as a harbor town for its more important neighbors Nola and Nuceria (Nocera) and for the smaller towns of the Sarno valley. But times were changing fast. The consolidation of Roman authority, the defeat of Carthage in the Second Punic War (218-201), and Rome's triumphant advance eastward into Greece, Asia Minor, and Syria opened up rich fields of economic enterprise of which the Campanians, with their mixed Graeco-Italic background, were ideally placed to take advantage. Puteoli (Pozzuoli) was now the principal port of Italy. Roman traders, prominent among them the Campanians, began to appear in large

The Amphitheater riot of A.D. 59
Naples Museum

numbers all over the eastern Mediterranean; and while a steadily increasing proportion of the financial capital was probably put up by wealthy Romans, there
were rich prizes for the Campanian merchants and middlemen and for those of
the Campanian landed gentry who had money to invest. By the second half of
the second century B.C. Pompeii was, as its monuments show, already a very
prosperous city.

The last century of the Roman Republic was a period of almost continuous
civil strife and deep social unrest, during which the political and economic
forces loosed by Rome's conquest of Italy, Carthage, and the Hellenistic king-
doms of the eastern Mediterranean battled their way to the new state of institu-
tional equilibrium that we call the Roman Empire. In such troubled times
Campania could not escape involvement: cities and individuals found themselves caught up in larger events, and many people lost their lives or property.
Pompeii itself was very far from being the happy small town without a history
that it is sometimes painted; but despite temporary ups and downs, it was still
able to maintain a surprising level of economic well-being. Because of its privileged economic position, Campania was better able than a great many parts of
Italy to adjust to the successive new situations, and when in 31 B.C. Caesar's
nephew and heir, Octavian (or Augustus, as he was to be known from 27 B.C.),
finally succeeded in reimposing peace and unified rule upon the Mediterranean
world, Pompeii was still a very prosperous town, well placed to take advantage
of the opportunities offered by the new Pax Romana.

From the earlier part of this period two closely related series of events stand
out as directly affecting the fortunes of Pompeii. One was the Social War of
90-89 B.C., in which Pompeii, with its fine walls, was one of the Campanian
strongholds of the Italian allies in their struggle to achieve full Roman citizen-
ship. There was heavy fighting, during which Herculaneum was occupied,
Stabiae captured and sacked, and Pompeii itself besieged by the future dictator,
Lucius Cornelius Sulla: one can still see the damage wrought by his artillery in
the walls near the Vesuvius Gate. We do not know the immediate local outcome

*Graffito of a triumphant gladiator, drawn by a
Pompeian after the riot of* A.D. 59: "*Campani
(probably the inhabitants of a suburb of
Pompeii) you too were destroyed in the victory
over the Nucerians*"

34

of those events, but the long-term result of the Social War was the unification of Italy south of the Po valley within the broad framework of the Roman polity.

The conclusion of the Social War did not, however, resolve the immediate local problems. It was left for Sulla to complete the Italian settlement after his return to Italy in 83 B.C. from Asia Minor at the head of a victorious army. Having eliminated all political opposition in Rome itself, he turned his hand to the larger problem with characteristic ruthlessness and efficiency. One of the most effective instruments to hand was the establishment of citizen colonies of loyal military veterans on land expropriated from past opponents. Many such colonies were planted in Campania, among them a group of possibly as many as two or three thousand families on the territory of Pompeii. It was a neat solution, satisfactory to all parties except the dispossessed, and, in extreme cases, it must have meant the virtual annihilation of the old Italic upper classes. At Pompeii, as we shall see, the long-term results were nothing like so drastic. But the immediate result was to give Pompeii and other similar colonies a new civic status, a new ruling class, and a new stake in the events of the world around them.

With the establishment of the Colonia Cornelia Veneria Pompeianorum in 80 B.C. we turn a page in the city's history. The historical perspectives shift, slightly but decisively. As a Hellenized Italic city Pompeii, though irrevocably involved in the fortunes of Roman Italy, had retained a certain measure of independence. Now, for better or for worse, she found herself a full partner in the great Roman adventure. For the next fifty years the death throes of the Roman Republic continued to offer the politically ambitious plenty of scope for direct involvement in larger events. We catch an occasional glimpse of such happenings in the pages of Cicero, who owned a property in the neighborhood: in 62 B.C. he successfully defended the founder of the colony, the dictator's relative Publius Cornelius Sulla, on a charge of involvement in the conspiracy of Catiline; in 49 B.C. Cicero himself, on his way to join Pompey in Greece, found himself approached by the commanders of the three cohorts stationed in or near the town (an offer he discreetly declined). Again, during the Servile War (73-71 B.C.), Spartacus' army remained for a long time in the countryside near Pompeii, and actually destroyed Pompeii's neighbor Nola. But such incidents were the inevitable by-products of troubled times. For the last century and a half of the city's existence, the inhabitants of Pompeii, in company with those of countless other colonies and municipalities in Italy, were fully engaged in reaping the material advantages of their new status.

From 80 B.C. onward the real history of Pompeii is that of the city and its inhabitants, and that can only be told in terms of the city's civic institutions, which are the subject of the section that follows. Here it must suffice to refer to the three remaining occasions on which Pompeii found itself front-page news outside Campania.

The first of these was the riot that took place in A.D. 59 after a gladiatorial spectacle in the Amphitheater, as a result of which a number of visiting spectators from Nuceria were killed or wounded. The matter reached the Senate in Rome, and as a punishment all spectacles in the Amphitheater were banned for a period of ten years—a sentence comparable today to a ten-year closure of the local football stadium. The scene is vividly portrayed in a contemporary picture, now in Naples Museum (see illustration), which was found in a house near the theater.

Then, on the fifth of February 62 there was a severe earthquake. Though

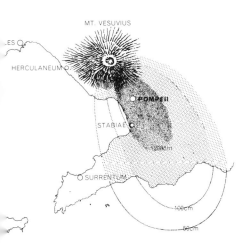

The area affected by the hail of pumice stones and the relative depths of ash ejected by Vesuvius in A.D. 79

nobody at the time knew it, this was Act One of the tragedy of A.D. 79, and like many earthquakes of a volcanic nature its effects were localized but intense, and Pompeii was the epicenter. The town was very badly damaged; quite how badly can be judged from the fact that when, seventeen years later, disaster hit again, only two of the city's public monuments (the Amphitheater and the Temple of Isis) and a handful of private houses had been completely restored. Of the Forum and the buildings around it, only in the Temple of Apollo was the work near completion; even allowing for the fact that after the eruption this whole area was ransacked for its metals, its marbles, and its building materials, it is quite evident that the only buildings where reconstruction work was not still in progress were those like the Capitolium, where it had not yet started—presumably because of plans to rebuild them in a more opulent, contemporary manner. In 79 the whole Forum area was a gigantic builders' yard. The same story is repeated all over the city: in the public bath buildings, the theaters, the Doric temple, the water supply, a great many of the private houses. As we shall see, this was not the only problem Pompeii was having to face in its last years, but the earthquake of 62 was in itself undoubtedly a major disaster.

The great eruption of Vesuvius of 24 August 79 came out of a clear sky. The volcano had been inactive since well before historical times and it was universally believed to be extinct. Villas and vineyards crowded up the slopes, and in a land where earthquakes are common the warning of A.D. 62 had passed unheeded.

For the course of the eruption, which followed a classic pattern, we have two contemporary sources: the analysis of the deposits of ash and cinders beneath which the whole city was buried, and the eyewitness account of Pliny the Younger, contained in two letters addressed to the historian Tacitus. At the time Pliny was staying with his uncle, the famous scientist and writer, who happened to be in command of the Roman fleet at Misenum, nineteen miles to the west, at the mouth of the Bay of Naples. It was about one o'clock in the afternoon when their attention was called to the cloud, shaped like a gigantic pine tree, which had appeared across the bay:

I cannot describe its appearance and shape better than as resembling an umbrella pine tree, with a very tall trunk rising high into the sky and then spreading out into branches. I imagine this was because where the force of the blast was fresh it was thrust upwards, but as this lost impetus, or indeed as the weight of the cloud itself took charge, it began to thin out and to spread laterally. At one moment it was white, at another dark and dirty, as if it carried up a load of earth and cinders.

(Pliny, *Letters* vi, 16)

Allied troops who witnessed the far less destructive eruption of March 1944 will at once recognize the description—nature's equivalent of the mushroom cloud released by an atomic bomb.

Summoning ships, the Elder Pliny headed straight for the coast near Herculaneum, where he found it already impossible to land. Instead he put in at Stabiae, at the coastal villa of a friend, Pomponianus, where he spent the night. In the small hours of the following morning a succession of violent earthquake shocks and the steadily falling ash drove the party down to the beach, where during the course of the morning of the 25th Pliny was overcome by the fumes and died. Meanwhile, Misenum was feeling the same earthquake shocks, and when a shift of wind into the east brought with it a cloud of darkness and falling ash the whole population took to the open countryside; it was not until the fol-

Facing page:
Volcanic Eruption, undated
Michael Wutky, Austrian, 1738–1822

lowing day that the ashes began to cease falling and that a fitful daylight broke through once more.

The eruption must have started between 10 and 11 o'clock on the morning of the 24th, and by the evening of that day some 6 feet of ash had already fallen on Pompeii. Here the first 8 or 9 feet of deposit consist of a thin scatter of lava pebbles (*lapilli*), the debris of the plug of solidified basalt that had for so long sealed the volcano, followed by successive layers of almost pure pumice. This represents the body of volcanic magma that was ejected up the throat as soon as it was clear, under conditions of great heat and enormous pressure, to a height of several thousand meters (the trunk of the "pine tree"); on reaching the upper atmosphere the drops of magma were able to expand, releasing some of the gases they contained, and to fall as a dense, spreading cloud of incandescent, gaseous pumice. More than two thirds of the deposits at Pompeii represent this first, cataclysmic series of events, after which the gases of the interior were free to escape upward with a much smaller admixture of pure magma, its place being taken by increasing quantities of alien material, as the old volcanic matter of the existing cone collapsed inward upon itself, causing a series of convulsive blockages and explosions. This was the peak moment of the eruption, involving a tremendous release of gaseous pressure and causing the earthquakes that destroyed Pomponianus' villa at Stabiae and spread panic at Misenum. But although the deadly rain of gas and cinders continued, the body of actual solid matter that fell was already tailing off rapidly. In terms of its power to destroy, by the afternoon of the 25th the eruption had already done its worst.

The city of Pompeii had ceased to exist, buried beneath twelve feet of lethal ash. We have no means of estimating the casualties, but in the town itself and the immediate countryside they must have run into many thousands. Those who got away did so in the first few hours, the lucky ones by sea, the rest striking inland before the roads were blocked and the air became unbreathable. Those who dallied to collect their valuables or who took shelter in the houses and cellars died miserably, some when the roofs and upper stories collapsed upon them under the weight of the ash, most of them suffocated by the steady accumulation of deadly, sulphurous fumes. The ash solidified around their bodies, leaving for posterity the pathetic record of their death agonies amid the darkness of that terrifying August day.

When something like normality had been restored a commission was sent to Campania to report, but there was nothing to be done. Herculaneum and many of the villas of the coast along the foot of Vesuvius had vanished from sight beneath an engulfing torrent of volcanic mud, washed down the mountainside by the torrential rains that accompanied the eruption. Pompeii and Stabiae were slightly better off in that the upper parts of many of the taller buildings were still visible above the mantle of ash. Here it was at least possible to do some salvage. The Forum area was ransacked for its bronze statues and its fine building materials, and many houseowners—and others—grubbed their way down into the houses, hunting for strongboxes and caches of valuables. But the town was beyond resurrection. The survivors drifted away or were settled elsewhere and, as has happened many times in Campanian history, nature took over and what had been Pompeii became once more rich agricultural land. The knowledge that there had once been a town here lingered on in folk memory: in the eighteenth century the area was still known as Città (*civitas,* or "city"). But as far as the learned world was concerned Pompeii, like Herculaneum, had been wiped off the map and had laboriously to be rediscovered.

THE TOWN: GOVERNMENT AND PEOPLE

Poster painted on the wall of House III, 2, 1, *advertising gladiatorial games to be given at the expense of Lucretius Satrius*

Lucius Caecilius Felix, father of Lucius Caecilius Jucundus Naples Museum

Marcus Holconius Rufus Naples Museum

A great deal of our information about life in Pompeii is derived from inscriptions. In addition to the ordinary everyday uses of writing that distinguish any advanced society, the Romans seem to have had a strong portion of the common human passion for self-commemoration. Three main categories of inscriptions may be distinguished. One is that of formal monumental epigraphy on stone or bronze, ranging from long, elaborate, formal texts down to the simple tombstones of the domestic slave and his family. To this category belong dedications to divinities and records of religious events; inscriptions in honor of members of the Imperial family and distinguished citizens; building inscriptions and funerary inscriptions. A second category is that of the inscriptions used in commerce and private life to denote the source of ownership of certain goods, or to facilitate accounting. These might be an integral part of the object inscribed, as were the maker's stamps on many sorts of pottery or lamps, or they might be scratched or painted on the object, as frequently for example on silver ware or the painted tally marks on amphoras. A third group, in which by the circumstances of its destruction Pompeii is unusually rich, is that of *graffiti* (literally "scratches"), a term that may be used to denote any sort of ephemeral sign or text scratched or painted on plaster or other appropriate surfaces. Many of these are the work of the inevitable idle scribbler, but a very unusual and important group consists of electoral posters painted on the fronts of the houses of the candidates or their supporters (see page 41). The evidence is not evenly spread: for the final period of the city we have a great deal of electoral propaganda, but few formal inscriptions setting out the names and careers of the successful candidates. Even so, as a Who's Who to the personalities of local politics it remains an invaluable source of information.

Another unusual group of inscriptions is that of the *tabulae ceratae,* the wax-surfaced wooden tablets upon which a local banker, Lucius Caecilius Jucundus, kept his business records. These were buried in the earthquake of 62 and never recovered; and not only do they throw light on aspects of contemporary life about which we normally hear very little, but they tell us a lot about the people involved. Because of the rigid rules of precedence prevailing in Roman society, even a list of witnesses can be an eloquent document.

Most of these inscriptions record the names of individuals, a great many of them in some public capacity, and to understand their significance it will be helpful at this point to glance briefly at the Roman rules governing the use of names, which fortunately for us were remarkably precise. By the end of the Republic it was standard practice for a Roman citizen to bear three names. Thus the full name of the most distinguished citizen of Augustan Pompeii was M[arcus] Holconius M[arci] f[ilius] Rufus. His middle name, Holconius, was that of the *gens,* the family of which he was a member, the equivalent of a modern surname. His first name (*praenomen*) was given to him at birth, and in normal Roman practice it was written in abbreviated form (A. for Aulus, L. for Lucius, Gn. for Gnaeus, etc.) and in official documents a man would normally also give his father's *praenomen*, which in the case of Holconius Rufus was the same as his own. In early Republican times two names had sufficed; but a developed society can carry only a limited number of plain John Smiths, and quite early it became the practice in aristocratic circles to add a third name, or *cognomen*, a practice that spread steadily down the social scale to all levels of citizen society. These *cognomina*, when first adopted, were very commonly descriptive (*Ahenobarbus,* "Brazenbeard"; *Calvus,* "Baldhead"; *Faventinus,* "from Faventia" [modern Faenza]), but they very soon became conventional names that ran in families. M. Holconius Rufus ("Redhead") was no more necessarily himself red-headed than his brother Celer ("Swift") was fast-moving. To his friends he was probably known as Rufus, although on this point there were no hard and fast rules. Cicero was M. Tullius Cicero, but Pliny the Elder was Caius Plinius Secundus, while his nephew on his sister's side, Publius Caecilius Secundus, whom he adopted, became Caius Plinius Caecilius Secundus (taking on his adopted father's family name but retaining his own [Caecilius] as a *cognomen*).

Women used a simpler form of the same system, usually at this period just their family name together with that of the father or husband whose legal dependents they were, while household slaves carried a single name, which was normally Greek, a convention that reflects the fact that the overwhelming majority of such slaves were of Greek-speaking extraction. Slaves, it must be remembered, were members of the family. If they were given their freedom (see below) they took their former master's name and forename, usually retaining their own slave name as a *cognomen.* A hypothetical slave of M. Holconius Rufus, named Narcissus, would have become officially M. Holconius M[arci] l[ibertus = freedman] Narcissus, whereas the son of the latter would have been (say) M. Holconius M. f[ilius] Primus, born free and from his name indistinguishable from any other freeborn citizen. There were innumerable possible nuances of the system, and with the passage of time names tended to become more complex and many fresh names came into circulation. But down to A.D. 79 the main rules still broadly applied.

From the inscriptions we learn that M. Holconius Rufus had been a *duovir* of the colony five times (the fourth time in 2/1 B.C.) and *quinquennalis* twice; he was a *flamen Caesaris Augusti;* he was an official patron of the colony; and he was one of the three known Pompeians to have been appointed a *tribunus militum a populo,* an honorary office that gave him equestrian rank in Rome, a position of privilege second only to senatorial rank. Together with his brother, Celer, he modernized the Large Theater after the model of the Theater of Marcellus in Rome. This was a very distinguished municipal career. What did these titles signify, and how did the system work?

When a Roman colony was founded it was given its own written constitution and, because the Romans were an orderly minded people, such constitutions tended to follow a broadly uniform pattern, with relatively minor variations to meet special local circumstances. There is no direct record of the law with which in 80 B.C. Sulla established the Colonia Cornelia Veneria Pompeianorum, but we do have fragments of several other late Republican or early Imperial constitutions, and it is evident that that of Pompeii followed conventional lines.

The colony was established initially by an official (*deductor*) who was appointed by the central government and who in this case was the dictator's relative, Publius Cornelius Sulla. His tasks included the appropriation and allocation of lands for the new settlers, the establishment of a municipal council, and the appointment of the first body of magistrates. The council, a body usually of some 80-100 members, was known corporately as the *ordo decurionum* and its individual members as decurions (*decuriones*). Decurions had to be freeborn citizens; certain professions were ineligible (an odd list, including innkeepers, auctioneers, comedy actors, gravediggers, gladiators, trainers) and others (shopkeepers and small traders) eligible only under conditions that at this date would have been prohibitive; tenure was for life, unless a holder was specifically disqualified for some breach of the conditions; and—a very important provision—there was a high property qualification. A decurion, and *a fortiori* a magistrate,

Election poster: "All the fruitsellers with Helvius Vestalis support the election of M. Holconius Priscus as duovir"

was expected to spend money on the community. The *ordo* in effect constituted a moneyed municipal aristocracy, and as long as money was plentiful membership was a valued privilege. It was a Roman senate in miniature, but— as Cicero remarks to a friend who had asked his support in getting his stepson appointed to the *ordo* of Pompeii— it was rather harder to get into.

The senior elected magistrates were a pair of *duoviri,* who between them presided over the meetings of the *ordo,* handled all important financial business, and administered local justice. Among other privileges certain senior priesthoods were reserved for members of the duoviral families, and a magistrate with good connections at the imperial court might aspire to the honorary but prestigious position of *patronus.* The *duoviri* were supported by a pair of junior magistrates, aediles, who dealt with such day-to-day administrative matters as the maintenance of streets and public buildings, the management of markets, and the issue of licenses and permits. These were young men at the beginning of their careers, and since election to a magistracy carried with it membership in the *ordo,* there was no shortage of candidates. Every five years the *duoviri* had special powers and were known as *quinquennales,* with the special task of carrying out a municipal census and of reviewing the qualifications of the members of the *ordo.* This last power must have greatly reinforced the tendency for municipal power to fall into the hands of a small self-perpetuating group of wealthy families. Only if things went badly wrong was central authority (i.e., from the time of Augustus onward, the emperor) likely to intervene. A properly qualified newcomer could in theory seek popular election, but in practice the only sure access was through marriage or adoption into the ruling families and the best key to that door was wealth.

The magistrates were elected annually by the whole body of free citizens, who were for the purpose divided into voting districts. As the electoral propaganda shows (most of it admittedly from the last period of the town's history, when the hold of the old families had largely broken down) this was a duty that the population entered into with gusto; and while many of the supporters were no doubt simply friends, neighbors, and clients of the candidates, others were organized bodies that may be presumed to have had a serious economic or social interest in the outcome. Religious associations such as the *Isiaci* and the *Venerii,* influential trade associations such as the fullers (*fullones*), bodies of people involved in agriculture or transport, the fishermen, the bakers, the goldsmiths, various sorts of small shopkeepers or stallholders, all of these are attested, together with a number of other groups of a less serious character— "the draughts-players," "the theatergoers," "the late drinkers," and so on. Elections were evidently lively affairs.

There were also a number of organizations of a partly administrative, partly social or religious character (the distinction is not always an easy one to draw), which offered an outlet to citizens or other residents who were not qualified to become ordinary magistrates. It has to be remembered that there were also substantial groups of resident foreigners. But although, slave or freeborn, a man's position was rigidly defined by his civil status, this was also a surprisingly fluid society. Not only could slaves of ability rise to positions of very considerable responsibility as stewards, bailiffs, managers of large estates, and the like, but slavery was actually one of the recognized roads to social advancement. A Roman citizen had the right of bestowing freedom upon any slave who had given faithful service, a right that was freely exercised; and although a freedman, or *libertus,* was debarred from holding certain positions that called for free

41

birth, his children born after he obtained his freedom were the equals at law of any other Roman citizen.

A great many of the domestic slaves came from the Greek-speaking East as prisoners of war, as the victims of a flourishing slave trade along and across the frontiers, or even as children sold into slavery by their families. Many of them had natural abilities and aptitudes in fields where the Romans were by temperament and position less qualified, and by the first century A.D. a very high percentage of the professional and commercial skills of a town like Pompeii were in their hands, either as trusted slaves working for their masters, or else as freedmen operating on their own behalf or as agents of their former masters. Doctors, teachers, accountants, secretaries, architects, decorators, barbers, cooks, small craftsmen and tradesmen of every sort, the overseers and technicians of commerce and industry, the staffs of the city offices: by the first century A.D. almost all of these would have been slaves or descendants of slaves, and, because of their natural ability and training, many of them were well-to-do and some of them were very wealthy. Trimalchio, the millionaire freedman of Petronius' *Satyricon,* is a caricature, but he is a caricature that everybody would have recognized as drawn from life.

It was, as we have seen, the regular practice for a freedman to adopt his former master's family name, and by the second generation it is often quite impossible to distinguish the descendants of freedmen from members of the parent family. Statistics elude us, but by A.D. 79 a very substantial proportion of the free urban population of Pompeii must have been descended from freedmen, and in many cases from the freedmen of freedmen. (In the countryside the proportion would have been less.) Much of the economy of the town was in their hands, and many of them were socially ambitious. The election posters of the last period include a lot of the old names, and although some of these were doubtless still the lineal descendants of the old Samnite and Roman families, a great many others were unquestionably the second- and third-generation products of this extraordinary ethnic melting pot.

For a vivid glimpse of the system at work we may turn to the inscription recording the rebuilding of the Temple of Isis after the earthquake of 62. The restoration was paid for by N. Popidius Celsinus, who bears the name of one of the most distinguished of the pre-Roman families of Pompeii, the Popidii. It must have cost a lot of money, at a time when the town was in serious financial difficulties, and in return the council was doubtless glad to elect him to their number. The only surprising feature is that at the time Popidius was a boy of six. The truth is, of course, that the real donor was the boy's father, N. Popidius Ampliatus, who happened to have been born a slave and who, being himself debarred from membership in the *ordo,* chose instead to buy his son's way into it. But for the eruption, Celsinus, with his family's wealth behind him, might well in due course have become the town's chief magistrate.

Inscription from the Temple of Isis (no. 10) Naples Museum

N POPIDIVS N F CELSINVS
AEDEM ISIDIS TERRAE MOTV CONLAPSAM
A FVNDAMENTO P S RESTITVIT HVNC DECVRIONES OB LIBERALITATEM
CVM ESSET ANNORVM SEXS ORDINI SVO GRATIS ADLEGERVNT

The case of the restoration of the Temple of Isis is obviously in some respects exceptional, but it illustrates admirably the intent behind the system. Without doing violence to the inherited Roman prejudices in favor of free birth and against most forms of direct commercial activity, a real effort was made to engage the loyalties of the socially underprivileged and to direct their energies and wealth into socially useful channels. One such outlet was in the local administration of the *vici* and *pagi,* the subdistricts into which the town and its territory were divided (see p. 92). There were bodies known as *ministri,* who were mostly freedmen, but who might include freeborn citizens and in some cases even slaves. In origin the duties of the *ministri* may have been mainly religious, but, as organized bodies, they constituted a useful peg on which to hang other local responsibilities; they carried status, and we find them contributing financially to such municipal enterprises as building and the provision of games. Another important outlet was provided by the institution of the imperial cult in the time of Augustus (see p. 86). Here again, although the forms were ostensibly religious, the objectives were in reality far wider. The *Augustales* in particular were recruited from the most prominent freedmen of the community. They ranked immediately after the members of the *ordo* and, in addition to a large statutory payment on election, they were expected to use their wealth liberally on behalf of the community. In A.D. 79 the golden age of the *Augustales* was still to come, but even so they were already a powerful force within the community.

At Pompeii as nowhere else outside Rome we can follow the issues of local politics in terms of the individuals directly involved, the man in the street as well as the candidate for whom he voted. We must be content, however, to summarize the broad conclusions that emerge from the study of this mass of detailed information, insofar as it illustrates the history of the town during the 160 years of its existence as a Roman colony.

The first fifty years (80-31 B.C.), as reflected in the names of those who held municipal office or who were candidates for office, were closely influenced by the play of events elsewhere in Rome and Italy: the shifts of power and of allegiance in Rome itself following the rise of Caesar and, striking deeper and more lastingly, the breakup of the old tribal Italy and the steady emergence of a more urbanized, more broadly based Roman Italy. In this respect the founder of the colony, P. Cornelius Sulla, seems to have acted with considerable statesmanship and foresight. Although the colony was in intention founded as a closed electoral society from which the old Samnite families were excluded, within barely a generation we find members of the latter already back in the *ordo,* and they were joined there by an increasing number of families from other parts of Campania or from the impoverished inland districts of central Italy. The pattern is a familiar one. The product of a society that was out of balance, with large sections of the population adrift socially and seeking fresh opportunities within the enduring framework of Italian geography, there are many analogies with modern times.

If the first fifty years were, therefore, a time of rather rapid change, the next sixty to seventy years were characterized by a no less remarkable stability. Toward the end of the previous period many of the newcomers seem to have been partisans of the future emperor Augustus, and with the firm establishment of central authority after his victory at Actium in 31 B.C. they found themselves very comfortably placed. For a couple of generations the control of Pompeii seems to have lain in the hands of the small group of closely interrelated families

43

to which M. Holconius Rufus and his brother belonged. As large landed proprietors, with profitable outlets in wine production, the tile industry, and sheep farming, much of the local economy was in their hands: their wealth is attested by the sums they spent on buildings, games, and other municipal amenities, and they had secured an almost complete monopoly of civic office. Because of their close ties with central authority—the establishment of the imperial cult and the institution of the *Augustales* are symptomatic—it was a period during which any lingering Campanian eccentricities (for example, the use of the old Samnite weights and measures) were quietly eliminated. As the ferment of the Civil Wars settled, the processes of Romanization begun in 80 B.C. came to fruition. By the death of Augustus' successor, Tiberius, in A.D. 37, Pompeii was as fully Roman a city as were Mantua, Sulmona, and Venusia (Venosa, in Apulia), the birthplaces of Vergil, Ovid, and Horace.

The last forty-odd years of the city's history were by contrast a period of change and of urban crisis. The earthquake of A.D. 62 was a serious aggravation of a difficult situation; another must have been the loss of imperial favor after the Amphitheater riot of A.D. 59. But the underlying causes were political and economic. For one thing, Italy in general and Campania in particular were beginning to lose out economically to some of the developing provinces overseas; for another, the monopoly of wealth formerly exercised by the old landed classes was facing ever-increasing competition from the emergent middle class to which the wealthy freedmen belonged. Exactly how the crisis developed and on whose authority it was resolved we do not know. There are signs of imperial intervention (the normal procedure when the affairs of a municipality got out of hand) and perhaps of a temporary suspension of the normal civic institutions during the forties. It is not until after the adoption of Nero by his stepfather, the emperor Claudius, in A.D. 50, that we begin once more to find records of appointments to the normal magistracies and priesthoods. But from then on the record is extensive, and the message is clear. It shows that there had been an almost complete break with the recent past and with the group of families that had virtually controlled the city for more than half a century. Instead, many of the office-holders of the last period are from families with no previous political record; others are from old families that had long been excluded from office, and yet others are manifestly of freedman descent.

The monopoly of local authority by the established landed families had gone, and its place was being taken by a society in which privilege and wealth were more widely spread, but which found it difficult to fill the gap left by the withdrawal of the old, comfortable municipal paternalism. Pompeii was still a busy city, but it had fewer resources. It is no accident that in A.D. 79, seventeen years after the earthquake, only two major public buildings had been completely restored or that many of the fine old houses were being subdivided and converted into commercial premises. Another generation, and a great deal more of the older, wealthier Pompeii would have vanished. If it was the city's destiny to be preserved for posterity as a monument to a way of life, the eruption of 79 came just in time.

THE TOWN: PLANNING AND ARCHITECTURE

The early history of Pompeii is faithfully reflected in its town plan. The original settlement, which occupied the southwest corner of the later town, was situated on a spur of higher ground, projecting from the lower slopes of Vesuvius and looking out over the mouth of the river Sarno and the Bay of Naples. It was defended by a circuit of walls that on the south and west sides followed the cliffs above the river mouth, and on the landward side faced out across the saddle that carried the coast road from Naples toward Stabiae and the Sorrento peninsula, following a curving line still clearly visible in the street plan of the later town. Within this circuit the early town was laid out on orderly, though not mathematically precise, lines. Of the early buildings, the positions of two can be established: the sanctuary of Apollo, which lay beside the reserved open space that was later to become the Forum, and that of Hercules (?), finely situated on a rocky spur that projected southeastward above the river (later the "Triangular Forum"), possibly outside the city walls. This early settlement covered some twenty-four acres, and the population is estimated at about 2,000 to 2,500 people.

With its command of local land and river traffic and its ready access to the sea, the settlement prospered and grew rapidly, and in the fifth century B.C. it was greatly enlarged northward and eastward, within a new circuit of defensive walls enclosing a roughly oval area of some 160 acres. These walls, several times strengthened and repaired, were to remain the effective boundary of the city throughout its subsequent history: any subsequent expansion (and the inscriptions and excavation confirm that there was such expansion) was into suburban areas outside the gates.

The new town was laid out in the Greek manner. This consisted ideally of long, narrow, rectangular residential blocks separated by narrow access-streets *(stenōpoi)* running at right angles to the main traffic avenues *(plateai)*, and it can be seen at its simplest and most orthodox in the area south of the Via dell'Abbondanza, toward the Amphitheater. Elsewhere there are many irregularities of layout, but all of them make good sense as a rationalization of the already existing road-system outside the walls of the early settlement: the main coast road running southeastward from the Herculaneum Gate and down the well-marked valley that led to the Stabian Gate; and, radiating outward, a web of roads heading for Naples and Herculaneum, the farms on the slopes of Vesuvius, Nola, and Stabiae and Nuceria. With a little tidying up at important intersections, it is all there, a classic instance of an orderly planning system superimposed upon an existing topographical situation in such a way as to cause a minimum of disruption to established suburban street frontages and property rights.

Of the architecture of the earliest town we have little more than the scanty remains of the two Greek temples, including the platform of one of them and a selection of the gaily painted terracotta architectural ornament that once covered the superstructures of both. The earliest substantial surviving structures belong to the turn of the fourth and third century B.C., and it is not really until the last century of Samnite rule, in the second century B.C., that we begin to get any coherent picture of the town as such. At this time there was still plenty of room: among the several wealthy houses of the period still standing in A.D. 79 was the House of the Faun, which occupied an area of some six acres, covering a whole city block. During this period there was also a lot of public building. The Forum was enlarged and monumentalized by the addition of enclosing porticoes; at the north end it was dominated by a large, upstanding temple of Jupiter, and off the southwest corner there now opened a grandiose new basilica.

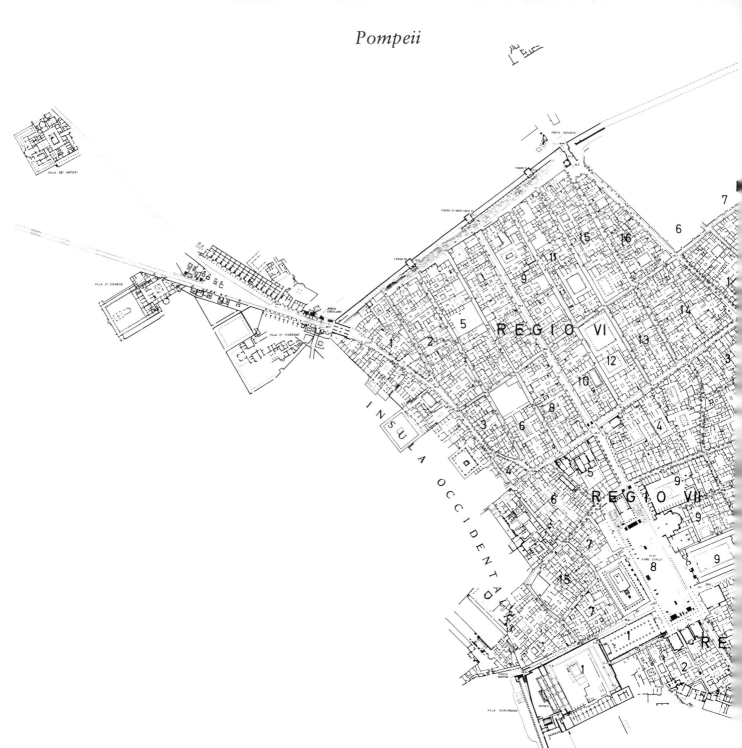

The original settlement at Pompeii

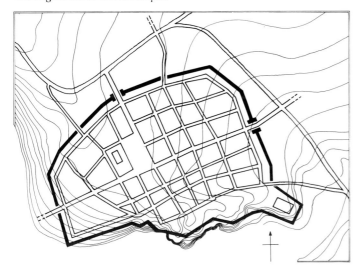

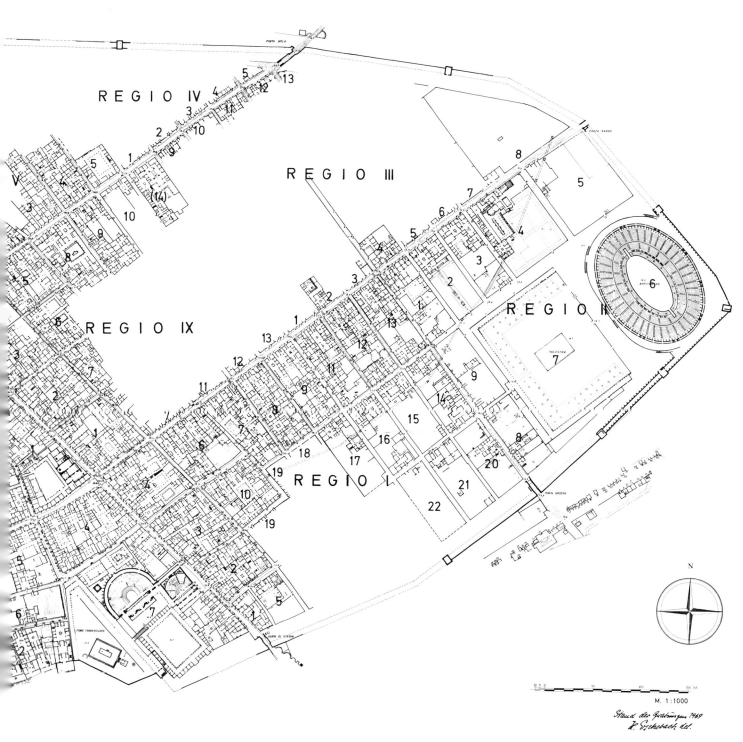

REGIO IV

REGIO III

REGIO IX

REGIO I

PALESTRA
7

M. 1:1000

Map of Pompeii
Courtesy of Hans Eschebach

1. *Forum*
2. *Temple of Venus*
3. *Forum Baths*
4. *House of the Tragic Poet*
5. *House of Sallust*
6. *Villa of Diomedes*
7. *Villa of the Mysteries*

8. *Temple of Fortuna Augusta*
9. *House of the Faun*
10. *Insula* VI, 13
11. *House of the Vettii*
12. *House of the Gilded Amorini*
13. *Fullery*
14. *House of the Silver Wedding*

15. *Central Baths*
16. *House of the Centenary*
17. *Bakery of Modestus*
18. *Stabian Baths*
19. *Temple of Isis*
20. *Theaters (see p. 87)*
21. *House of the Menander*

22. *Caupona of Euxinus*
23. *House of the Ship "Europa"*
24. *House of Julius Polybius*
25. *House of Pinarius Cerialis*
26. *House of "Loreius Tiburtinu*
27. *"Praedia" Julia Felix*
28. *Palaestra*

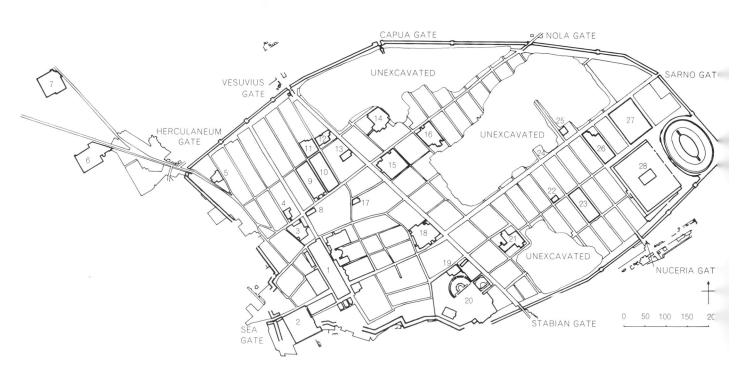

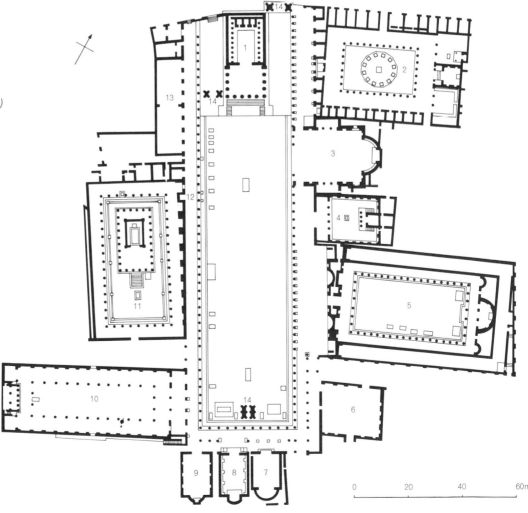

Aerial view of the Forum from the south, showing also the houses terraced out over the town walls.

The Forum

1. Temple of Jupiter
2. Provisions market (macellum)
3. Sanctuary of the City Lares
4. Temple of Vespasian
5. Cloth traders hall (Eumachia Building)
6. Voting hall (comitium)
7. Chief magistrates' (duovirs') office
8. Council chamber
9. Junior magistrates' (aediles') office
10. Basilica
11. Temple of Apollo
12. Control of weights and measures
13. Cereals market
14. Commemorative arches

49

To this same period belong also the first bath buildings of the new Roman type, the Large Theater in its original form, the elegant Doric colonnades of the Triangular Forum, and, very probably, the predecessors of such later temples as those of Venus, of Zeus Meilichios, and of Isis. Typical of this late Samnite-period architecture are the use of the brown tufa stone of Nocera, especially for house frontages, and of the First Style ("Masonry Style") painted stucco ornament to cover all the more important interior wall surfaces.

Although the establishment of the Sullan colony in 80 B.C. was achieved without any radical change to the existing urban structure, it was, as one would expect, followed by considerable building activity. The city walls were repaired; the temple at the head of the Forum was rebuilt and rededicated in honor of the Roman Capitoline triad, Jupiter, Juno, and Minerva; the Stabian Baths were enlarged and modernized; and a number of new public buildings were erected, including a smaller, covered theater (*theatrum tectum*) beside the existing open-air theater, an amphitheater (inaugurated in 70 B.C.) and a second public bath building, near the Forum. The list is an interesting one, illustrating as it does not only the initial contribution of the new colonists, but also their rapid assimilation to local ways. For all its top-dressing of Roman colonial forms, Pompeii was still a Campanian city.

Full Romanization came only under Augustus and his immediate successors, a process neatly symbolized by the formal adoption of the Roman system of weights and measures in place of the old Sabellian system, which the Sullan colony had retained. Once again, however, it was a process of organic development and mutual assimilation within the existing framework rather than one of radical change. The Forum was progressively modernized by the addition of a meat and fish market (*macellum*), a group of city offices, and a voting precinct; by the construction of the "Eumachia Building" by the patroness of the most powerful of the city's trade associations, the wool merchants; and by the rebuilding in limestone of the Forum porticoes—this last still in progress at the time of the earthquake of A.D. 62. Other major public works of this period include provision for the newly established imperial cult; the creation of a huge exercise ground (*palaestra*) near the Amphitheater; an elaborate remodeling of the old Samnite-period theater, undertaken by the wealthy brothers Holconius (see p. 40) in conscious imitation of the Augustan Theater of Marcellus in Rome; and the building of an aqueduct and a city-wide system of public water points. To this same period, between 80 B.C. and the middle of the first century A.D., belong most of the large private houses, with their elaborate schemes of Second and Third Style painted decoration. Both in the public and the private sector, this was a time of great and varied architectural activity.

By contrast, the last thirty years before the eruption were a time of economic stress and of gathering urban crisis. After the earthquake many of the large private houses were abandoned as residences; seventeen years later only two public monuments (the Amphitheater and the Temple of Isis) had been completely restored and there was little or no new public building. In 79 the Forum was a vast builder's yard, and even the water supply was still under repair. Of the few exceptions, the building usually identified as a public *lararium*, in honor of the city's protecting divinities, and the small temple in honor of Vespasian, could both have been considered necessary acts of propitiation toward religious and secular authority, following the disaster of A.D. 62. The only major new project of a utilitarian nature was a large new bath building, the Central Baths, still incomplete in A.D. 79.

A street in Pompeii (The paving stones are made of hard gray lava.)

In its use of building materials and construction techniques the architecture of Pompeii lies rather on the fringes than at the center of contemporary Italian building history—rather surprisingly so when one considers that the event that changed the face of classical architecture, the discovery of the unique properties of the mortar based on the volcanic sand of west central Italy, took place little more than 20 miles away, at Puteoli (Pozzuoli), and that some of the outstanding early manifestations of its use are still to be seen at Baiae. At Pompeii there was evidently a considerable prejudice in favor of the familiar Greek construction traditions still to be overcome. It was only in such frankly innovating building types as the amphitheater and the bath building that the arch and the vault (the forms in which the new Roman "concrete" found its ideal expression) could be used freely and explicitly without doing violence to the conventions of established monumental taste. Viewed in context, the amphitheater in particular appears as one of the outstanding early examples of the emergence of an architectural aesthetic based on the candid exploitation of the visual properties of the arch. At the time this was something quite new in classical architecture.

Another conspicuous innovation, in this case well represented at Pompeii, was the emergence during the last two centuries B.C. of a number of the new building types that were to figure so prominently in the later history of Roman architecture. Pompeii, though surely not a major creative center in its own right, was in this respect right in the mainstream of progressive architectural thinking. The stone-built Amphitheater, the upstanding Roman-type theater, the Basilica, the bath building, the market building with a circular pavilion of the type here represented beside the Forum: all of these important and distinctive architectural types seem first to have taken monumental shape in southern Italy rather than in Rome itself, and to have been products of the new social needs and opportunities created by Roman wealth and power operating within a setting of sophisticated local building skills and technical know-how. Although the amphitheater as an institution came from central Italy, Rome itself did not have a permanent amphitheater building until 29 B.C.; the first permanent theater in the capital dates from 55 B.C. and the first public bath building not before 19 B.C. There had been a basilica, the Basilica Porcia, beside the Roman Forum as early at 184 B.C.; but even in this case there is good reason to believe that the prototype came from South Italy, and the Basilica beside the Forum at Pompeii is the earliest example surviving anywhere. In this respect Campania during the second and first centuries B.C. was fertile soil, and by the accident of its preservation Pompeii offers us a unique vision of Imperial Roman architecture in the making.

THE POMPEIAN HOUSE
AND GARDEN

No survey of the art of Pompeii can be complete without some knowledge of the wealthy houses in which so much of it found its natural place. Buildings such as the House of the Faun, the House of the Menander, and the House of the Vettii figured as prominently in the local artistic life of their time as they do today in the itinerary of the modern visitor. They were not, of course, the only type of urban dwelling. There were many small, simpler family houses; there were modest upper-story apartments, particularly in the later period; and there were one-room or two-room *tabernae* that opened directly off the street, and served both as workshops and as living quarters for the poorest families. But, given the family-centered nature of traditional Italic society, the large, well-to-do houses did in fact bulk far larger than their equivalents would do in any advanced modern society, or indeed in the later urban architecture of Rome itself; the owners of these houses constituted the major source of patronage for local artistic enterprise.

As an architectural form the Pompeian house was very much a phenomenon of its age and place, occupying a midway position between the great hall of archaic Italic practice and the luxurious town residences of the wealthy Roman families of the Imperial age. Like any such term, "the Pompeian house" represents an abstraction, a convenient label for a page of architectural history torn from what was in fact a continuously developing historical narrative: but the use of this term may be justified by the strong element of formal continuity that runs right through the three centuries and more separating the earliest from the latest surviving examples. It does, moreover, greatly simplify description. Although by the end of the period the names and functions of some of the rooms were changing or had become obsolete (as in our own times such names as "parlor," "powder room," and "cloak room"), it is still broadly possible to use the same terminology to describe the individual members of the whole series.

As late as the early second century B.C. a typical Pompeian atrium house such as the House of Sallust (VI. 2, 4) was still essentially an inward-facing building, enclosed by bare walls and lit almost exclusively from within. The dominant feature of the plan was a large centrally lit hall, the *atrium,* the roof of which might in earlier times still have taken on one of the several forms described by later writers, although by the second century B.C. it seems invariably to have been of "compluviate" form, sloping downward and inward toward a rectangular opening (*compluvium*) situated above a rectangular basin (*impluvium*), so as to admit more light and at the same time to replenish the cisterns that were the house's principal water supply.

Grouped around the atrium were the other rooms of the house. The entrance was originally set back within an entrance porch (*vestibulum*) beyond which lay a short corridor (*fauces*). To right and left were service rooms (in the House of Sallust their place was already taken by shops facing outward onto the street), and along the two longer sides of the atrium itself a series of small, square bedchambers (*cubicula*), in which the position of the couch was usually marked by the pattern of the floor and often also by the shape of the ceiling. Along the fourth side two lateral wings (*alae*) extended outward, giving access to a range of rather larger rooms. In the center, opposite the entrance and structurally open toward the main hall, from which it could be closed off by a wooden screen or a curtain, lay the *tablinum.* This was the principal reception room of the house and, unlike most of the other rooms, it was often lit by a window, which opened onto the garden plot (*hortus*) beyond. Of the two rooms on either side of it, one was often used as a dining room or *triclinium,* so named from the ⊓-shaped

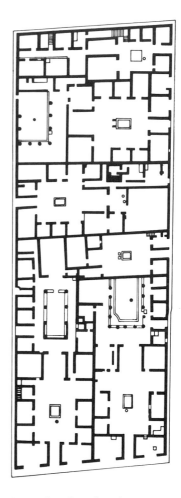

A typical residential insula (city block) VI, 13

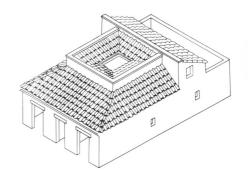

Restored view of an early atrium house

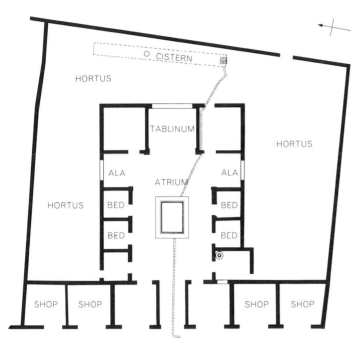

House of Sallust, second century B.C.

House of Sallust, A.D. 79

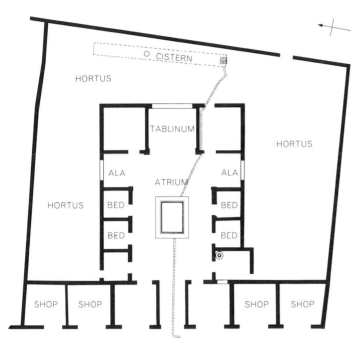

Atrium in the House of the Silver Wedding

arrangement of three couches (*klinai*) that constituted the normal dining pattern in classical times, and like the *cubicula* often identifiable from the layout of the floor patterns. Within the atrium one would have looked for such features as the family strongbox and the household shrine (*lararium*). Furnishing was by modern standards scanty, but it might include wooden couches and cupboards and small tables of wood or later of marble, as well as wooden doorways and screens. After dark the rooms were lit by means of oil lamps, often on tall bronze stands, and they were heated by braziers of bronze, iron, and terracotta.

This was the basic pattern of the atrium house, and with the passage of time it was developed and elaborated in a number of ways. The precise forms and layouts of such development obviously depended upon the particular circumstances of each house in relation to its neighbors, but once again the process can conveniently be summarized in terms of what was clearly felt to be a normal type.

The most important single innovation was a direct result of the ever-increasing exposure of Campania to the sophisticated civilizations of the Hellenistic world, where the standard type of wealthy house was one built around a rectangular, cloister-like, colonnaded courtyard known as the peristyle. These Hellenistic contacts made themselves felt at every level, notably in the character and wealth of the architectural detail and in the transformation of the old cavernous atrium by the incorporation of columnar supports for the central opening, at first four columns and later whole colonnades, until in extreme cases it came to resemble a miniature peristyle. But the most dramatic and far-reaching innovation was unquestionably the conversion of the old garden area beyond the house into a formal peristyle complex, accessible from the atrium by a corridor or corridors leading past the *tablinum*, which itself tended also to be opened up toward the peristyle.

For much of the year the rooms around the peristyle offered far more agreeable living conditions than the small, rather cramped rooms around the atrium, and there was an inevitable tendency for the main living rooms to migrate outward. One recurrent form, known as an *oecus* (a Greek name, which suggests that it was introduced in the same context as the peristyle itself), was an elaborately decorated room open toward the portico and often used as a fair-weather dining room. Another common innovation was the introduction of a private bath suite; yet another, wherever the slope of the ground involved a measure of terracing, was the introduction of a crypto-portico, a long, narrow, vaulted chamber or chambers, lit obliquely from above and useful for storage, or even as a hot-weather residential amenity. Above ground the open area of the peristyle was regularly equipped with fountains and pools, and with formal gardens in which plants and trees alternated with statuary and garden furniture.

The atrium-peristyle house needed plenty of space, and in the second century B.C. most of the wealthy householders could still achieve this by building out over their existing gardens. But in parts of the town one can already detect signs of what was to be a growing problem, that of increased population pressures and rising property values. Galleries and upper stories began to be added along the façade and around the atrium and, as street frontages became more valuable, more and more of the service rooms on either side of the main entrance were converted into independent single-room shops (*tabernae*) opening directly off the street, just as has happened to the frontages of so many of the palaces of post-medieval Italy, and for identical reasons.

Peristyle garden in the House of the Gilded Amorini (VI, 16, 7)

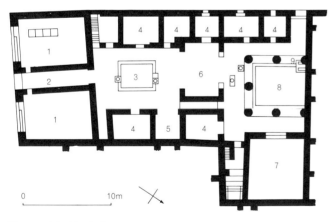

House of the Tragic Poet (VI, 8, 3),
an early peristyle plan

1. *Shops*
2. Fauces
3. *Atrium*
4. *Bedrooms*
5. Ala
6. Tablinum
7. Oecus
8. *Peristyle garden*
9. Lararium

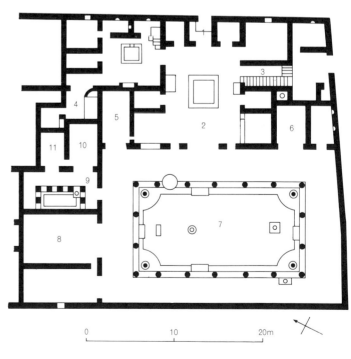

House of the Vettii, (VI, 15, 1),
a late peristyle plan

1. *Vestibule*
2. *Atrium*
3. *Staircase to upper story*
4. *Kitchen*
5. *Dining room (triclinium)*

6. *Dining room (triclinium,
    "Pentheus room")*
7. *Peristyle garden*
8. *Oecus*
9. *Small peristyle*
10. *Dining room/sitting room*
11. *Bedroom*

A third and more insidious change was inspired by the villas of the contemporary countryside. One of the more attractive aspects of Roman culture was its appreciation of natural beauty and of landscape. The town houses perforce looked inward toward their gardens, but by the second century B.C. it was already customary among well-to-do Romans also to maintain a country house (*villa*) — or indeed several of them. Although these were normally working farms (*villae rusticae*), many of them were also equipped to serve as occasional residences, and we regularly find these villas situated and designed so as to take full advantage of their setting, with terraces and garden rooms facing outward over the adjoining landscape. Within the towns scope for such development was obviously limited, but both at Pompeii and at Herculaneum we do find in the later period a number of fine houses terraced out over the walls so as to take full advantage of the views over the Bay of Naples, and during the first century B.C. the seaward façade of the Villa of the Mysteries was remodeled in the same sense. In practical terms, this opening up of the house was greatly facilitated by the widespread introduction of window glass, and although its full effects would not be felt in urban architecture until after A.D. 79, it was already a factor in the later planning of Pompeii.

Seaside villa landscape, in the House of Marcus Lucretius Fronto

The villas on the slopes of Vesuvius, at Boscoreale, for example, and at Boscotrecase, were of the sort described, centers of working estates that were also residences. But there were also the *villae marittimae*, the luxurious seaside residences that studded the coastline of the Bay of Naples ever since, in the first century B.C., Campania had become the preferred playground of the wealthy Roman. Inevitably their proximity affected standards of luxury and taste in the neighboring towns. Moreover, they were picked up by the painters of the Third Style wall paintings and used as one of the stock subjects for the smaller secondary panels of their large wall compositions. The seaside villa landscapes that one sees on the walls of a house such as that of Marcus Lucretius Fronto (see illustration) were *genre* pieces, but it was a *genre* rooted in actuality. Waterside villa platforms, jetties, harbors, single-storied or two-storied colonnaded façades with projecting wings or outcurving *belvedere* rooms, towers and balconies, temples and rustic shrines, grottoes, fountains, and statues: these were the commonplaces of a landscaped architecture as rich in contrived fantasy as any eighteenth-century English park. One of the sources of such paintings was undoubtedly a real, three-dimensional, luxury architecture, which itself owed much to what was obviously a very widely felt contemporary taste for romantic landscape — a taste that turns up again in the so-called sacro-idyllic landscapes and again in the conventions of the popular Egyptianizing "Nilotic" idiom. In painting we meet it already in the mythological landscapes of the late Second and early Third Styles of painting — the same trees and rocky outcrops, the same grottoes, the same towers, the same rustic shrines. Whatever the ultimate source of the individual motifs, these were all very much part of a contemporary Roman artistic fashion that affected architecture and painting alike.

Finally, a word about the gardens. In origin no doubt these were simply those parts of the individual building plots that were left over after the building of the houses, and were planted with fruit and vegetables for domestic consumption. In A.D. 79 there were still, behind the built-up street frontages, surprisingly large areas of open green, notably within the southeastern perimeter of the city, on either side of the Amphitheater and the Palaestra (which had no doubt been sited here because of the available open space). Here, as recent excavation behind the House of the Ship Europa (1, 15, 1) has shown, there were large

The upper garden terrace in the House of "Loreius Tiburtinus"; at the far end is the open-air dining room.

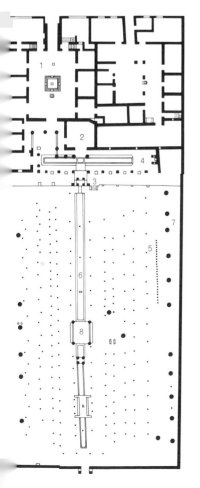

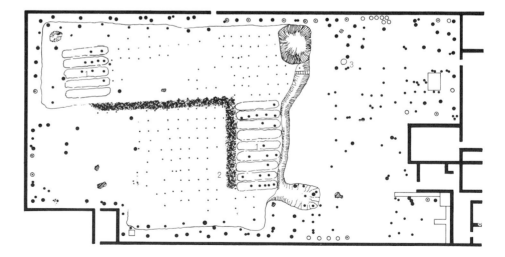

Plan of the House of "Loreius
Tiburtinus"

1. Atrium
2. Oecus
3. Peristyle garden terrace
4. Open air dining area
5. Line of plants in pots
6. Ornamental water channel
7. Large trees
8. Small pavilion

0   10   20m

Market garden in the House of
the Ship "Europa" (1, 15, 1).
Small dots indicate grapevine
roots; black circles indicate
roots of various sizes; empty
circles indicate plants in pots.
1. Vegetable gardens
2. Path
3. Water cistern

0   10m

stretches of market garden, in which vegetables were combined (as they still are in Campania today) with orderly rows of fruit trees and areas for bedding out young plants; there was also at least one sizable vineyard, in the block immediately north of the Amphitheater.

With time, however, and in the more densely populated quarters, there was an inevitable tendency for the garden to be absorbed within the architectural complex of the house itself. At one extreme were small, tree-planted courtyards, areas of shaded green upon which the occupants of the *tablinum* and the *triclinium* could look out: this was the logical development of the old Italic *hortus*. And at the other extreme, from the second century B.C. onward and, it seems, like the peristyle itself a newcomer from the Hellenistic East, we have the sort of highly organized, formal garden that one finds in the peristyle courtyards of such buildings as the House of the Vettii and the House of the Gilded Amorini.

It has long been known that these gardens were lavishly planted with trees and shrubs, and recent work is beginning to tell us a great deal not only about the layouts but also about the actual plants used. Not surprisingly, these included a great many of those still familiar in Campania today: olives, lemons, soft fruits, pomegranates, walnuts and filberts, chestnuts, and vines grown on trellises. Vegetables leave fewer traces that are readily identifiable, but here we have the evidence of wall painting and, most recently, a beginning of the results of the analysis of pollen remains. Paintings such as the garden room at Prima Porta (page 96) show that there were also cultivated garden flowers, but not, it seems, on any very substantial scale.

Perhaps the most surprising result of recent work is to show how large many of the trees were. Modern replanting has tended to follow the model of the later "Italian" garden, with low trimmed hedges and shrubs; and in the formal peristyle gardens, where the plants were a setting for fountains and statuary, something of the sort might indeed seem reasonable. But many of the smaller, courtyard gardens evidently followed simpler, more luxuriant patterns, including substantial trees. This has been demonstrated in the recently excavated House of Julius Polybius (IX, 13, 1-3), and also at Oplontis.

Within the town there was little room for landscaping: that had to be left to the villas of the seaside and the suburbs. But we do get a glimpse of it in the garden of the House of "Loreius Tiburtinus" (II, 1, 2), which sloped downhill from the Via dell'Abbondanza toward the open ground within the southern walls. Here the whole rear frontage of the house opened onto a transverse terrace, with a marble-lined water channel and a trellised pergola. At the east end of this terrace there was an open-air dining room, while a fountain in the middle dropped its water into a second, architecturally embellished water channel that ran down the length of the garden. Terrace and fountain basins were adorned with statuary, while serried lines of trees carried the eye down the garden toward the view across the Sarno plain and the mountains of the Sorrento peninsula beyond—a fine example of a studied formal design used to emphasize the beauties of natural landscape.

THE ECONOMY:
AGRICULTURE
AND INDUSTRY

Terracotta plaque set into a wall north of the Forum, showing two men carrying an amphora strung from a pole

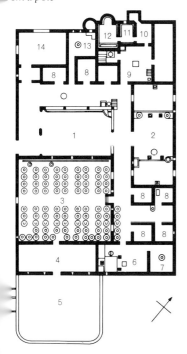

…n of a villa rustica at Boscoreale

  . Courtyard
  . Wine presses
  . Wine vats
  . Barn
  . Threshing floor
  . Oil press
  Olive crushing room
  Bedrooms
  Kitchen
  -12. Baths
  Bakery
  Dining room

The economy of Pompeii was based primarily on two factors: the boundless fertility of the Campanian soil and the town's position as the harbor for the whole area south and east of Vesuvius. Although industry was mainly geared to local needs, the proximity of large numbers of wealthy seaside villas must at the same time have furnished a steady market for surplus produce, for everyday tools and equipment, and for building materials. In addition to these local possibilities, Campanian prominence in the markets of the eastern Mediterranean offered rich outlets for spare capital, as well as numerous fringe opportunities for the smaller operators in which this region has always abounded and still abounds.

Fruits and vegetables of almost all sorts familiar in the area today (except, of course, for such post-Roman intruders as the potato and the tomato) are attested in the wall paintings and in many cases by the organic remains recovered during the recent excavations. In these, as in grain and other market produce, the city would have been self-sufficient. But the two outstanding agricultural products were undoubtedly wine and olive oil. Both of these, particularly the former, were widely exported, and they must between them have furnished a high percentage of the wealth of the rich landed families. Large numbers of wine amphoras have been found in southern France bearing the name of two of the prominent indigenous families, the Lassii and the Eumachii. Another of the leading local families, the Holconii, gave its name to a special quality of vine, while another prized vine was known simply as the Pompeian Vine (*vitis pompeiana*). The best known local wines came from the Sorrento peninsula and from Vesuvius; those of Pompeii itself were said to leave a hangover. The only surviving ancient picture of Vesuvius, from the household shrine of the House of the Centenary (see illustration), does portray the god of wine, Dionysus, decked with grapes, and beyond him the lower slopes of the mountain covered with trellised vines; the remains of the villas recovered on these slopes, like those of Boscoreale and Boscotrecase (see plan), show that they were not only the occasional residences of their rich owners but also the centers of working estates, equipped with all facilities for pressing wine and oil. Even within the city, excavation has recently revealed small vineyards, and the huge oil-storage jars are everywhere a familiar feature.

The one major exception to this predominantly agricultural, or agriculture-oriented, economy was the production of woolen goods. The wool was produced in the highlands of Samnium and Lucania, where some of the indigenous families still had ties and where many wealthy Romans had acquired large absentee estates. The family of M. Numistrius Fronto, for example, who was chief magistrate (*duovir*) in A.D. 2/3, evidently came from Numistro in northern Lucania (Muro Lucano, near Potenza) in the heart of the sheep-rearing country; and it was his widow, Eumachia, the heiress to a big local family, who built the large courtyard building near the southeast corner of the Forum to serve as the headquarters of the trade association (*collegium*) of the wool-traders and fullers. It was used among other things as a cloth market, and periodic auctions of raw wool were held in the forecourt, toward the Forum. The continuing importance of this woolen industry even after the earthquake of A.D. 62 is shown by the number of fulleries (*fullonicae*) that have been found in the city, some of them installed in what had previously been well-to-do private residences. The election posters, too, reveal the members of the association of fullers as active and influential supporters of the candidates for municipal office.

Dionysus and Vesuvius
Naples Museum

Feltmakers at work (painted on the outside wall of a shop on the Via dell' Abbondanza)

0   10m

Plan of a fuller's workshop installed in a private house (VI, 14, 21–22)

1. *Shop with treading vats and fuller's press*
2. *Kitchen*
3. *Atrium*
4–7. *Living quarters*
8. *Corridor full of fuller's earth*
9. *Peristyle with three large basins (A–C) for soaking the cloth, on three different levels, water draining from one to the next. D is a high walk at level of top of basins from which steps lead into the basins. E. Treading vats.*

The same election posters give us the names of a great many other trade associations, and these confirm the impression left by the excavated remains, namely that within Pompeii commerce was geared very largely to local needs. The associations named include agricultural laborers and smallholders, men engaged in various types of transport, dealers in poultry, fruit and vegetables, fishermen, bakers, goldsmiths. The list is not exhaustive—there is no mention, for example, of the important building and decorating trades—but it helps us to people the markets and the small one-room workshops in which, in the immemorial Mediterranean manner, many of them earned their livelihoods. A few local specialities went further afield. Cato, who farmed in northern Campania, advises sending to Pompeii for oil mills, or to Rufrius' yard at Nola. The building stone of the Sarno valley was shipped extensively to sites around the Bay of Naples, while the amphoras made in the local potteries traveled wherever their contents took them, including Spain, Gaul, and North Africa.

About industry it is less easy to generalize in terms that are readily comprehensible today. In the absence of mechanical power the factory even for a product with a world market, such as the red-gloss "terra sigillata" pottery of Arretium (Arezzo, in eastern Tuscany), was little more than a large group of related workshops, differing from those that supplied the local markets mainly in their number and organization. The only Campanian industry organized on this sort of scale about which we hear in the sources was the fine bronzework produced under the late Republic in and around Capua. It awaits detailed study, but it was evidently based on Greek experience and technical know-how, as already practiced in several well-known South Italian centers, notably Tarentum (Taranto), supported by ready access to the output of the Spanish mines, made available by Rome's defeat of Carthage in the Second Punic War. Already in the second century B.C. Cato advises going to Capua or Nola for bronze pails, water-jugs, and urns for oil or wine; and for a couple of centuries this area supplied much of the western Mediterranean, spreading its products up into central and northern Europe, often far beyond the Roman frontiers. At Pompeii itself considerable traces of bronze working have come to light outside the Vesuvius Gate; the Capuan factories and their Campanian subsidiaries must have been the source of a great deal of the fine bronzework in local circulation. Pottery was another flourishing local industry, both for domestic use and to supply the containers (*amphorae*) in which wine, oil, *garum,* and other local products could be stored and shipped.

Such in outline was the economy on which the manifest prosperity of late Republican and early Imperial Pompeii was based. But there are many signs that by the middle of the first century A.D. things were changing, and changing fast: the earthquake of A.D. 62 hastened, but was not itself the root cause of, what could well be termed a state of urban crisis. The prosperity of the recent past, based on Campania's privileged position in the markets of the Mediterranean world, was being rapidly eroded by the growing prosperity of many of the provinces. Spanish and North African oil were beginning to dominate the markets of the West. Gaul too was beginning to develop not only its own vineyards but also its own industries. Henceforth the bronzework of Capua found itself competing with workshops established in Gaul and, for the Danube market, in North Italy. A dramatic illustration of what this process of devolution could mean is provided by a crate of South Gaulish red-gloss pottery that was found at Pompeii, newly imported and not yet unpacked. Under Augustus the prototypes for such wares had been shipped from Italy all over the known world, from Britain to the Indian Ocean. But already under Tiberius an enterprising potter from Arezzo had set himself up in South France, nearer to his markets, and by A.D. 79 these South Gaulish wares were beginning to be shipped to Italy.

The results of this economic decline inevitably made themselves felt also in the social sphere. The established landed families were rapidly losing their virtual monopoly of local wealth and, with it, of local political office. During the last period of Pompeii we find their place increasingly taken by new men, many of them of quite recent servile origin. As we have seen (p. 44), awareness of some aspects of the process goes back at least to the beginning of the century; but while many of the new men no doubt retained their newly won family connections (it was common for patrons to invest capital in the enterprises of able freedmen), or indeed set about establishing themselves as landed proprietors, in the last phase of Pompeii there clearly was a considerable shift in both the distribution and the use of property. Some of the new men were very well-to-do: witness the reconstruction of the Temple of Isis after the earthquake at the expense of a man who had been born a slave. Nevertheless a surprising number of the old town houses were abandoned as residences and were being taken over piecemeal for commercial purposes. Of the private houses in the insula that contained the House of the Menander only one was actually being used as a private residence at the time of the eruption. The gentry were moving out. There was still vitality in the processes of municipal life, as the election posters show, but by A.D. 79 new social patterns were rapidly emerging.

Painting of a baker's shop
Naples Museum

Bakery of Modestus (VII, 1, 36)

CULTS AND BELIEFS

Lararium in the atrium of the House of the Menander

As might be expected in a society that was in a state of rapid transition, the religion of Pompeii during the last century and a half of its existence was a stream of many currents. The traditional state religion was one of practice rather than of religious experience. It satisfied certain enduring everyday needs both of the individual and of society; but in the absence of any consistent body of doctrine or of any fount of written authority comparable to the Bible, to the Koran, or to the works of Karl Marx, for example, it had little or nothing to offer those in search of higher truth. An old order was passing away, an order that was rooted in the needs of the family and of a simple agricultural community; and the new order that was to replace it, an order geared to the needs of the multinational society that came into being as a result of Alexander the Great's conquests, had still to take definitive shape. Everywhere we are confronted by a confusion of beliefs and practices. All that we can hope to do is to single out a few of the more consistent threads that went to make up the larger pattern.

One such thread was that of the popular beliefs and practices, many of them inherited from a remote past, which were, and were to remain, one of the enduring aspects of Mediterranean society. At one end of the scale there were the great gods of Olympus and their Italian counterparts, divinities whom the accidents of history and a powerful literary tradition had singled out for universal dominion; and at the other end there were the countless little local gods who so often lurk behind the well-known names. Great and small, together they represented the classical world's first attempt to come to terms with the forces of nature and the vagaries of human society. Like the local saints of Christian Italy (who were so often their lineal successors) they were the intermediaries to whom men turned when confronted by the hazards and seeming irrationalities of the world around them.

By comparison with this heritage from an older, simpler past the mystery religions were relatively recent. Classical Greece had had its Mysteries, but in the forms in which the Mystery religions made themselves most powerfully felt at Pompeii and elsewhere in contemporary Italy, they represent a fund of oriental religious experience to which the classical world fell heir as the result of Alexander the Great's conquest of the ancient East. More recent again, though derived ultimately from the same eastern sources, was the institution of the cult of the emperor as the symbol and formal embodiment of the well-being of the Roman state.

Few if any classical sites can equal Pompeii for the light they throw on religion at its popular, grass-roots level. The household shrines (*lararia*) that are such a prominent feature of the houses represent religion at its simplest and least articulate and yet, because it was obviously so much a part of everyday life, also at its most real. Traditional Roman religion was concerned with success, not sin: as Cicero remarks, "Jupiter" is called the Best and Greatest (*Optimus Maximus*) not because he makes us just or sober or wise, but because he makes us healthy, rich and prosperous." At every level of society religion was a matter of observance, not doctrine.

By Cicero's time the public face of religion was entirely in the hands of colleges of priests, prominent citizens who were elected or appointed to perform the proper ceremonials and rituals on behalf of the community they represented. Domestically the father of the family fulfilled the same office on behalf of the household under his care, offering daily prayers and gifts at the *lararium,* within which were displayed the figures of the traditional household gods, the *Lares* and the *Penates,* and of such other divinities as the family might hold in special

Terracotta wall plaques with a phallus

Priapus painted on the vestibule wall of the House of the Vettii

honor. Here too were performed the rituals associated with important family events, such as a boy's coming of age. These simple rituals were a part of daily life that no prudent Roman would have willingly neglected.

Yet another aspect of primitive religion that lived on into historic times was an emphasis on fruitfulness and reproduction, an idea closely associated in popular belief with that of good and evil fortune as active forces that had to be no less actively fostered or diverted. The Italian peasant who hangs a pair of horns at his roof tree, or who makes a gesture with his hand to ward off the evil eye, is acting out traditions that go right back to the patterns of belief natural to a primitive agricultural society, in which survival and fruitfulness are virtually synonymous. Many of the oldest Latin gods, such as Faunus, Silvanus, and Flora, had been concerned with aspects of agricultural or pastoral plenty; objects such as wreaths of fruit or horns of plenty (*cornucopiae*) were among the enduring commonplaces of religious symbolism; and the *phallus* (the extended male reproductive organ) is apt to turn up in (to modern eyes) the most disconcerting contexts: on a plaque at a street corner, on the statue of a minor rustic divinity, in the entrance lobby of a wealthy villa. The owner of the House of the Vettii, one of the wealthiest houses of the last period of the city's history, saw nothing incongruous in displaying in the entrance a figure of Priapus with a gigantic male organ being weighed in a pair of scales, as a symbol and safeguard of the prosperity of his house. Fruitfulness was an accepted and important fact of life.

Man's devotion to the little gods, even when they bore great names, is easy enough to understand. But what of the great Olympian gods—Zeus, Aphrodite, Apollo, Poseidon, and their fellows—whose quarrels and whose amatory exploits fill the pages of classical literature, and who figure so prominently on the walls of Pompeii? The Romans freely identified them with the gods of their own pantheon. But could any intelligent society take them seriously as divinities? Or were they little more than literary and artistic conventions, comparable to Milton's nymphs and shepherds or the Venuses of Botticelli and Correggio?

There is no simple, all-embracing answer. The old, anthropomorphic religion of the Greek Olympian gods was in truth long dead, killed finally by the collapse of the institutions that had given it life, and buried forever beneath the elaborate edifice of mythology that literature and art had built up around it. But despite the massive Hellenization of Roman educated society, and the consequent transference to many of the old Italian gods of the attributes and characteristics of their Greek counterparts, so far as the traditional religion of Italy was concerned these were superficial changes. Jupiter might be portrayed in the guise of Zeus, but it was as the time-honored guardian divinity of Rome, whose temple on the Capitol was at once the symbol and the enduring guarantee of Roman prosperity, that he continued to head the Roman pantheon. When in 80 B.C. a colony of Roman citizens was established at Pompeii, one of the first acts of the new regime was to convert the existing temple of Jupiter (Zeus) at the head of the Forum into a temple of Jupiter Optimus Maximus Capitolinus. This was not just a token of Roman political dominion: in terms of traditional Roman belief, it was the obvious and natural way of ensuring the continued welfare of Pompeii within the larger polity of Rome, of which Pompeii had now become a part.

[*text continues on page* 81]

Facing page:
208
Statuette of Aphrodite with Priapus
Fine white, translucent marble, possibly from Paros
Height 62 cm
Found on a table in the *tablinum* of House II, 4, 6

The group represents Aphrodite preparing to bathe (see No. 209), raising her left foot to remove her sandal and resting her left forearm on the head of a small figure of the god Priapus; a tiny Eros sits below her foot. Aphrodite's left hand, now missing, was carved in a separate piece of marble. The group is remarkable for th extensive remains of gilding as well as some traces of paint. In addition to her necklace, armbands, a bracelet, and gilded sandals, Aphrodite wears an exiguous, bikini-like harne Her eyes are inlaid with cement and glass paste The hair and pubic hair of both main figures were once gilded (the dark red paint now visibl was the underlay), and there are traces of red paint on the lips of the goddess and on the tree stump that supports the group; of green on Priapus' pedestal; and of black on the base.

The statuette was found in the large comple of rented accommodation, including a bath-ho and tavern, known as the villa of Julia Felix. *Graffiti* and other finds suggest that this part o the complex may have served as a brothel in th last years of the town's history.

156
Dionysiac scene in marble intarsia
Slate and colored marbles
Length 67 cm, height 23 cm
From the House of the Colored Capitals
(VII, 4, 31–51)

One of a pair of Dionysiac scenes found in the *tablinum,* where they were probably used on the walls as panel pictures *(pinakes).* On the left a maenad dances in ecstasy, with torch and *tympanon;* on the right a satyr clutches a *thyrsus* and is waving a goat skin; and in the center is a small shrine.

The technique is that of intarsia, a sophisticate variant of *opus sectile,* composed of shaped and inscribed pieces of colored marble (*giallo antico* from Africa, *fior di persico* from Euboea, and *paesina verde* and *palombino* from Italy) cut out and fitted into a slate panel. Third quarter of the first century A.D.

247
Wall painting: entertainment after a meal
Width 46 cm, height 44 cm
From House I, 3, 18 at Pompeii

The central panel picture (now rather faded) of a Third Style wall.

Facing page:
192
Wall painting: Dionysiac cult objects
Height 46 cm, width 46 cm
From Pompeii

Along a narrow ledge at the top of a small flight of steps are, from left to right: a tambourine; a wicker basket, on which are a drinking horn draped with a panther skin, a drinking cup, and a *thyrsus;* and a second, taller drinking cup decorated with vine leaves. On the steps are a spray of bay, a pair of cymbals, and a small panther grappling with a snake. All these object are associated with the cult of Dionysus.

141
**Wall painting: medallion with busts of
Dionysus and a Maenad**
Diameter 44.5 cm
From Herculaneum

Dionysus, god of wine and of ecstatic liberation,
is shown with a wreath of grapes and vine leaves;
in his right hand he holds a drinking cup
(cantharus) and in his left, resting against his

shoulder, the characteristic Dionysiac staff, or
thyrsus. Behind him, her hand on his shoulder,
is one of his attendant devotees, a maenad; she
wears a mantle and earrings, with flowers in
her hair.

52
Wall painting: Phaedra and Hippolytus
Width 1.03 m, height 1.04 m
from Herculaneum

Phaedra, wife of Theseus, King of Athens,
had conceived a guilty passion for her stepson,
Hippolytus, a passion that he rejected; whereupon Phaedra accused him of trying to seduce
her. He was subsequently killed while out hunting, and she hanged herself. In this painting
Phaedra's old nurse tells Hippolytus of her mistress's love, as he is setting out for the hunt. The
scene, of which there were several variant copies
at Pompeii, is based on a Hellenistic original,
which in turn was inspired by Euripides' tragedy
Hippolytus.

143
Wall painting: Pan and Hermaphroditus
Width 1.25 m, height 74 cm
From the atrium of the House of the
Dioscuri (VI, 9, 6)

Part of the upper zone of a Fourth Style scheme,
from above the doorway leading from the *fauces*
into the atrium. Hermaphroditus, one of the
more curious by-products of Greek mythology,
was a minor divinty of bisexual form, with
female breasts and male genitals. In this picture
he is seated by a pool, and Pan, aroused by his
apparently female charms, has just discovered
his mistake. Beyond Pan is a tower within a
square enclosure, set in a rocky landscape. On
the right is a statue of Priapus, standing on a
pedestal and holding a cornucopia.

299
Wall painting of a chariot race
Height 57 cm, length 92 cm
Probably from the House of the Quadrigae
(VII, 2, 25), although the inventory books say
from Herculaneum

The picture, which is bordered below by a
red line but is certainly incomplete above and
to the left, shows four four-horsed racing
chariots (quadrigae) and, top left, the legs of
the horses of a fifth. The drivers (aurigae)
stand, as was customary, on a very light two-
wheeled frame, dressed in short tunics. For protection in the event of a crash (and these were
common) they wear tight-fitting leather helmets
and a harness of leather thongs on body and legs.
On the white ground below the picture there
are faint traces of an inscription painted in
large letters, which suggests that it comes from
a street-front, perhaps of a shop or tavern.

There was no provision for chariot-racing
at Pompeii itself, but many cities both in Italy
and in the provinces did possess a *circus* or
hippodrome, and as a spectator sport it rivaled
and eventually superseded gladiatorial contests.

It was organized into teams, or factions, the
support for which was Empire-wide. At first
there were only two factions, the Reds and the
Whites, but early in the first century A.D. two
more were added, the Greens and the Blues. In
the long run this proved to be too much for the
Romans, who at heart were as clearly two-
faction in racing as the Americans and the
British are two-party in politics, and by the end
of the second century A.D. the Blues had absorbed
the Reds, and the Greens the Whites, a situation
that greatly facilitated the expression of rival
enthusiasms. It was a clash between the Blues
and the Greens that in January 512 reduced the
center of Constantinople to ashes, leaving at
least thirty thousand dead behind it — an all-time
record for active spectator participation.

Following page:
199
**Wall painting from a household shrine
(lararium)**
Width 1.83 m, height 1.28 m
Found 6 June 1761 in VIII, insula 2 or 3

The painting is divided into two registers.
In the upper register, below three garlands, is a
scene of sacrifice. The *genius,* or presiding
divinity of the household, with head veiled and
bearing a cornucopia, symbolic of plenty, holds
out a dish (patera) over a marble altar. He is
attended by a small boy carrying a fillet (a wreath,
with ribbons for tying) and a platter; opposite
him a musician plays the double pipes, beating
time with a wooden clapper beneath his left foot,
while a slave brings forward a pig for sacrifice.
On either side stand the two Lares of the household, pouring wine from a drinking horn, or
rhyton, into a small wine bucket, or *situla.* In
the lower register two serpents approach the
offerings (of fruit?) upon an altar. Together with
the setting of rich vegetation, they symbolize the
fertility of nature and the bounty of the earth
beneath.

241

Large painted panel with still life (right half)
Height 74 cm, width 114 cm
From the *triclinium* on the west side of the
garden, which lies within the property *(praedia)*
of Julia Felix (II, 4, 3)

This still life, which is unusually large, comes
from the upper part of the Fourth Style walls of
a dining room.

A raised block carrying a large glass bowl full
of fruit (apples, pomegranates, grapes, figs). At
a lower level, a pottery vase containing dried
fruit (prunes?) and, leaning against it, a small
amphora-shaped jar, its lid tightly sealed by
means of cords attached to the handles.

238

Fish mosaic
Originally about 90 cm square
From House VIII, 2, 16

A studio piece made of very fine tesserae, laid
within a tray-like frame of terracotta, for use as
the central panel *(emblema)* of a larger, less delicate pavement, the design of which is not know
It probably belonged initially to House VIII, 2,
and was reused when this was rebuilt in the ear
Empire and incorporated in this much larger
House VIII, 2, 16.

Against a black background is displayed a
gallery of edible sea creatures, portrayed with
a lively naturalism that enables most of them to
be identified, in almost all cases, with species
still found and fished in the Bay of Naples. Am
the more familiar are octopus, squid, lobster,
prawn, eel, bass, red mullet, dogfish, ray, wrass
and a murex shell. The inclusion in the left margin of a small stretch of rocky landscape, which
is quite out of character, is perhaps to be explained as a fill-in taken from a different source

240
Four still life panels
Width 154 cm, height 37 cm
From Herculaneum

Each of these panels was originally the center-piece of a large panel in a Fourth Style wall, as in the peristyle of the House of the Dioscuri. After being cut out, they were framed together to form a frieze. The first two are very different in style from the other two.
a. A plucked chicken or turkey, hung by its feet, and a rabbit hung by one forepaw.
b. Left, strung from a ring by its beak, a partridge. Right, a pomegranate and an apple.
c. Upper shelf, thrushes. Lower shelf, six pink mushrooms.
d. Upper shelf, two birds, probably partridges. Below, two eels.

242
Three painted still life panels
Width 129 cm, height 41 cm
From Herculaneum

Each of these panels was originally the center-piece of a large panel in a Fourth Style wall (cf. No. 241). After being cut out they were framed together to form a frieze.
a. Young bird and a light-colored pottery jug, over the mouth of which is placed a glass beaker with rilled decoration of a type frequently found in Campania and possibly manufactured at Puteoli (Pozzuoli). On the shelf above are in-distinct objects: leaves, material, or possibly sheets of tripe.
b. Silver vase, with a small bird perched on its tall handle; a trident; seafood and shellfish *(frutta di mare)*, including murex shells; and a large crayfish. On the shelf above, two cuttlefish.
c. A rabbit nibbling at a bunch of grapes and a dead partridge hanging from a ring. In the window, a large red apple.

43

**Composite picture made up of four separate
fragments taken from Fourth Style walls**
Width 49 cm, height 43 cm
The writing materials and the still life came
from Herculaneum, the other two from somewhere in the Vesuvius area.

A silver urn, probably from the upper zone
of a wall.

Left, two book-scrolls of papyrus, one half-
unrolled; the titles, on little tags, hang from the
wooden baton on which the papyrus is rolled.
Right, a diptych, or wooden two-leafed writing
tablet (as No. 17).

Landscape: a rustic shrine with figures.

Half of a still life panel, similar to Nos.
240–242: an apple, a pear, and a pomegranate.

302
Terracotta statue of an actress
Height 1.11 m
Found with No. 301

The mask, shown fastened on with a band decorated with little flowers, is that proper to a courtesan in tragedy. The figure, whose left hand was already damaged in antiquity, was colored. There are extensive remains of the white underlay and traces of brown paint on the hair and of blue and red on the drapery.

Facing page:
309
Wall painting: tragic mask of a youth
Length 62 cm, height 62 cm

One of four theatrical masks from the House of the Stags at Herculaneum, where they constituted the lower parts of four of the vertical members dividing the middle zone of the Fourth Style scheme into panels. Each is shown placed at the head of the steps leading up onto a stage, within a frame of garlands with Dionysiac attributes.

[*text continued from page 64*]

Facing page:
305
Mosaic panel: rehearsing for a Satyr Play
Width 55 cm, height 54 cm
From the *tablinum* of the House of the Tragic
Poet (VI, 8, 5)

The rehearsal for a Greek Satyr Play, the characteristic postlude for a Greek dramatic trilogy. The action takes place in front of an Ionic portico hung with *oscilla* (see No. 69) and draped with wreaths and fillets, above which is an attic façade decorated with pilasters, four large golden vessels, and a pair of herm-like musicians. The bald and bearded figure wearing a Greek mantle (*himation*) and sandals is the chorus master, possibly the dramatist himself. He watches two actors wearing goatskin loincloths, who appear to be rehearsing dance steps to the notes of the double pipes played by a richly robed and garlanded musician (who would himself have appeared on the stage). On the right an attendant is helping another actor into a shaggy Silenus costume. Behind the seated figure, on a pedestal, is a male tragic mask, and at his feet a female tragic mask and a Silenus mask.

What had changed was not the substance of traditional Roman religion, but the outward symbols by which its meaning could be expressed, whether in art or in literature. When Augustus built a state temple in honor of his own chosen guardian divinity, Apollo, or of the divinity who personified the military might of Rome, Mars the Avenger, it was as natural to have the cult statue carved in terms of contemporary Hellenizing taste as it was for Donatello or Carpaccio to portray Saint George as a youthful knight in contemporary armor. We meet the same phenomenon all the way down the social scale. Trimalchio, the parvenu millionaire of Petronius' *Satyricon,* had himself portrayed on the walls of his house as protected and sustained by Mercury, the god of commerce; at Pompeii we have an actual illustration of just such a situation. On the two doorposts of a dyer's establishment in the Via dell'Abbondanza are shown, respectively, Mercury and Venus, of whom the latter was doubly appropriate, both as the patron of a business that dealt in feminine adornment and as the patron goddess of Pompeii. Mercury is shown in the traditional guise of the Greek Hermes, staff and money-bag in hand, stepping from his temple to bring his blessings to the house; Venus, on the other hand, appears in one of her more exotic manifestations, as Aphrodite-Isis, riding in triumph in a chariot drawn by four elephants and escorted by the personification of the city bearing horns of plenty. The familiar images of the old gods, and of some of the newer gods too, had become a conventional language in which anybody might express his own individual hopes and interests; and it was because of the very familiarity of those images that they were able to convey their meaning.

With the mystery religions we enter a very different world of ideas. Whereas traditional religion had been a matter of influencing the higher powers through a discreet mixture of propitiation, flattery, and ritual observance, the mystery religions all in varying degrees envisaged the possibility of man's entering into some more direct relationship with the sources of divine power, and thus of obtaining special favor in either this world or the next, or both. To achieve this state one underwent some form of initiation, at which a "mystery" was revealed, and through which one became a member of an inner communion, with all its privileges and its obligations.

In the classical world, as elsewhere, the basis for such a relationship had existed since long before the dawn of written history. In any agricultural society one of the earliest subjects of religious speculation was almost bound to be the cycle of the seasons and of the death and rebirth of the crops upon which man's whole existence depended: the notion of the seasonal death or rebirth of some divine embodiment of these events is one of the commonplaces of primitive religion everywhere. In Greece the central figure in this annual drama was Demeter, goddess of crops and in particular of corn, whose daughter Kore, or Persephone, was abducted by the god of the underworld, whence through the intervention of Zeus she was each year restored for a spell of life in this world. The center of the cult of Demeter was Eleusis in Attica, where each year at the appropriate seasons the story was enacted symbolically in the famous Mysteries. The archaeological evidence at Eleusis appears to indicate continuity since Mycenaean times; the story (and by clear implication the Mysteries themselves) had already taken near-definitive shape by the time it first appears in literature in the Homeric *Hymn to Demeter,* composed probably around 600 B.C.

At what stage and in what measure the notion developed that the individual initiate himself underwent some form of divine rebirth and an assurance of a blessed afterlife it is very hard to determine. To ourselves, the heirs to a Christian

Temple of Jupiter Capitolinus at the northern end of the Forum

Aphrodite-Isis riding in an elephant quadriga

Isis-Fortuna from the cookshop IX, 7, 21/22
Naples Museum

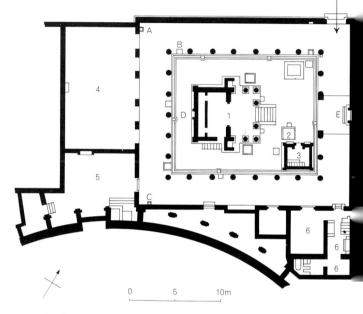

0   5   10m

Temple of Isis   1. *Temple*
2. *Main altar*
3. *Building with water tank*
4. *Meeting hall*
5. *Initiation chamber*
6. *Priests' lodging*

A. *Statue of Venus*
B. *Statue of Isis (no. 191)*
C. *Herm of Norbanus Sorex*
D. *Statue of Dionysus*
E. *Shrine of Harpocrates*

culture within which the concept of individual redemption is central, it is not easy to envisage the attitudes of mind of a world where such a concept was alien; but the weight of evidence is that at Eleusis it was in fact quite a latecomer, probably introduced by assimilation with the ideas of the other mystery cults. The Eleusinian story plays only a very modest part in the funerary art of Rome, which is our richest single source for the strength and nature of such beliefs in later antiquity. Instead, we are confronted by the stories and the symbols of the mystery cults of Asia Minor, Syria, and Egypt: the Great Mother (Cybele) and Attis, Dionysus (in one of his several aspects), Sabazios, Aphrodite-Astarte and Adonis, Isis, Mithras, and a host of lesser divinities.

The content and moral tone of these religions varied greatly, and Christian apologists both in antiquity and since have been at pains to emphasize the differences between Christianity and the mystery religions. There were indeed substantial differences, but there were also a great many resemblances. Jesus' reply to his disciples when they asked him why he taught in parables: "Because it is given unto you to know the mysteries of the kingdom of Heaven, but to them it is not given" (Matthew XIII.II); or Saint Paul's, "Behold, I show you a mystery . . . the trumpet shall sound and the dead shall be raised incorruptible" (I Corinthians XV. 51) — these were words that would have been immediately intelligible to the followers of many other cults. Sacramental rites, including initiation and ritual meals; a theology based on the death and resurrection of a member of the divine family; belief in the readiness of divinity to intervene on behalf of those human individuals who were ready to accept divine authority, a belief often coupled with an emphasis on purity and morality rather than on the performance of ritual acts — in a great many respects Christianity and the mystery religions followed parallel paths.

The most obvious and significant difference was that Christianity, the child of Judaism, held itself rigidly apart from all other creeds, whereas most of the mystery religions happily gathered in all and sundry as manifestations of one and the same divine spirit. One of the most moving passages in classical literature is where Lucius, the hero of Apuleius' second-century A.D. romance, the *Metamorphosis,* calls in his trouble upon the Queen of Heaven (Isis), "whether thou art Ceres . . . or Venus . . . or Diana . . . or Proserpine . . . by whatever form of divinity, by whatever ritual, in whatever shape it is right to call upon thee." In her reply Isis acknowledges these and many other forms of her godhead, adding that "It is the Egyptians who call me by my true name, Isis." Here, out of the welter of ancient cults, we see the emergence of the concept of a single, ecumenical, all-embracing divinity. Christianity chose a simpler, more direct road to monotheism. But in the event, as it matured, even Christianity had to develop such doctrines as the Trinity, the special status of the Mother of God, and the communion of the saints. Old beliefs have their own ways of creeping back. As the heirs to a Christian culture, we ourselves have no difficulty in understanding the contemporary appeal of the mystery religions.

It was no doubt to her readiness to merge with the established forms of traditional religion that Isis owed something of her popularity at Pompeii. In the household shrines (*lararia*) it is exceptional for Isis and her co-divinities to usurp altogether the place of the traditional household gods, but they do very commonly occupy a place side by side with them. Isis in particular, in the guise of the Roman Fortuna, is found watching over every aspect of daily life. In a cookshop in Region IX (insula 7, 21/22) the owner, not content with the traditional *lararium* in front, had a second shrine painted on the wall leading to the

83

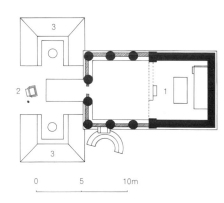

Temple of Dionysus, at S. Abbondio, near Pompeii

1. *Temple*
2. *Altar*
3. *Ritual banqueting couches*

lavatory, in which we see the two serpents characteristic of such shrines, a gracious Isis-Fortuna, and the figure of a man relieving himself. At its most elementary, Roman popular religion could indeed be severely practical.

For a truer assessment of the significance of the mystery religions, we do of course have to look to their more organized manifestations, and here there can be no possible doubt that of the mystery religions current in Italy in the period before A.D. 79 the most popular and widely practiced was that of Isis and her consort Serapis (the Egyptian Osiris). Although the existing buildings of the Iseum at Pompeii all date from the period between A.D. 62 and 79, they followed closely the lines of a predecessor that was already established there before the foundation of the colony in 80 B.C. It took the form of an enclosed precinct, within which the temple, a rather exotic stuccoed and gaily painted version of a small classical temple, stood on a high platform, facing eastward down the axis of a peristyle courtyard toward a shrine in honor of the third member of the divine family, the child god Harpocrates (the Egyptian Horus). In the southeast corner of the courtyard there was a smaller building, with access to a subterranean vaulted chamber in which there was a tank, thought to have contained holy water from the Nile. Opening off the south portico, behind this building, there was a lodging for the resident priest, and at the far west end, behind the temple, two rooms that had evidently been added at some later date, at the expense of the Samnite-period *gymnasium*. The larger of these was elaborately decorated and served probably as a place of reunion and, very possibly, for the service of the ritual meals, which constituted an important part of the cult. The smaller, entered by a small separate door, seems to have been used at night (in it were found eighty-four small lamps), and it may well have been the scene of the dramatic initiation ceremonies that played an important part in this and other mystery cults.

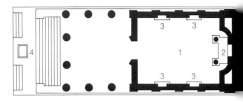

Temple of Fortuna Augusta

1. *Temple*
2. *Cult statue*
3. *Statue niches*
4. *Altar*

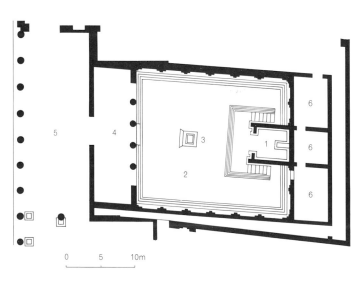

Temple of Vespasian

1. *Temple*
2. *Courtyard*
3. *Altar*
4. *Vestibule*
5. *Forum portico*
6. *Sacristies and storerooms*

Altar carved with a scene of sacrifice (no. 3 on plan)

At the moment of excavation in 1764-1765 the walls of these buildings were still covered with paintings (the illustration is one of many sad reminders of how much was lost in that early work) and although the cult statues had been removed, the altars and most of the temple vessels and fittings were still in place. The central mysteries of Isiac spiritual experience are probably lost forever. But the Isiac religion was also one of elaborate ceremonial observance; here for once, in the temple at Pompeii, classical literature and the archaeological remains converge to give us a vivid glimpse of the daily rituals of one of the most powerful precursors and rivals of early Christianity.

Campania's mercantile connections and the large numbers of resident slaves and freedmen of Greek or Asiatic origin together made it fertile ground for the introduction of non-Italian religions, and there are in fact at Pompeii scattered traces of many such (for example, Cybele and Sabazius). But the only one to have taken a hold at all comparable to the cult of Isis was that of Dionysus (Bacchus) who, though long an adopted member of the classical Greek pantheon, was in origin a stranger from the lands to the north and east of the Aegean (Thrace and Phrygia) and one who had far too many disturbing overtones ever to be fully absorbed within it. Visitors to the "Thracian Gold" exhibition will recall the opulent drinking services of the Thracian devotees. But although Dionysus is best known as the god of the grape and of wine, he did in fact represent a very wide variety of religious experience, ranging from the uninhibited, ecstatic possession so vividly portrayed in Euripides' *Bacchae* to the sort of fine-drawn mystic experience to which so much later Roman art bears witness. His was a complex religious personality, and an aspect of it that bulks very large in art is its intimate association with the origins of Greek drama. It was in the Theater of Dionysus, on the slopes of the Acropolis at Athens, that the plays of Aeschylus, Sophocles, and Euripides were first performed, and the repertory of later classical art of all periods is filled with motifs that derive from this association.

In the absence of any substantial body of doctrinal or liturgical Dionysiac writing, the precise meaning of any particular archaeological manifestation can often only be a matter of informed guesswork, but it does seem that at Pompeii one would have encountered several distinct layers of Dionysiac belief and practice. One was that of domestic religion. In a town whose prosperity was so closely linked with the wine trade, it is hardly surprising that many individuals should, like the owner of the House of the Centenary (IX, 8, 3), have chosen to put themselves under the personal protection of the god of wine. Another aspect of Dionysiac worship, based presumably on the rituals inherited from Greece, was that practiced by the community of believers who established the small temple found and excavated outside the walls at S. Abbondio. At yet another level of sophistication were the rites and rituals of which the walls of the Villa of the Mysteries offer so tantalizing a glimpse. Here the worship of Dionysus was plainly a "mystery" based upon one of the primeval aspects of his personality, as a god of vegetation, of seasonal death and rebirth, and of reproduction. Common to all these layers of observance and belief was a symbolic language that was remarkably durable and pervasive. Grapes and vine scrolls, pine cones, ivy leaves, satyrs and maenads, panthers, theatrical masks, certain forms of drinking vessels: these are among the commonplaces of Pompeian art, so common indeed that they often seem to have been used as almost purely decorative motifs, with very little reference to their symbolic meaning.

What of Jews and Christians? Of Saint Paul, voyaging from Malta to Rome in A.D. 62, it is recorded that ". . . on the second day we came to Puteoli. There we found brethren, and were invited to stay with them seven days" (Acts 28.13-14). Members of this harbor-town Jewish community could well have had connections in Pompeii, and it is just possible that among them there might have been Christian sympathizers. But that is really as much as one can say. If there were, they have left (and indeed at this early date they could have left) no tangible trace that we can recognize. The romantically minded will do better to rest content with the pages of Bulwer Lytton.

The third strand in the religious life of Pompeii in its later years was that of the Imperial cult. The notion of the ruler as a divine being may seem strange to modern thinking, but it was one very widely held in antiquity, and it was one with which the Hellenistic monarchs had found it both prudent and profitable to come to terms. For a society within which the formal observances of state religion were a necessary condition of the welfare of the community, it was indeed a logical function of kingship to have a direct line to the sources of divine authority, and in the eastern provinces Roman rulers, from Caesar onward, accepted divine honors as a matter of course. Italy, with its long republican traditions, was not yet ripe for the overt, direct worship of the reigning emperor, but it was very ready to accept the sort of polite fictions of which Augustus was master. By getting divine honors conferred upon the dead Caesar, he became himself the son of, and successor to, a god; and within a generation cults in honor of his *genius,* his *numen,* and other similar personifications of his position as head of the Roman state were springing up all over Italy. At Pompeii the building shortly before 2 B.C. of an official temple in honor of the Divine Providence (*Fortuna*) of Augustus is typical, and there is an inscription (*CIL* X. 896) that records the building of a second shrine, dedicated in this case, it seems, to Augustus himself.

The establishment of these cults was clearly in the first instance a demonstration of loyalty, which might reasonably be expected to yield a dividend of Imperial favor; and it is significant in this respect that one of the very few new buildings put up in Pompeii in the difficult times following the earthquake of A.D. 62 was a small temple beside the Forum in honor of Vespasian and the new Flavian dynasty. But they also served another purpose. Whereas the major priesthoods were, in effect, elected magistracies and were held by such prominent citizens as Marcus Holconius Rufus (page 39) and his brother Celer, who were among the first priests (*sacerdotes*) of the Augustan cult, the day-to-day administration of the cult could be put in the hands of freedmen (and in one instance also of trusted slaves), at first as clients of the wealthy families, but before long as well-to-do citizens in their own right, thus providing a healthy outlet for the social ambitions of a new and rapidly growing class in the body politic—and a means of tapping their new-won wealth for the benefit of the community. The freedmen *Augustales* occupied a position of status and privilege second only to that of the municipal senate, the *ordo decurionum.* The *ministri Augusti* and the *ministri Fortunae Augustae* were smaller fry. Two of the three men named as *ministri Augusti* in a Pompeian inscription were still slaves. Their appointment throws a vivid light on Rome's extraordinary ability to attract and absorb the talents and loyalties of a potentially troublesome minority.

ENTERTAINMENT, SPORT, AND LEISURE

Hot room (caldarium) *in the Forum Baths, Pompeii*

Terracotta *telamons flanking cupboard niches in the walls of the warm room* (tepidarium), *Forum Baths*

The public provision for exercise and entertainment at Pompeii faithfully reflects the city's mixed Greek and Italic heritage. At one end of the scale we have the public exercise grounds (*palaestrae*) that were the direct successors to the Greek *gymnasia*, that is to say places where a young man might pursue the physical excellence that was such an important part of his education. At the other extreme we have the Amphitheater, an arena for brutal spectator sports, which took formal architectural shape in Campania, but embodied far older Italic traditions to which Greece was a stranger; in between the two we have such buildings as the theaters and the bath buildings, which represent Greek traditions modified to suit Italic and Roman ways.

The old Samnite-period *palaestra*, beside the Theater, was in all but name a Greek *gymnasium*—a rectangular courtyard surrounded by elegant Doric porticoes, with a row of rooms opening off one short side. At some later date one end of it was annexed to allow for an extension of the Temple of Isis, but by this time its place had been taken by the vast new *palaestra*, undated but almost certainly an Augustan building, which lay immediately to the west of the Amphitheater. This was a huge rectangular open space, three acres in extent and enclosed on three sides by porticoes. It was shaded by orderly rows of large plane trees and in the center there was a swimming pool (*natatio*), the whole complex forming a magnificent public setting for such athletic sports as running, jumping, throwing the discus, wrestling, and swimming. There was a *palaestra* of comparable proportions at Herculaneum but, before the time of Nero, nothing of the sort in Rome. This was a specifically Campanian innovation.

Another, and in Roman terms more orthodox, development from the old Greek *gymnasium* was its incorporation within the newly evolving type of the Roman bath building—"Roman" because it was the Romans who completed its development and carried it with them to the remotest corners of the empire. But we now know that both the technology of the Roman bath building and the social habits of which it was an expression first took shape in Campania. The first public bath building in Rome was not built before 19 B.C., whereas there were already two in Samnite Pompeii a century earlier. Recent excavations

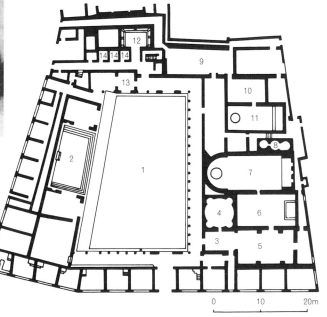

Plan of the Stabian Baths

1. Palaestra
2. *Swimming pool* (natatio)
3. *Entrance hall*
4. *Cold bath* (frigidarium; *formerly a hot sweating room,* laconicum)
5. *Undressing room* (apodyterium)
6. *Warm room* (tepidarium)
7. *Hot room* (caldarium)
8. *Furnaces*
9. *Women's* apodyterium
10. *Women's tepidarium*
11. *Women's caldarium*
12. *Latrine*
13. *Bath supervisor's office*
14. *Individual "hip bath" cubicles*

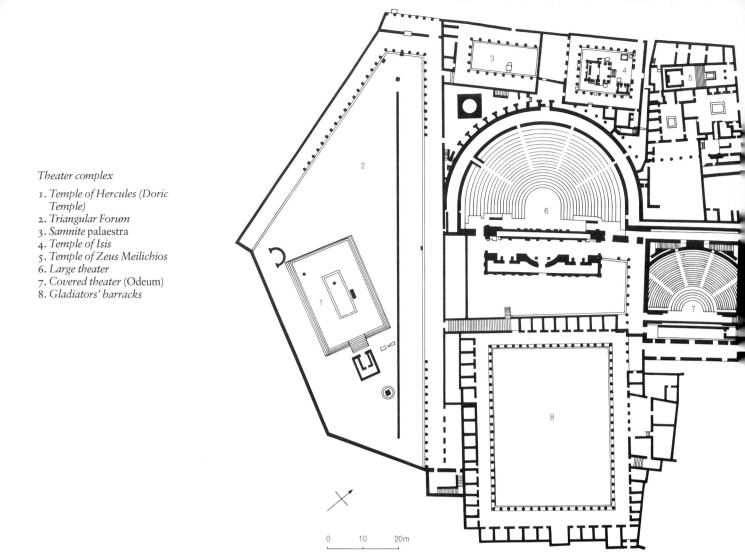

Theater complex

1. *Temple of Hercules (Doric Temple)*
2. *Triangular Forum*
3. *Samnite* palaestra
4. *Temple of Isis*
5. *Temple of Zeus Meilichios*
6. *Large theater*
7. *Covered theater (Odeum)*
8. *Gladiators' barracks*

0   10   20m

Small Theater

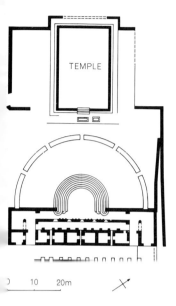

TEMPLE

0   10   20m

Theater at Pietrabbondante

within the Stabian Baths have documented in detail the gradual transformation of what had been a typical Greek establishment (as represented, for example, at Olympia), with small individual "hip bath" cubicles, into a fully fledged Roman bath, with chambers of varying temperatures heated by the passage of hot air beneath the floors and up through the flues in the walls, and equipped with hot-water and cold-water plunges—in effect what today we would call a Turkish bath, but with certain additional facilities. One of these was the addition of a *palaestra* for the taking of exercise before bathing. As the inscription that records the modernization of the Stabian Baths soon after 80 B.C. records, there was already a *palaestra* in the old Samnite Baths, and it was to remain an important part of the establishment down to A.D. 79.

The theaters of Pompeii (see plan) represent a comparable merging of Greek, Italic, and Roman traditions, once again with Campania playing a prominent part in shaping the merger. As regards both the forms of classical drama and the highly specialized buildings that grew up to house them, the classical theater was, of course, a purely Greek invention. It evolved steadily over the centuries; but it retained an extraordinarily durable hard core of continuity, as one sees very clearly, for example, in the visual conventions of the Roman theater, which were still steeped in Dionysiac symbolic imagery—an association that goes right back to the very origins of Greek drama, in the dances and sacred rituals connected with the cult of Dionysus. The original Samnite-period theater at Pompeii had been a Greek-style building terraced into the slopes overlooking the Stabian Gate. Later it was almost totally remodeled in the Roman manner, by building up the seating and by reshaping the relation of seating to stage and the form of the stage building itself; but one can still get a very good idea of what the earlier building would have looked like from the recently excavated second-century B.C. theater at Pietrabbondante (*Bovianum Vetus*), a sanctuary deep in the mountain country of western Samnium. This, it must be remembered, was a century or so earlier than the first permanent theater in Rome itself, the Theater of Pompey, built in 55 B.C. Beside the large open-air theater at Pompeii was later added a smaller, covered theater (*theatrum tectum*) or Odeum. This was built soon after 80 B.C. by the same pair of chief magistrates as built the Amphitheater. Except for the subsequent addition of marble paving in the *orchaestra* and the facing with marble of the front of the stage building (originally decorated with Second Style painting) the remains in this case are still those of the original building. It had an unsupported roof span of 20.6 meters, a good indication of the technical skills of the Campanian architects of the Sullan period.

What sort of performances would these theaters have staged? For the more serious cultural occasions there was the Covered Theater, occasions such as concerts, lectures, readings of verse, or the displays of visiting rhetoricians in which antiquity took such a perverse pleasure. The Large Theater was, by contrast, a place of popular entertainment, and Rome was not the only society to discover that patronage based on popular taste does not make for a very high level of theater. It is not improbable that in its more serious moments the Large Theater may have staged the comedies of Plautus and Terence, perhaps even the tragedies of Pacuvius (who came from south Italy and bore an Oscan name) and Accius. But in the long run the Roman dramatists of the second century B.C. were to prove more important for the history of Latin literature than for the creation of a flourishing dramatic tradition. A single anecdote will serve to show what they were up against. Even in his own lifetime Terence, who died in 159 B.C., saw the first performance of one of his plays ruined by the rival

Amphitheater

*Marble relief from a tomb outside
the Stabian Gate*

attractions of a rope dancer and a boxer, and, at the second attempt, by rumors of a gladiatorial combat. By the first century B.C. tragedy had become an almost exclusively literary form, written for declamation or private performance; and although comedy was more robust (the texts of some of the plays of Plautus have survived because they were performed) it too was fast losing ground to simpler, more popular forms of entertainment.

It is difficult to present a coherent picture of this popular entertainment, for several reasons. One is that, being nonliterary or at best sub-literary, it has left all too few traces in the written record. Another is that at this level of perform-ance the element of improvisation tended to be high and the demarcation lines correspondingly fluid. If we accept the distinctions made by classical writers, at least three well-known types of entertainment were certainly presented in the Theater at Pompeii: the Atellan Farce, the Mime, and the Pantomime.

The Atellan Farce would have found a ready audience. Named after Atella, near the modern Aversa, between Naples and Capua, it was a Campanian spe-ciality, played in Oscan. Like the later Italian *Commedia dell' Arte,* or (to take a modern analogy) like many strip cartoons, it portrayed scenes of small-town life, revolving around the incongruous adventures and buffoonery of a few stock characters—Maccus the greedy clown, Pappus the gaffer, and a few others. Rendered in Latin, it had a brief semiliterary vogue in late Republican Rome, but it was really popular, grass-roots entertainment, bawdy, topical, and wholly lacking in sophistication.

Of all the forms of Roman theatrical entertainment, the Mime was at once the most elementary and the most enduring. Such formal shape as it assumed was derived from many sources, including no doubt the Atellan Farce and (another, slightly earlier Campanian specialty) the *phlyax* players of the fourth and third centuries B.C., who seem to have specialized in ribald burlesques of mythological subjects; but above all from the companies of strolling performers, the forebears of "I Pagliacci," who for centuries past had been dancing, singing, juggling, and playing their way from town to town, wherever they could drum up an audience. By Roman times, at any rate, they seemed to have abandoned the masks of Greek theatrical tradition, since the lead player, the *archimimus,* evidently relied heavily on facial expression. Like the Atellan Farce, the Mime had a brief literary vogue in late Republican Rome, but it was really, and it remained, a sub-literary form, deriving its vitality and lasting popularity pre-cisely from its impromptu adaptability to the changing demands of local taste and of contemporary fashion.

The most sophisticated of the popular art forms was the Pantomime, which was introduced to Rome in 22 B.C. from the eastern Mediterranean, and which soon achieved enormous popularity. To modern ears the name calls up visions of the old-fashioned Christmas pantomime, but the classical pantomime was in fact something totally different, far more closely resembling modern ballet, involving the acting out of some traditional story in wordless gesture. The main difference was that almost the entire action was in the hands of a single player, the *pantomimus* (literally, "one who imitates all things"), supported by a chorus and musicians. A top-ranking *pantomimus* was the pop star of his day, the idol of the public, and often the intimate of emperors. A typical career was that of L. Aurelius Pylades, "the first *pantomimus* of his time," who had been born a slave and, after a successful acting career, was freed by the emperors Marcus Aurelius and Lucius Verus (A.D. 161-166). He retired to Puteoli, where, as a wealthy gentleman of leisure, he became a prominent local benefactor. At Pom-

Phlyax players

peii, as the *graffiti* make clear, the ratings of rival *pantomimi* were followed eagerly and the visit of a successful *pantomimus* was a major event.

The level of theatrical performance at Pompeii may not have been very exalted, but the Theater did undoubtedly play a lively part in local life. This is brought vividly home to us by a bronze bust, on a herm, which dates from about the turn of the first centuries B.C. and A.D. and which is now in the Naples Museum (inv. no. 4991; inscription *CIL* X. 1, 814). It was found in the Temple of Isis and it commemorates one Caius Norbanus Sorex, described as a player of second parts, a descendant (probably the grandson) of the well-known *archimimus* of the same name who had been a personal friend of the dictator Sulla. "To play second parts" was, in Roman terms, "to play second fiddle"; the Pompeian Norbanus Sorex was no David Garrick. Moreover, in the eyes of the law acting was one of the dishonorable professions, whose members were disqualified from holding public office. And yet here we have one of a pair of honorary herm-portraits (the shaft of the other was found in the Eumachia Building) set up in a popular public temple with the formal approval of the town council (*ex decurionum decreto*), by the *magistri* of the *pagus Augustus Felix suburbanus,* a body that one might loosely translate as the parish council of one of the country sub-districts outside the walls of Pompeii—not perhaps a very large pond, but in it a Norbanus Sorex could be quite a large fish and, by implication, a substantial public benefactor. Once again we are reminded that Pompeii was not Rome, and that, whatever the law might say, a successful local actor could be an honored member of the community.

The amphitheater was an Italian creation, in which Campania, with its hybrid Hellenized Italic culture, played a leading part. Rather surprisingly, Rome itself did not have a permanent arena until 29 B.C., and even then it was built of timber on masonry footings, not unlike the seating for the open-air opera in the Baths of Caracalla in present-day Rome. Before 29 B.C. displays of gladiators or of exotic beasts had had to take place under makeshift conditions in such open spaces as the Roman Forum or the Circus Maximus. This was a costly business, and it could be dangerous, as when the elephants displayed by Pompey in 55 B.C. took fright and stampeded. Keeping performers and mobs of excited spectators apart is no new problem in popular spectator sport. The problem was resolved, and it was resolved in Campania, by the creation of the *amphitheatrum* (literally "a place for viewing from all sides") consisting of an oval arena separated by a barrier from rising tiers of stone benches. The Amphitheater at Pompeii, built soon after the foundation of the colony in 80 B.C., lacks the grandeur and sophisticated planning of the later giants at Capua and Puteoli, or the Colosseum in Rome. But it has an honored place in architectural history. It is the earliest surviving example of an architectural form that is still in worldwide use today. It is also one of the first public buildings in Roman Italy to have used the arcade as a monumental feature in its own right. Campania at this time was way out in front as a center of lively architectural invention.

Although the Amphitheater could be used for any form of large spectacle, in practice what the crowd expected was blood, in the form either of gladiatorial combats or of performances involving the pitting of ferocious wild beasts against human victims or against each other. The provision of "games" (*ludi*) was a ready passport to popular favor, and one of the formal requirements of public office at Pompeii was the expenditure of a large sum either on public building or on public entertainment. The human performers were either condemned criminals exposed to some form of sophisticated butchery, or else trained gladia-

tors, who might be either the unwilling victims of circumstance (slaves, prisoners of war, lesser criminals) or else tough, voluntary professionals. They were organized into schools (*familiae*) under private or public ownership (in Rome itself they very soon passed into Imperial hands), one of the earliest and most famous of such schools being that at Capua from which Spartacus and seventy-seven other gladiators made their historic escape in 73 B.C. The possession of an amphitheater was a valuable civic asset, bringing in spectators from all the nearby towns. The disastrous Amphitheater riot of A.D. 59 was sparked off by the presence of large numbers of fans from Nuceria, a neighboring city that, in the best Italian tradition, was also Pompeii's deadly rival. It was natural that Pompeii, with its fine arena, should set up its own gladiatorial establishment. This was installed after the earthquake of A.D. 62 in what had been a large porticoed foyer behind the Theater (see plan, page 88). By A.D. 79 it was already partly occupied, and in it were found some of the fine armor and weapons now in the Naples Museum.

Every gladiator was a specialist, belonging to one of a number of conventional categories clearly distinguished by their armor and weapons and bearing conventional names. These names appear regularly in the literature and in the advertisements, and at any given time and place the fans would certainly have known exactly what to expect (and how to lay their bets) when a *myrmillo* from such-and-such a training school, with twenty-five wins to his credit, was matched against a less experienced but well spoken of *Thrax* from such another school. We today cannot follow all the nuances; when one recalls how even in as conservative a game as cricket the positioning of players in the field and the naming of those positions have changed quite substantially in the last fifty years, it is hardly surprising that the evidence from antiquity is not always consistent. Most of the main types seem to have been first established by the introduction of prisoners of war wearing their native armor and weapons, beginning with the "Samnites" in the third century B.C., and followed by the "Gauls" and "Thracians" and, possibly introduced by Julius Caesar from Britain, gladiators fighting from chariots (*essedarii*). Broadly speaking, they may be divided into the group of heavily armed fighters that evolved from the original "Samnites"; a somewhat more mobile, less heavily armed group of which the "Thracian" was typical; and a number of more specialized types, of which the most colorful was the *retiarus,* or net-thrower, who was very lightly armored (alone among gladiators he fought bare-headed) and who was armed only with a net, a fisherman's trident, and a dagger, relying entirely on his own greater speed and mobility. He was normally matched against a *myrmillo* (so named from the representation of a fish, the *morimylos,* which he wore on his helmet) or a *secutor* ("chaser").

The games followed an established ritual. After a public banquet the evening before, in which all the contestants participated, they started off with a procession (*pompa*), which was heralded by trumpets and horns, and which included the sponsor of the games and all the fighters, dressed in splendid costumes and wearing armor, which they would later change for their actual fighting equipment. After a series of rather tame preliminaries (mock fights, fights with wooden weapons, etc.) the serious business of the day began with a war trumpet (*tuba*) sounding for the first pair of gladiators, who proceeded to fight to the death, although there was a reasonable chance of a good loser being allowed to live to fight another day. About midday there was a slack period, filled with more mock fighting, assorted displays, and the executions of criminals, after

93

*A bar counter on the Via
dell' Abbondanza*

Caupona of Euxinus (I, II, 10)
1. *Bar*
2. *Kitchen and latrine*
3. *Open air dining/drinking area*
4. *Vineyard*

which the afternoon would be devoted to *venationes*, in which wild animals
were pitted against each other or against trained animal-fighters (*bestiarii*).
Throughout the day there was a more or less continuous accompaniment from
trumpets, horns, pipes, drums, water organs and, possibly, from voices. The
whole performance is vividly portrayed in a marble triple frieze found outside
the Stabian Gate (see illustration, p.90), probably from a large tomb: in the upper
register, the procession; in the middle, on a larger scale as befits the major
attraction, five scenes of gladiatorial combat; and below, incidents from the
venationes.

To conclude this section about leisure activities, a few words about eating
customs.

The Roman's single main meal of the day (*cena*) was taken in the evening after the afternoon bath. In polite society one dined on a couch reclining on one's left elbow. The average dining room took its name (*triclinium*) from the fact that it held three couches (*klinai*, or *lecti*), though a wealthy house might have several *triclinia* for different seasons, including one for *al fresco* dining in the garden; for a really large dinner party several might be used at once—carefully graded socially, if we are to believe the contemporary satirical writers. The couches faced inward upon three sides of a square, within which stood the tables and from which the food and drink were served. Three courses were customary, each consisting of several different servings, and wine (normally but not invariably mixed with water, and in some contexts served hot) was drunk both with and after the meal. The details varied greatly according to the taste of the host and the degree of formality. Frequently the meal was accompanied or followed by some form of entertainment such as music, dancing, acrobatics, or, if the host had literary pretensions, readings from poetry. Petronius' *Satyricon,* for all its element of parody, offers a brilliant picture of the sort of dinner that might have been served by a wealthy vulgarian in mid-first-century Pompeii.

For the man in the street and for visitors there were numerous bars and eating houses (*cauponae*), many of which also provided lodging, with or without female company. The Caupona of Euxinus will serve as an example. It was one of a number situated near the Amphitheater to cater for the crowds of visitors who came from all the neighboring towns whenever there was a show. On the façade was a painted inn-sign, with a figure of a Phoenix and two peacocks and the words *Phoenix felix et tu* ("You too will enjoy the Happy Phoenix"), and below it were two electoral posters painted up on the orders of the innkeeper, Euxinus, whose name and address are attested also by the inscriptions on three wine amphoras found in the bar: *Pompeiis ad amphitheatr(um) Euxino coponi* ("to Euxinus the innkeeper, near the amphitheater, Pompeii"). The premises were large: on the street corner a bar, with a typical L-shaped counter, a store, large jars for keeping food hot, and traces of a wooden rack for storing wine amphoras; behind the bar three other rooms, a storeroom, and a lavatory; and on it to the right a large open courtyard, which did double duty as a vineyard and, as in many a *trattoria* today, a place for open-air drinking and dining and, no doubt, gaming. At the far end of the garden was a painted *lararium* and stairs leading to some upper rooms; there was more accommodation in the adjoining house.

The *graffiti* found on the walls were characteristic, including representations of Dionysus and Priapus and tags of verse. One of these ran:

"Blondie bad me hate the dark ones. If I can I will. If I cannot, all unwilling I will love them still."

Tablinum *wall in the House of Sallust (First Style)*

Cubiculum *in the House of the Silver Wedding (Second Style [IIA])*

Cubiculum *in the Villa of the Mysteries (Later Second Style [IIB])*

Cubiculum *in the House of the Epigrams (from a drawing) (Late Second Style [IIB])*

Garden Room, Villa of Livia

Tablinum *wall in the House of M. Lucretius Fronto (Late Third Style)*

PAINTING

The standard classification of Pompeian wall painting into four successive "Styles" was first enunciated by August Mau in 1882, and it still provides the best framework for any outline survey of the two hundred-odd years of painting presented on the walls of Pompeii itself and of the neighboring towns and country villas.

The First, or "Masonry," Style followed closely the conventions of the decoratively jointed stone masonry of which it was a gaily colored representation. Very similar work has been recorded from sites as far afield as Macedonia, Asia Minor, and Israel, and by the second century B.C. it was evidently already a commonplace of both public and domestic interior decoration throughout the Hellenistic world. At Pompeii it was already giving place to the Second Style when the interior of the Capitolium was decorated shortly after the foundation of the Roman colony in 80 B.C., and very soon after that it was generally replaced by the Second Style. The House of Sallust (see illustration) is one of the relatively few examples that survive in good condition. Relying as it did for its effect upon the patterns of the painted surfaces, which imitated in stucco the cornices and plinths, blocks and slabs of real ornamental masonry, it was essentially a style that emphasized the real solid qualities of the walls it adorned.

The Second, or "Architectural," Style began to come in soon after 80 B.C., reflecting the widening cultural perspectives created both by the foundation of the Roman colony and by Italy's ever-increasing involvement with the established centers of the arts in the eastern Mediterranean. The element common to all its very varied manifestations was a development of the wall surfaces in seeming depth, usually within a framework of simulated architecture; where the First Style had emphasized the tangible solidity of the wall, the Second Style did all it could to play down that solidity and to create an illusion of receding space. In its earlier stages (Style IIA), before the middle of the first century B.C., this took the form simply of making the main wall surface appear to be set back behind a framing order of painted Corinthian columns, which looked as if they stood upon a projecting plinth and supported a projecting cornice (see illustration). This was a direct two-dimensional imitation of a real architectural device already current in the earliest concrete-vaulted architecture of Campania and of Latium, and the resulting simulation of reality by every known trick of illusionistic perspective and lighting was to remain characteristic of the Second Style in all its manifestations.

At first the wall surfaces "behind" the framing architectural colonnade continued to be treated much as in the previous period. But quite soon (for example, in the secondary rooms of the Villa of the Mysteries, ca. 60–50 B.C.) this began to be accompanied by an opening-out of the upper part of the wall, as if the lower part were merely a screen over the top of which one could glimpse the open sky framed by receding architectural vistas. This search for visual escape from the sense of enclosure imposed by the inherited traditions of a compact, inward-facing urban architecture was to remain one of the dominant trends of Roman domestic architecture throughout the Pompeian period. The best known of all Pompeian paintings of this period, the Hall of the Dionysiac Mysteries in the Villa of the Mysteries, is in this respect an exception, Second Style in date but not in its composition. Not only does it omit the columns of the architectural framework but it also portrays the figures of the frieze itself as if they were acting out their parts in front of a neutral background rather than moving into and out of it. It is only in the small bedchambers (*cubicula*) that one finds the characteristic glimpses of open spaces beyond the wall (see illustration). In this respect the great figured frieze of this villa, like the Aldobrandini Wedding frieze in the Vatican Museums, is an intruder for which the precedents must be sought outside Italy in the Hellenistic world. Within less than a generation, however, this alien tradition had been captured and assimilated, and it is thus that we find it, displayed within a conventional Second Style architectural framework, on the walls of the Villa of Publius Fannius Synistor at Boscoreale on the slopes of Vesuvius. Despite its numerous and continued borrowings from, and links with, the larger Hellenistic world, the Second Style was evidently already an established Italian phenomenon, created for the houses and villas of wealthy Romans in the capital and in Campania, and faithfully reflected on the walls of the well-to-do citizens of Pompeii.

In the third quarter of the first century B.C. the Second Style (Style IIB) took a turn that was to affect the whole subsequent history of wall painting at Pompeii. The painted architectural framework, which had at first faithfully conformed to the simple rectangular shapes of the rooms it adorned, began to take on a life of its own, with each individual wall treated as a separate compositional unit, symmetrically balanced about the central bay within the larger symmetry of the rooms' three main walls. Both the painted architectural foreground and the wall surfaces it framed lent themselves admirably to such treatment. Among the many recurrent schemes one may note the development of the whole wall as an elaborately three-dimensional architectural façade articulated about three large doors, as in the Villa of P. Fannius Synistor at Boscoreale; the portrayal of a porticoed courtyard enclosing some central feature such as a circular *tempietto* (*tholos*) glimpsed between the columns and curtains of an ornately baroque columnar screen, as in the large painted *triclinium* at Oplontis; or, prominently displayed within the central bay, a large representation of a panel picture, usually depicting some mythological subject (see illustration).

Scholars have expended much erudition and ingenuity in tracing the sources of these compositions: in contemporary stage design, for example; in the fantasy architecture that graced the courts of the Hellenistic monarchs (and particularly that of the Ptolemies of Egypt); and in the elaborately contrived landscape architecture of the villas of Campania itself. That there was any single, all-embracing source is in fact doubtful; this was the expression of an aspect of late Hellenistic taste that no doubt found many outlets. But, making every allowance for an element of painterly exaggeration, it does seem clear that a great deal of what we see portrayed on the walls of Pompeii was rooted in real three-dimensional fantasy architecture. When, in one of the rare surviving passages of classical literature that indulges in contemporary art criticism, the architectural historian Vitruvius, writing about 25 B.C., roundly condemns this style for its "unreality," it is clear from the context that the reality with which he contrasted it was the sober functionalism of traditional classical architecture. Not for him the heady baroque fantasies favored by the avant-garde decorators of Rome and central Italy.

Two other famous surviving Second Style paintings must be mentioned because of their importance for what follows. One is the frieze illustrating scenes from Homer's *Odyssey* within the setting of a continuous landscape. Found on the Esquiline in Rome, it is now in the Vatican Museums. Scholars are divided as to the extent to which the "Odyssey Landscapes" reflect lost Hellenistic originals, but there can be no doubt about the degree to which this tradition of naturalistic landscape with figures had already taken root on Italian soil. In this case the landscape is shown as if glimpsed between the columns of a typical columnar order. In the Garden Room from the Villa of Livia, wife of Augustus, at Prima Porta just outside Rome (see illustration), even this formal restraint is lacking: the four walls simply flow outward, portraying in loving detail the trees and shrubs, the birds, and flowers of a formal garden laid out beyond a low fence. In this respect the Second Style could go no further.

If we have lingered over the Second Style, of which relatively few Pompeian examples were to survive another century of rebuilding and redecorating (and of which it is in consequence, very hard to convey any real impression from the few fragments available for exhibition), it is because this was the great creative period of Roman wall painting. This was when the basis of most of the subsequent repertory was established. It is common to speak of the Third and Fourth Styles as if they represented an orderly sequence of development. Development there certainly was, but much of it was achieved in terms of a repertory of inherited patterns and motifs, and it was punctuated by frequent references back to the recent past, the products of which were still there on the walls of the older houses for all to see.

The dominant characteristic of the Third Style was its renunciation of the search for an illusion of three-dimensional depth and its concentration instead upon the purely decorative possibilities inherent in the formal schemes it had inherited from the previous period. It retained the rigid horizontal symmetry of the later Second Style, with its two flanking panels leading the eye in toward the panel picture framed by the central *aedicula;* but although the formal vocabulary of the latter was still largely that of Second Style fantasy architecture, it was increasingly an architecture without substance, little more than a frame for the picture that had become the focus of the whole composition. At the same time there was a steadily increasing emphasis upon the fields of color and upon the patterns presented by the surrounding wall surfaces. Slender candelabra, trailing tendrils, arabesques of delicate foliage, abstract geometrical motifs— all these were used with an elaborate inner logic to create a formal unity covering the whole wall surface (see illustration). A good example of this can be seen in the Villa of the Mysteries, in the black *tablinum.*

Vertically too there was the same movement away from the illusion of real architecture characteristic of the Second Style toward two-dimensional schemes of balanced pattern. The plinth, the middle register of the wall, and what had been the zone opening out above this middle register, became three rigidly distinct horizontal bands of composition, linked by little more than the shared tripartite symmetry of the overall design. The gable of the central *aedicula* was flattened and compressed downward into the middle zone, to the upper and lower borders of which added emphasis was given by the introduction of secondary bands of small, elongated horizontal panels; the plinth became an independent strip of color set along the base of the wall and with its own independent ornament, while along the upper register were ranged groups of delicate, architectural fantasies, as far removed in spirit from the illusionistic Second Style fantasy architecture of which they were the offspring as the former had been from the "real" architecture with which Vitruvius so contemptuously contrasts them.

A third and very important component of the Third Style was its use of color to emphasize the formal divisions, and in particular the vertical divisions, of the design. A typical color scheme is that of the *oecus* of the House of the Menander, with its black dado, its green middle zone punctuated by black vertical members, and its white upper zone. To such wall schemes must be added the sober white

House of the Red Walls (VIII, 5, 37) *(Early Fourth Style)*

House of the Centenary, detail of wall in the white dining room (Early Fourth Style)

House of "Loreius Tiburtinus" (II, 2, 2–5)

House of the Apollo (VI, 7, 23)

South triclinium *in the House of the Vettii* (VI, 15, 1)

Large landscapes on the garden wall of the House of the Small Fountain (VI, 8, 23)

Hercules in the Garden of the Hesperides *(from the* triclinium *of the House of the Priest Amandus)*

or black and white of the mosaic or marble floors and the patterned polychrome tracery of the stucco vaulting. These were carefully studied, often sophisticated effects. To modern eyes much of the coloring may seem rather overpowering, but there was nothing indiscriminate about its application.

Insofar as it is possible to draw an arbitrary dividing line between two stages of a single, developing artistic phenomenon, the line between the Second and Third Styles appears to fall around 15 B.C., and the Third Style may reasonably be regarded as a direct reflection of the rather formal classicism that characterizes the official art that was just then taking shape at the court of Augustus. The earliest and finest Third Style paintings in Rome itself come from just such a milieu, a villa in Trastevere (near the present Villa Farnesina), which was probably the residence of M. Vipsanius Agrippa, the colleague and designated heir of Augustus, after his marriage in 19 B.C. to Augustus' daughter, Julia. If that is correct, the link with Pompeii is clear. The child of the marriage was Agrippa Postumus, born shortly after his father's death in 12 B.C.; it was in a villa belonging to this son found in 1902 at Boscotrecase on the slopes of Vesuvius, two miles from Pompeii, and reburied by the eruption of 1906, that a number of paintings were found, so close in style and content to those of the Villa Farnesina that they may well have been painted by one of the artists who had worked there (see illustration). This sort of thing, though we can rarely document it so precisely, must in fact have been common practice in the wealthy patrician villas of the Bay of Naples; when one sees how many such villas there were within a ten-mile radius of Pompeii (see page 16), it is easy to understand how, in style if not always in quality, the walls of this small provincial city came to reflect so faithfully and so rapidly the art of Rome itself.

The latest manifestations of the Third Style proper date from the middle of the first century A.D. (an unusually well-preserved example is the *tablinum* of the house of M. Lucretius Fronto ([V, 4, 9; see illustration]) and once again it was changes of taste at court that ushered in the fourth and last phase of Pompeian wall painting, in the years immediately preceding the earthquake of A.D. 62. This is conventionally known as the Fourth Style, but it might in fact better be described as a chronological phase embodying a number of concurrent stylistic trends, some of which reflect the extravagant innovations of taste introduced into the art of the capital by Nero, while others hark back to the recent past of Pompeii itself.

Space permits us to illustrate only a few of the more striking aspects of this Fourth Style. At one extreme we find rooms like those in the House of the Red Walls (VIII, 5, 37) and in the House of the Centenary (IX, 8, 6; see illustration), in which the walls are treated as a single sheet of color, upon which is overlaid a delicate patterned tracery; there is a marked tendency to reduce the size of the panel pictures, or even to omit them altogether. A favorite conceit within this *genre* is to balance a "White Room" against a "Black Room," as in the House of the Centenary and in the recently excavated House of Julius Polybius (IX, 13, 19 – 26). At the other extreme we find a reversion to the illusionistic architecture of the Second Style, this time, however, treated as a continuous architectural backdrop to the main action of the composition, which is portrayed as if taking place on a stage. Good examples of this are in the House of Pinarius Cerialis (III, 4, 4) and in the House of Apollo (VI, 7, 23). Between these two extremes lie a large number of rooms that are formally no more than an ultimate phase of the Third Style, more or less combined with elements derived from the Second Style or from other types of Fourth Style practice. A room such as the south *triclinium* of the House of the Vettii (see illustration) quite obviously incorporates elements derived from both the preceding styles.

Because this was the sort of painting current at the time of the city's destruction it bulks large in the surviving remains, yet its wider artistic significance is less. For one thing, the last years of Pompeii were a time of marked economic and social decline, a decline that was inevitably reflected in the levels of patronage and, in consequence, of artistic standards. For another, wall painting as an important art form was on the way out, to be replaced by marble paneling and, in really wealthy circles, wall mosaic. In this respect the eruption was nicely timed. Another few years, and there would have been little left of the older, finer Pompeii.

And what of the mythological panel pictures that were the most prominent features of so many Pompeian walls and that, torn from their context, have for so long dominated the modern image of the Roman painter's art? Very early on in the excavations it was realized that they were in some sense "Old Master Copies," based on well-known Greek originals, and for a very long time it was almost exclusively as evidence of these lost originals that they captured the imagination of scholars. It is only quite recently that they have begun to be studied in their own right as paintings that, though presented in terms of certain inherited conventions, are in many cases as Roman as the walls they adorned.

That they represent free variations upon the themes established by the originals, and not merely straight copies of them, is apparent the moment one compares the different versions of one of the more familiar myths. There are, for example, ten versions of the story of Theseus and the Minotaur derived from at least three different originals. The competence varies greatly, and those who wish to demonstrate the artistic superiority of the lost originals have no difficulty in finding telling examples; this was after all the work of house decorators doing their best to furnish their clients with a "Greek" art that was not their own, but that social convention demanded. But a more fruitful line of inquiry is that of the extent to which these panel pictures reflect developments in contemporary Roman painting. Here their real quality emerges; there can be little doubt that one of the most significant of such developments lay in the field of landscape painting, and in particular of the sort of landscape with figures of which Second Style "Odyssey Landscapes," referred to above, afford such an eloquent foretaste.

Although many of the standard motifs of Second Style landscape paintings and stuccoes—isolated trees, towers, rustic shrines, altars, columns, rocky outcrops—do seem to derive from a preexisting Hellenistic tradition of painting or stuccowork, few today would question that a painting such as the *Rescue of Andromeda* in the House of the Priest Amandus (1, 7, 7) represents a fresh and specifically Italian version of that tradition (see illustration). This painting occupies the center of the lefthand wall of a *triclinium* redecorated in a version of the Third Style that is variously attributed to the middle of the first century A.D. or to the years just before A.D. 79. Comparable figured landscapes, portraying respectively the Fall of Icarus and the story of Polyphemus and Galatea, occupy two of the other walls, while the fourth wall displays a painting of Hercules in the Garden of the Hesperides, which is a reasonably competent, if to modern eyes rather dull, copy of a Greek original (see illustration). The differences between this last picture and the other three leap to the eye. In it the figures are isolated against a neutral background very much in the manner of the figures of a carved classical relief; the orange tree, illustrated because it is an essential feature of the story, stands in the same plane, without the slightest attempt to convey

Rescue of Andromeda
(from the triclinium *of the House of the Priest Amandus)*

Wild beasts on the garden wall of the House of the Epigrams
, 1, 18)

any illusion of an actual garden setting. This was the classical Greek tradition. The other three pictures are quite different in mood, composition, and treatment. It is the landscape that dominates, with its all-encompassing sense of real space, and the conventions used in its portrayal foreshadow to a startling degree those of later Roman narrative art. This is truly Roman painting. Ironically, but predictably, it was the "Greek" picture that got the post of honor. The educated Roman, hypnotized by the prevailing taste for Greek art, was notoriously blind to his own country's very real artistic achievements.

Much the same qualities emerge in the smaller decorative panels and other accessories that figure so largely on the walls of the Third and Fourth Styles. Still lifes, architectural landscapes, the Egyptianizing, or Nilotic, scenes that constitute the Roman equivalent of *chinoiserie*: painted in the broad, impressionistic technique of which Roman painters were the masters, they have an assurance and a directness that cannot fail to appeal to modern taste. This too was an art that had achieved a distinctively Roman personality.

One final question before we leave these mythological pictures. Was there any logic behind the choice of scenes? Did they carry a message, or were they simply the stereotypes of phil-Hellenic artistic fashion?

That many of the individual scenes carried widely accepted overtones of religious or philosophical interpretation there can be no doubt. Used in combination with each other and with the secondary motifs by which they were regularly surrounded (a great many of which had themselves entered the artistic repertory in the context of religious symbolism), they constituted a visual language that could be used to convey a remarkably clear and explicit message. Thus, the paintings from the villa of Publius Fannius Synistor at Boscoreale have been very plausibly interpreted as showing that the owner was an initiate into the mysteries of Aphrodite (Venus) and Adonis. In such a context the language of symbolism could be as subtle as it was eloquent, because it was addressed to people who understood what it was saying. At a more generalized level of communication, the mythological pictures are commonly used in what appear to be significant pairs, or trios, and some of these too may have been chosen because they illustrated the stories of the divinities to whose protection and good will the owner of the house aspired. Others (for example, the Trojan cycle in *Ala* 4 of the House of the Menander) may simply reflect the owner's literary or artistic tastes, although here too it would have been quite easy to read into them overtones of moral or philosophical meaning.

It does not, on the other hand, follow (as is sometimes claimed) that all of the mythological paintings at Pompeii carried a deliberate message. It is implicit in the language of symbolism that the more widely it is used, the more the precision of its meaning tends to get blunted. The terms become so familiar that they need a context to give them precise meaning, and in such a situation meaning tends increasingly to lie in the eye of the beholder. The workshops of Pompeii were not laboratories for the portrayal of belief. Under sophisticated patronage they could be so used, and at a more commonplace level any householder might select the current models that best suited his own personal tastes and convictions. But they remained essentially workshops, repositories of a body of established models, patterns, and skills; what they produced was determined by the fashions of contemporary taste, which to many citizens must have been largely a matter of keeping up with the Joneses. In the matter of giving more esoteric meanings to these paintings one has to take each case on its own merits.

We have dealt at some length with the formal painting that, by the very fact of its survival in such quantity, constitutes Pompeii's unique contribution to the history of classical art, and that, because it operated within a very precise range of conventions, does need some such explanation to be intelligible. By the same token we can be very brief in presenting the other facet of Pompeian painting, namely the popular art that adorns the gardens, domestic shrines, bars, and shopfronts. Simple, unsophisticated, direct, it tells its own story.

Much of this popular art was concerned with the portrayal of the well-known things of daily life: the shop of a baker (see page 62) or a potter, fuller or felt-makers at work (see page 61), a ship, scenes of tavern life, or of daily life in the Forum (see illustration, page 105). Occasionally it gives us a glimpse of larger contemporary events, as in the well-known scene of the Amphitheater riot of A.D. 59 (see illustration, page 34), but for the most part it was the work of simple craftsmen giving direct expression to what they saw around them. Even so, it was curiously selective: it was rarely used without some practical purpose.

It is at this level of meaning that one can most intelligibly draw a rational distinction between the spheres of formal and of popular Pompeian art. Although, as we have seen, the former could be used in sophisticated hands to express the religious, philosophical, or literary preferences of an individual patron, it was in itself no more than a repertory of motifs and styles of which the common denominator was the norms imposed by contemporary artistic taste. Popular art, on the other hand, like the popular religion of which it was so often an expression, tended to operate at a far simpler, more direct level of human experience. Nothing could be more stridently "popular" than the painted household shrines (lararia) with their great curling serpent figures and many of the street-front paintings were placed directly under the protection of the owner's patron divinity; advertisements of his activities, it may be, but also at the same time tangible insurances against the changes and chances of a capricious providence. This was a grass-roots art, shaped not only by its use of everyday themes but also by its expression of everyday attitudes of mind.

As in most such classifications, the distinctions between formal and popular Pompeian art tend to get a bit ragged at the edges. One sees this very clearly in many of the gardens. Here, side by side with formal Third and Fourth Style rooms are rooms and garden walls treated in a wide variety of other styles. Many of the subjects are borrowed from the small, secondary panels of the house itself—landscapes, scenes of hunting, animal landscapes, occasional mythological figures—but they tend to be treated in a far more relaxed manner, and often on a very much larger scale; typical examples are the huge landscapes in the House of the Small Fountain (VI, 8, 23-24; see illustration), the very large animal frieze on the garden wall of the House of M. Lucretius Fronto (IV, 2, 1), and the birth of Venus in the House of the Venus (11, 3, 31). Occasionally the influence was in the other direction, the garden influencing the house. Some miniature garden panels patently derive ultimately from such famous originals as the early Third Style garden room of the Villa of Livia at Prima Porta, while plants were freely copied on the dadoes of formal Fourth Style compositions, as, for example, in the House of the Silver Wedding (V, 2, Mau E). There was a marked tendency for the garden, its fountains, and its plants to invade the paintings of the adjoining walls. At the same time, the influence of wall mosaics was just beginning to make itself felt. The last phase of Pompeian art was one of transition toward a future that Pompeii itself was never to see. In it what had been "popular" art was rapidly acquiring a fresh, more monumental dimension.

SCULPTURE

*Equestrian statues in
the Forum
Naples Museum*

The early history of Roman sculpture in Campania is largely shaped by the fact that by the first century B.C. there were few wealthy or influential Romans who did not possess luxurious country residences on the Bay of Naples. These were the people who, under the late Republic, were busy amassing private collections of sculpture inspired by the huge galleries of Greek loot on display in the temples and public buildings at Rome. Original works were naturally in short supply and contemporary Greek workshops in the old sculptural centers of the eastern Mediterranean were quick to take advantage of the growing demand for replicas and adaptations of old masterpieces. The letters of Cicero (who had two, if not three, properties in Campania, one near Pompeii) provide us with an entertaining picture of the lengths to which an educated Roman would go in order to furnish his country retreats with suitable statuary. The amazing array assembled by Lucius Calpurnius Piso Caesoninus, a rich but not exceptionally wealthy Roman, in his villa near Herculaneum (see page 110) vividly demonstrates the size and quality of one of these early collections. Most of the eighty-three pieces were acquired between 60 and 40 B.C., the products of various workshops. Among the many close copies and freer interpretations, which reveal Caesoninus' preference, in common with most of his contemporaries, for Archaic and Classical Greek originals, was a series of eighteen busts, herms and statues of Greek philosophers, orators and poets, and an impressive group of portraits of Hellenistic kings and generals. There were only two portraits of Romans, both of them historical personalities whose identities are in dispute, but no portraits of the family itself. Despite their relative prosperity the wealthy citizens of Pompeii could not compete on this level, but small-scale echoes are found in such bronzes as the Dancing Faun from the House of the Faun (Naples Museum, inv. 5002), the statue of Perseus from House v, 3, 10 (Naples Museum, inv. 126170), the statue of an ephebe adapted to a lamp-holder from a fourth-century B.C. original and found in the House of Cornelius Teges (1, 7, 10; Naples Museum, inv. 143753), to which may now be added a similar conceit from the House of Fabius Rufus.

It was not until the political stability that accompanied the reestablishment of central authority by Augustus that the erection of public municipal statues in honor of members of the Imperial family and of prominent local citizens became part of the everyday life of a small town like Pompeii. Once launched, the fashion caught on rapidly. But for the earthquake of 62 and the salvage operations that followed the eruption, a visitor to the Forum would have been confronted by a forest of statues. Three very large bronze statues, probably of members of the Imperial house, occupied most of the space at the southern end, and among the eighteen equestrian statues that stood on bases marshaled along the front of the western portico, in front of the Temple of Jupiter and elsewhere, must have been that recorded on the tombstone of the wealthy *garum* manufacturer and chief magistrate of Pompeii, Aulus Umbricius Scaurus (*CIL* x. 1024). Perhaps his is among those portrayed in a scene of the Forum from the Villa of Julia Felix (Naples Museum, inv. 9068; see illustration). About fifty other standing figures wearing the toga, the majority probably in marble, commemorated the services of other local worthies. In the surrounding public buildings and temples, here and elsewhere in the town, were numerous other opportunities to indulge this new craze. Among the few survivals are the herm portrait of Norbanus Sorex (Naples Museum, inv. 4991; see page 92) in the Temple of Isis (of which a duplicate stood in the Eumachia Building) and those of such conspicuous benefactors and donors of public buildings as Eumachia herself (Naples Museum,

*Bronze portrait busts
Naples Museum*

inv. 6232), Marcus Tullius (Naples Museum, inv. 6231), and Marcus Holconius
Rufus (Naples Museum, inv. 6233), who were responsible for the fullers' hall,
the Temple of Fortuna Augusta, and the rebuilding of the Large Theater,
respectively.

It is at this period that portrait statues of family members begin to join the
other sculptures in the Villa at Herculaneum, and portraits appear on semipublic
display in private houses at Pompeii. Fine examples of these are the bronze busts
of a man and a woman placed in an *ala* of the atrium in the House of the Citharist (Naples Museum, inv. 4992; see illustration) and the series of portraits on
herm shafts found placed at the entrance to the *tablinum* in several of the larger
houses. The most famous is that of the banker L. Caecilius Felix (better but
mistakenly known as Caecilius Jucundus; see illustration, page 39), but there
are also good-quality marble examples portraying successful businessmen who
were well known in the town: Vesonius Primus from House VI, 14, 20 (Pompeii
Antiquarium, inv. 407-4), Cornelius Rufus from VIII, 4, 15 (Pompeii Antiquarium, inv. 403-4), and the portrait of an old man (no. 26). Styles and techniques
are so closely related to those found in public statuary that presumably, and not
surprisingly, they were produced by the same workshops.

Such "display" portraits must be distinguished from the purely private aspects
of family portraiture that already had a long history, among them stylized
funerary statues executed by local craftsmen in local materials. The series begins
about the time the Sullan colony was established and continues until the eruption. Another aspect is exemplified by the shrine of the *imagines maiorum* in the
House of the Menander (see illustration). These are little more than puppet
heads carved in the traditional materials of wood or wax, taken to represent the
probably generalized and purely symbolic portraits that formed part of the
ancestral cult. That this was still a living portrait form and not an extraordinary
survival from a much earlier period is shown by the still unpublished wooden
heads, on a larger scale, from Herculaneum, the best preserved of which appears
to represent a woman of Augustan or later date. There was obviously an element
of the population who, whatever it may have thought of the developing, strongly
Hellenized style in vogue for public statuary, preferred to uphold, in a funerary
context at least, the established conventions of an older tradition. Once again
we see the "popular" forms and those more sophisticated trends influenced by
the larger world existing happily side by side.

One of the saddest losses is that of all but a few fragments of the cult figures
of the temples, among which must have been some of the earliest and finest
pieces of sculpture that the town possessed. All the statues of divinities that have
survived are secondary dedications within the temple precincts or from private
houses, such as a Venus from a blue-painted shrine in the garden peristyle of
House I, 2, 17 (Naples Museum, inv. 6412) and an Artemis (no. 4), all copyist
works of varying quality and almost all produced in the early Empire.

With garden decoration we are again in the familiar world of Hellenistic imagery, and here one cannot help being struck by the extraordinary dominance of Dionysiac themes. These included all the rustic members of Dionysus' company and of course brought in all the characters of ancient theater. It looks as though there was a very strongly established convention in this field that the suppliers and their clients were content to follow. The only major exceptions appear to be the various animal figures allowed as appropriate to fountains.

There is nothing in the surviving works at any level to support the idea that Pompeii had its own school of sculpture. Undoubtedly a number of local jobbing workshops produced much of the simpler sculpted ornament on public fountains, wellheads, less extravagant tombs, and the odd figured group in local tufa like the naively conceived gladiator and Priapus commissioned by a tavernkeeper (Pompeii Antiquarium, inv. 11739). Some experienced craftsmen must have been charged with the daily maintenance and occasional repairs required by the growing quantities of municipal and official statuary. One or two workshops specializing in funerary sculpture of the traditional type — a type found all over Campania — could have supplied the needs of the town in this context. But most of the major commissions, if not imported as finished works from Rome or Greece, would have been executed by the workshops based at Puteoli, where a steadily growing body of evidence attests the considerable activities of marble workers and sculptors.

*Marble head of a woman from
a statue
Naples Museum*

THE OTHER ARTS

In a society that made no distinction between fine arts and craftsmanship, the "minor arts" were bound to play an important role. Although some of the pieces here exhibited were heirlooms or luxury pieces imported from other parts of the Roman world, the majority were made locally in Campania, which is known to have been an important center for the production of metalwork and glass, and which was almost certainly largely self-supporting in such things as jewelry, the engraving of seals and gems, stuccowork, and mosaic.

In the second and first centuries B.C. the long-established Campanian bronze industry, centered on Capua but with workshops probably in many of the neighboring towns, was exporting all over the Roman world, and although by the first century A.D. it was losing ground to new centers established in northern Italy, Gaul, and probably elsewhere in the provinces, in A.D. 79 it was still a flourishing industry. Its products await detailed study, but it is clear that they went in very large quantities to the European market, both in the provinces and beyond the frontiers. Although it was famed particularly for its large wine vessels (*situlae*) and other fine bronze tableware, it was certainly producing bronzework of many other kinds, including household furniture of all sorts, heating and lighting equipment, small-scale statuary, and statuettes. Several Pompeian families had connections with the Capuan industry, among them the Hordionii and the Nigidii, one of whom, M. Nigidius Vaccula, presented a large bronze brazier to the Stabian Baths and a bronze bench to the Forum Baths. Small workshops established in the town to undertake repairs may also have produced some of the simpler domestic utensils. Two *graffiti* mention coppersmiths (*fabri aerarii: CIL* IV, 3702 and 4256) and a bronze strainer found at Boscoreale is inscribed *pertudit Pompeis Felicio* ("pierced by Felicio at Pompeii"). In 1899 a partially excavated site outside the Vesuvius Gate produced quantities of scrap bronze, two plaster models of heads, a statuette of an ephebe brought in for repair, and a number of little bronze-workers' anvils. The coppersmith seen at work in one relief (no. 276) was evidently producing fresh work as well as undertaking repairs, and he was surely resident in Pompeii. Priscus the engraver *(caelator)* who greeted Campanus the gem-cutter in a *graffito* on the wall of the Palaestra (*Priscus caelator Campano gemmario fel*[*iciter*]) (*CIL* IV, Suppl. 8502) could have worked either in bronze or in silver.

The Roman passion for collecting silver plate was first fostered by the enormous wealth of treasure brought back by the victorious generals of the early second century B.C. from the Greek cities of southern Italy and from Greece itself and the East. At first it was available only to the very rich, who bought the booty sold at public auction, but silversmiths were soon established in Rome, producing plate in ever-increasing quantities, until by A.D. 79 we find even quite modest households possessing one or two pieces. Sets of eating silver (*argentum escarium*) and drinking silver (*argentum potorium*), together with one or two show pieces that were treasured as family heirlooms, were proudly displayed on special tables, such as that painted in loving detail on the precinct wall of the tomb of the young aedile C. Vestorius Priscus outside the Vesuvius Gate at Pompeii (see illustration).

Individual pieces from such services had been found in Pompeian houses ever since the excavation began, but a great many of the larger collections had doubtless been recovered after the eruption, and it was not until 1895 that a complete set of silver plate, 109 pieces in all, was found in a *villa rustica* at Boscoreale, two miles northwest of Pompeii. It had been deposited in a vat in the wine-press room (see plan, page 59), together with gold jewelry and over

"*Imagines maiorum,*"
House of the Menander

Mosaic emblema *of a Nilotic landscape (House of the Menander)*

display of silver plate painted on the wall of the tomb of Vestorius Priscus

one thousand gold coins, and beside it lay the skeleton of a woman. The collection had been made very largely in the early years of the first century A.D., but it also included a dish over three hundred years old and there were some later purchases. As well as drinking cups and eating dishes there were also some display pieces and toilet mirrors.

In 1930 this hoard was matched by the discovery of a similar treasure in an underground room of the House of the Menander (see plan, page 48), where it had been stored for safekeeping in a large wooden chest, reinforced with bronze, each piece carefully wrapped in a cloth and neatly arranged in series. It comprised 118 pieces, weighing a total of just under 53 pounds (24 kilograms). Alongside it was found the family jewelry, which included a *bulla* and a number of gold and silver coins, carefully chosen (as is customary in such stores of reserve coinage) from issues that, because of their gold or silver content, were secure against the inflation that was already steadily eroding the value of ordinary contemporary coinage. Most of the vessels were probably produced by the workshops in Rome, but there were silversmiths from southern Italy and Greece resident in Neapolis and Puteoli who could as easily have supplied the more strongly Hellenistic forms. The carefully executed repairs made to some of the silverware found would certainly have been done locally.

Goldsmiths and gem-cutters were among the small craftsmen of Pompeii. The *aurifices* declared themselves as supporters of an electoral candidate, and Campanus, a *gemmarius,* is hailed by the metal-engraver (*caelator*) Priscus. A dealer or cutter of gemstones, Pinarius Cerialis, lived in a house (III, 4b) on the Via dell'Abbondanza, in which were found some engraving tools and a box containing 114 cut and partially worked carnelians, sardonyx, amethysts, and agates.

Most of the fine glass found in Pompeii probably came from Puteoli, where glassblowing was a major industry. No glass furnaces have yet been found at Pompeii itself, but these would in any case have tended to be located outside the residential districts in areas as yet only very summarily explored. There are, moreover, several rather simple forms—a particular type of plain beaker, for example, and a special form of squat, handled wine jug (*askos*)—that appear to be peculiar to Pompeii. It seems likely that, like jobbing bronze-workers, small potters, and lamp-makers, there were also glass-workers catering for the simple everyday needs of the town.

Among the other craftsmen active at Pompeii, there were a great many painters, mosaicists, and stuccoists. The almost total absence of any reference to them in the inscriptions and in the *graffiti* does, however, suggest that, as at many other periods of history, such men tended to travel wherever their skills were required, and that most of them were based elsewhere in Campania. There was also a measure of centralized workshop production for some of the finest pieces, such as the mosaic *emblemata* that constituted the highly prized centerpieces of many of the best pavements (as in the House of the Menander; see illustration) and that were made in specially transportable trays. The same would have applied to the painted *pinakes* that, being on wood, have almost all perished. In both cases one thinks naturally of Neapolis, that great local center of conservative Greek culture, the Roman-period archaeology of which is probably lost to us forever.

HERCULANEUM

Herculaneum lay on the coast, on a spur projecting from the foot of Vesuvius, about five miles east of Neapolis (Naples) and ten miles west of Pompeii. The ancient coastline is today so overlaid by later deposits that it calls for a strong effort of the imagination to picture Herculaneum as it is described by the first-century-B.C. historian Sisenna, namely as a small city set on a headland between two inlets that served as harbors. Dionysius of Halicarnassus refers to the excellence of these harbors, and Strabo refers to it as an unusually healthy place. To judge from the few references in ancient literature (and archaeology has as yet barely touched the earlier levels) its early history was very similar to that of Pompeii. Founded probably as a fortified Greek trading post, it passed with Pompeii under Samnite rule. During the Social War it was occupied by Sulla's troops in 89 B.C., but there is no evidence to indicate that, like Pompeii, it was refounded as a Roman colony. Instead, at about this time it seems to have acquired the status of a municipality (*municipium*), a status that involved the establishment of municipal institutions closely akin to those of a *colonia,* but without any expropriations of property or the introduction of fresh citizens from outside. Though badly damaged in the earthquake of A.D. 62, Herculaneum made a more rapid recovery than Pompeii. Within the area excavated much is rebuilt or redecorated, but there is little unfinished work. In broad essentials the two cities continued to have much in common, enough certainly to justify the use of exhibits from Herculaneum wherever, for one reason or another, comparable material is not available from Pompeii.

There were, however, also significant differences, of which two in particular deserve mention here. One is that whereas Pompeii, thanks to its position at the mouth of the river Sarno, became a prosperous local port and market town, Herculaneum developed on more exclusively residential lines. Some local commerce it did of course have: the main coast road ran straight across the town, of which it was one of the principal transverse streets, and the harbor was the natural outlet for the vineyards of the southern slopes of Vesuvius. But one has only to walk through the streets of the excavated quarter to sense the difference of atmosphere: almost exclusively residential, with shops and bars grouped along two of the main streets and very little trace of local industry. Herculaneum's role was that of a miniature Brighton, profiting from its salubrious climate and from the proximity of many wealthy villas. One of these, the Villa of the Papyri, the property of L. Calpurnius Piso Caesoninus, the father-in-law of Caesar, lay just outside the west gate. Here, eighteenth-century tunneling brought to light a unique series of late Hellenistic bronze sculptures and a library of more than a thousand papyrus rolls, most of them—such are the ironies of archaeological survival—the works of minor Epicurean philosophers. The area of the city so far uncovered, running southward from the main cross-street toward the southeastern part of the sea frontage of the promontory, is laid out on a street grid of Greek type. Among the public buildings excavated, or explored by tunneled galleries in the eighteenth-century manner, are a small but richly adorned theater; a building opening off the main street that may or may not prove to have been a basilica; two public bath buildings, one within the town and akin to the Stabian baths and a more modern building outside the walls; and on the east side of the town a large *palaestra* similar to that near the Amphitheater at Pompeii. Still to be located, but known from inscriptions, are a market building (*macellum*), a temple of Isis, and a temple of Magna Mater, the predecessor of which had been destroyed by the earthquake and was restored in A.D. 76 through the bounty of the emperor Vespasian.

Herculaneum

A second and to ourselves very important distinction between Pompeii and Herculaneum is the very different manner in which they were hit by the final catastrophe, a circumstance that has materially affected the nature and condition of the surviving remains. Whereas Pompeii was slowly but inexorably engulfed by layer upon layer of airborne, sulphurous debris, at Herculaneum the destruction took place in two sharply distinguishable stages. The initial bombardment of incandescent pebbles and rocks resulting from the first explosion may well have been more intense than at Pompeii; it will be recalled (see page 37) that a few hours later Pliny the Elder was already unable to put ashore here and had to coast down to Stabiae. But there was not much ash, and most of the inhabitants seem to have been able to make good their escape up the road to Naples. Relatively few bodies have been found within the city. Then came the second stage, in which the town was engulfed by a horrendous avalanche of liquid mud, swept down the mountainside by the torrential rains that frequently accompany an eruption, and channeled toward Herculaneum by the valleys of which the city's two harbors were the mouths. A wall of mud flooded through the streets and into the houses, bringing down the roofs of some and filling up others. When the area became once more accessible, the coastline had changed beyond all recognition. The city lay buried beneath a mantle of deposit in places as much as sixty-five feet deep, which was rapidly hardening into the solid rock through which well-diggers in the early eighteenth century chanced upon the Roman theater, and upon which the houses of the modern Resina now stand.

This sequence of events had several important consequences. One is that whatever was not destroyed by the first impact of fire and mud was securely sealed against all intrusion until modern times. At Pompeii few of the public buildings or the wealthier houses escaped the post-eruption attentions of their owners or of looters. They could be located because many of the taller landmarks were still visible, and although it was dangerous work (and some of the bodies found are certainly those of looters rather than of eruption victims), there were rich prizes to be won. The Forum area was stripped of its bronze statuary and much of its marble and fine building stone, and private houses were ransacked for their treasure chests and other valuables. At Herculaneum all that was not removed during the first few hours of the eruption was preserved for posterity. Sadly, the eighteenth-century treasure hunters destroyed far more than they recovered, but even so we have a unique body of public statuary found as and where it was used in antiquity. Another consequence was the preservation not merely of the impressions of organic objects, but also in many cases of the actual carbonized remains of the objects themselves, such things as furnishings and woodwork, doors and screens, foodstuffs, or the papyrus rolls referred to above. Such objects are, alas, too fragile to travel, but they have added very materially to our knowledge of many aspects of daily life in antiquity, which in normal circumstances are irrevocably lost.

BIBLIOGRAPHY

1. Periodicals and reference works cited in the catalogue in abbreviated form

AA	Archaeologischer Anzeiger (in JdAI), Berlin.
AJA	American Journal of Archaeology, New York.
Annali dell'Inst	Annali dell'Instituto di Corrispondenza Archeologica, Rome.
AZ	Archäologische Zeitung, Berlin.
BdA	Bollettino d'Arte, Florence.
BJb	Bonner Jahrbücher, Bonn.
BMC Gems	H. B. Walters, Catalogue of the Engraved Gems and Cameos . . . in the British Museum, 2nd ed., London 1926.
BMC Lamps	H. B. Walters, Catalogue of the Greek and Roman Lamps . . . in the British Museum, London 1914.
BMFA	Bulletin of the Museum of Fine Arts, Boston.
Bronzi di Ercolano	Le Antichità di Ercolano esposte, vols V-VI (= I Bronzi di Ercolano 1-2), Naples 1767 and 1771.
Bull Inst	Bullettino dell'Instituto di Corrispondenza Archeologica, Rome.
Ceci	Museo Nazionale, Naples, Piccoli bronzi del Real Museo borbonico . . . descritte e disegnata da Carlo Ceci, 2nd ed., Naples 1858.
CIL	Corpus Inscriptionum Latinarum.
Daremberg & Saglio	C. Daremberg and E. Saglio, Dictionnaire des antiquités grecques et romaines, Paris 1877-1919.
EAA	Enciclopedia dell' arte antica, classica e orientale, vols I-VII, Rome 1958-1966.
ILS	H. Dessau, ed., Inscriptiones Latinae Selectae, 3 vols, Berlin 1892-1916.
JdAI	Jahrbuch des deutschen archaeologischen Instituts, Berlin.
JRS	Journal of Roman Studies, London.
Kraus & von Matt	T. Kraus and L. von Matt, Pompeii and Herculaneum: Living Cities of the Dead, New York 1975 (English translation of Lebendiges Pompeji, Cologne 1973).
MAAR	Memoirs of the American Academy in Rome, Rome.
MB	Real Museo Borbonico, 1st ed. in 16 vols, Naples 1824-1857; subsequent ed. with major alterations, in 9 vols, Rome 1837-1845.
MdI	Mitteilungen des deutschen archäologischen Instituts (1948), Berlin.
MemErc	Memorie della Regale Accademia Ercolanese di Archeologia, Naples 1840-1848.
MemLinc	Memorie dell'Accademia nazionale dei Lincei, Rome.
Mon Pitt	Monumenti della pittura antica scoperti in Italia, Rome.
Muse	Muse, Annual of the Museum of Art and Archaeology, University of Missouri-Columbia.
Neue Forschungen	Neue Forschungen in Pompeji, ed. B. Andreae and H. Kyrieleis, Recklinghausen 1975.
NSc	Notizie degli scavi di antichità communicate alla (Reale) Accademia dei Lincei, Rome.
PAH	Pompeianorum Antiquitatum Historia, ed. G. Fiorelli, 3 vols, Naples 1860-1864.
Pitture di Ercolano	Le Antichità di Ercolano esposte, vols I-V (= Le Pitture di Ercolano, 1-5), Naples 1757-1779.
Pompeiana	Pompeiana. Raccolta di studi per il secondo centenario degli scavi di Pompei, Naples 1950.
RAAN (Rend Nap)	Rendiconti dell'Accademia di Archeologia, Lettere e Belle Arti di Napoli.
RendLinc	Rendiconti della R. Accademia dei Lincei.
Rev Arch	Revue Archéologique, Paris.
RM	Mitteilungen des deutschen archäologischen Instituts. Römische Abteilung, Rome (commonly referred to as Römische Mitteilungen).

2. General bibliography, listed in alphabetical order under author's name. Any abbreviations used in the catalogue are given below in parentheses following the individual entries.

Andreae, B. "Rekonstruktion der grossen Oecus der Villa des P. Fannius Synistor in Boscoreale," in Neue Forschungen 71-92.

Andreae, B., and others. Pompeji: Leben und Kunst in den Vesuvstädten [catalogue of exhibition Villa Hügel Essen]. Recklinghausen 1975 (Andreae, Pompeji).

Andreau, J. Les affaires de Monsieur Jucundus. Ecole Française de Rome, 1974 (Andreau).

Augusti, S. "La tecnica dell'antica pittura parietale pompeiana." Pompeiana 1950, 313-354.

Barnabei, F. La Villa Pompeiana di P. Fannio Sinistore scoperta presso Boscoreale. Rome 1901.

Barnabei, F. Pompei e la regione sotterrata dal Vesuvio nell'anno LXXIX. Naples 1879.

Beloch, J. Campanien im Alterthum. 2nd ed. Naples 1890.

Beyen, H. G. Über Stilleben aus Pompeji und Herculaneum. The Hague 1928 (Beyen, Stilleben).

Beyen, H. G. "The Workshops of the 'Fourth Style' at Pompeii and in Its Neighbourhood." 1. Studia archaeologica G. Van Hoorn oblato. Leiden 1951.

Bianchi Bandinelli, R. Rome: The Centre of Power. Roman Art to A.D. 200. London 1970 (Bianchi Bandinelli).

Bieber, M. History of the Greek and Roman Theater. Princeton 1939 (Bieber, Theater).

Blanckenhagen, P. H. von, and Alexander, M. The Paintings from Boscotrecase. Heidelberg 1962 (Blanckenhagen and Alexander, Boscotrecase).

Boyce, G. K. "Corpus of the Lararia of Pompeii," MAAR XIV, 1937 (Boyce).

Breglia, L. Catalogo delle oreficerie del Museo di Napoli. Rome 1941 (Breglia).

Carrington, R. C. Pompeii. Oxford 1936.

Carrington, R. C. "Studies in the Campanian 'Villa rusticae'." JRS 21 (1931), 110-130.

Casella, D. "Frutta nelle pitture pompeiane." Pompeiana 1950, 355-386.

Castrén, P. Ordo Populusque Pompeianus: Polity and Society in Roman Pompeii (Acta Instituti Romani Finlandiae vol. VIII). Rome 1975 (Castrén).

Chiurazzi, Società anonima, fonderie-ceramica-marmeria, Napoli. Catalogo, compilato da Salvatore Chiurazzi. Naples, n.d. (Chiurazzi).

Coarelli, F., ed. Guida archeologica di Pompei. Verona 1976.

Made possible by grants from
The National Endowment for the Humanities
and Xerox Corporation

Comparetti, D., and De Petra, G. *La Villa Ercolanese dei Pisoni, suoi monumenti e biblioteca*. Turin 1883.

Cosenza, G. *Stabia: Memorie storiche ed archeologiche*. Castellamare di Stabia 1890.

Cosenza, G. *Studi archeologici topografici e storici su Stabia*. Trani 1907.

Croisille, J. M. *Les natures mortes campaniennes* (Coll. Latomus, LXXVI). Brussels 1965 (Croisille).

Curtius, L. *Die Wandmalerei Pompejis*. Leipzig 1929; reprinted Darmstadt 1972 (Curtius).

D'Arms, J. H. *Romans on the Bay of Naples*. Cambridge, Mass. 1970 (D'Arms).

Dawson, Ch. M. "Romano-Campanian Mythological Landscape Painting." *Yale Classical Studies* 9, 1944 (Dawson).

De Franciscis, A. *The Pompeian Wall Paintings in the Roman Villa of Oplontis*. Recklinghausen 1975.

De Franciscis, A. *Il ritratto romano a Pompei*. Naples 1951 (De Franciscis).

Della Corte, M. *Case ed abitanti di Pompei*. Pompei Scavi 1954.

Della Corte, M. *Pompei: I nuovi scavi e l'anfiteatro*. Pompeii 1930.

De Ridder, A. *Les bronzes antiques du Louvre* II, *Les Instruments*. Paris 1915.

Di Capua, F. "Sacrari Pompeiani." *Pompeiana* 1950, 60-85.

D'Orsi, L. *Come ritrovai l'Antica Stabia*. Milan 1962.

Elia, O. "Nota per uno studio della decorazione parietale a Pompei." *Pompeiana* 1950, 97-110.

Elia, O. "Le pitture della casa del Citarista." *MonPitt: Pompei*, fasc. 1, Rome 1937.

Elia, O. "Le pitture del Tempio di Iside." *MonPitt: Pompei*, fasc. 3-4. Rome 1942 (Elia, *MonPitt*).

Elia, O. *Le pitture di Stabia*. Naples 1957.

Elia, O. *Pitture murali e mosaici del Museo Nazionale di Napoli*. Naples 1932 (Elia).

Eschebach, H. "Feststellung unter der Oberflache des Jahres 79 n. Chr. im Bereich der Insula VII, I – Stabianer Thermen – in Pompeji" in *Neue Forschungen* 179-190.

Eschebach, H. "Die stadtbauliche Entwicklung des antiken Pompeji." *RM* Ergänzungsheft no. 17. Heidelberg 1970.

Etienne, R. *La vie quotidienne à Pompei*. Paris 1966.

Fienga, F. "Esplorazione del pago marittimo pompeiano." *Atti del III Congresso Nazionale di Studi Romani*. Bologna 1934, 172-176.

Fiorelli, G. *Catalogo del Museo Nazionale di Napoli, Armi antiche*. Naples 1869 (Fiorelli, *Armi antiche*).

Fiorelli, G. *Catalogo del Museo Nazionale di Napoli, Raccolta pornografica*. Naples 1866 (Fiorelli, *Raccolta pornografica*).

Fiorelli, G. *Gli scavi di Pompei dal 1861 al 1872*. Naples 1873 (Fiorelli, *Scavi*).

Gell, W., and Gandi, J. P., *Pompeiana: The Topography, Edifices and Ornaments of Pompeii*. 2 vols. London 1817-1819.

Gigante, M. "La cultura letteraria a Pompei." *Pompeiana* 1950, 111-143.

Gusman, P. *Pompéi: La ville, les moeurs, les arts*. Paris [1899?]; English ed. *Pompeii: The City, Its Life and Art*. London 1900 (Gusman).

Harden, D. B. "The Glass," in Hawkes, C. F. C., and Hull, M. R. *Camulodunum*, 287-306. Oxford 1947 (Harden, *Camulodunum*).

Helbig, W. *Untersuchungen über die campanische Wandmalerei*. Leipzig 1873.

Helbig, W. *Wandgemälde der vom Vesuv verschutteten Städte*. Leipzig 1868 (Helbig).

Héron de Villefosse, V. "Le Trésor de Boscoreale." *Monuments Piot* v, 1899.

Higgins, R. A. *Greek and Roman Jewellery*. London 1961.

Ippel, A. *Der dritte pompejanische Stil*. Berlin 1910.

Isings, C. *Roman Glass from Dated Finds* (Archaeologica traiectina II). Groningen 1957 (Isings).

Jacono, L. "Note di archeologia marittima. I. Il Porto di Pompei?." *Neapolis* I, 1913 fasc. III-IV, 353ff.

Jashemsky, W. F. "The Caupona of Euxinus at Pompeii." *Archaeology* XX (1967) 36-44.

Jashemsky, W. F. "The Discovery of a Market Garden Orchard at Pompeii." *AJA* 78 (1974) 391-404.

Jashemsky, W. F. "Excavation in the Foro Boario at Pompeii." *AJA* 72 (1968) 69-73.

Jashemsky, W. F. "From Vesuvius' Dust: Pompeii Emerges a City of Gardens, Vineyards." *Landscape Architecture*, May 1976, 224-230.

Jashemsky, W. F. "A Large Vineyard Discovered in Ancient Pompeii." *Science* 180 (1973) 826.

Jashemsky, W. F. "Pompeian Gardens Yield Their Secrets." *American Horticultural Magazine*, spring 1970, 54-63.

Jashemsky, W. F. "Tomb Gardens at Pompeii." *Classical Journal* 66 (1970-71) 97-115.

Johannowsky, W. "Contributi alla topografia della Campania antica." *RAAN* n.s. XXVII 1952, 83-146.

Kapossy, B. *Brunnenfiguren der hellenistischen und römischen Zeit*. Zurich 1969 (Kapossy, *Brunnenfiguren*).

Kirschen, F. *Die Stadtmauern von Pompeji* (Die hellenistische Kunst in Pompeji VII). Berlin 1941.

Kluge, K., and Lehmann-Hartleben, K. *Die antiken Grossbronzen*. 3 vols. Berlin and Leipzig 1927 (Kluge-Hartleben).

Laidlaw, A. "A Reconstruction of the First Style Decoration in the Alexander Exedra of the House of the Faun," in *Neue Forschungen* 39-52.

Lauter, H. "Zur Siedlungsstruktur Pompejis in Samnitischen Zeit," in *Neue Forschungen* 147-154.

Lauter-Bufe, H. "Zur architektonischen Gartengestaltung in Pompeji und Herculaneum," in *Neue Forschungen* 169-173.

Lehmann, P. W. *Roman Wall Paintings from Boscoreale in the Metropolitan Museum of Art*. Cambridge, Mass. 1953.

Lepore, E. "Orientamenti per la storia sociale di Pompei." *Pompeiana* 1950, 144-166.

Levi, A. *Le terracotte figurati del Museo Nazionale di Napoli*. Florence 1926 (Levi).

Maiuri, A. *La casa del Menandro e il suo tesoro di argenteria*. 2 vols. Rome 1933 (Maiuri, *Menandro*).

Maiuri, A. *Ercolano: i nuovi scavi (1927-1958)*, vol. 1. Rome 1958 (Maiuri, *Ercolano*).

Maiuri, A. "Geologia ed archeologia ad Ercolano ed a Pompei." *RAAN* n.s. XXII 1942-1946, 113-140.

Maiuri, A. "Gli scavi di Pompei dal 1879 al 1948." *Pompeiana* 1950, 9-40.

Maiuri, A. *Herculaneum*. Paris 1932.

Maiuri, A. "Le pitture delle case di M. Fabius Amandio, del Sacerdos Amandus, di Cornelius Teges." *MonPitt: Pompei*, fasc. 2, Rome 1938.

Maiuri, A. *L'ultima fase edilizia di Pompei*. Rome 1942 (Maiuri, *L'ultima fase*).

Maiuri, A. *La Villa dei Misteri*. Rome 1947.

Mau, A. *Geschichte der decorativen Wandmalerei in Pompeji*. Berlin 1882.

Mau, A. *Pompeji in Leben und Kunst*. 2nd ed. Leipzig 1908; supplement to 2nd ed., Leipzig 1913.

Mau, A., and Kelsey, F. W. *Pompeii, Its Life and Art*. New York 1899 (Mau-Kelsey).

Mustilli, D. "Botteghe di scultori, marmorarii, bronzieri e caelatores in Pompei." *Pompeiana* 1950, 206-229.

Mustilli, D. "La villa pseudo-urbana ercolanese." *RAAN* n.s. XXXI 1956, 77-97.

Niccolini, F. *Le case ed i monumenti di Pompei designati e descritti*. Naples 1854-96 (Niccolini).

Nissen, H. *Pompeianische Studien zur Städtekunde des Altertums*. Leipzig 1877.

Noack, F., and Lehmann-Hartleben, K. *Baugeschichtliche Untersuchungen am Stadtrand von Pompeji* (Denkmäler antiker Architektur II). Berlin and Leipzig 1936.

Onorato, G. O. "La data del terremoto di Pompei: 5 febbraio 62 d.C." *RAAN* ser.8, IV 1949, 644-661.

Overbeck, J. *Pompeji in seinem Gebäuden, Alterthümern und Kunstwerken.* Leipzig 1884.

Packer, J. "Middle and Lower Class Housing in Pompeii and Herculaneum: A Preliminary Survey," in *Neue Forschungen* 133-146.

Palombi, A. "La fauna marina nei mosaici e nei dipinti pompeiani." *Pompeiana* 1950, 425-455.

Pernice, E. *Gefässe und Geräte aus Bronze* (Die hellenistische Kunst in Pompeji IV). Berlin 1925 (Pernice IV).

Pernice, E. *Hellenistische Tische, Zisternenmundungen, Beckenuntersätze, Altare, und Truhen* (Die hellenistische Kunst in Pompeji V). Berlin 1932 (Pernice V).

Pernice, E. *Pavimente und figürliche Mosaiken* (Die hellenistische Kunst in Pompeji VI). Berlin 1938 (Pernice VI).

Peters, W. J. T. *Landscape in Romano-Campanian Mural Painting.* Assen 1963 (Peters).

Presuhn, E. *Pompeii: Les dernières fouilles de 1874-1878.* Leipzig 1878.

Pugliese Carratelli, G. "L'instrumentum scriptorium nei monumenti pompeiani ed ercolanensi." *Pompeiana* 1950, 266-278.

Reuterswaard, P. *Studien zur Polychromie der Plastik: Griechenland und Rom.* Stockholm 1960 (Reuterswaard, *Polychromie*).

Richardson, L. "Pompeii: The Casa dei Dioscuri and Its Painters." *MAAR* XXIII, 1955 (Richardson).

Rittmann, A. "L'eruzione vesuviana del 79." *Pompeiana* 1950, 456-474.

Rizzo, G. E. *La pittura ellenistica-romana.* Milan 1929.

Rocco, A. "*Pompeiana supellex.*" *Pompeiana* 1950, 278-287.

Rodenwaldt, G. *Die Komposition der pompejanische Wandgemälde.* Berlin 1900.

Rostowzew, M. "Die hellenistische-römische Architekturlandschaft." *RM* XXVI (1911) 1-186 (Rostowzew, "Architekturlandschaft").

Roux Aîné, H. *Herculanum et Pompei: Recueil général des peintures, bronzes, mosaiques, etc.* 8 vols. Paris 1870-1872.

Ruesch, A., ed. *Guida illustrata del Museo Nazionale di Napoli.* Naples 1908 (Ruesch).

Ruggiero, M. *Degli scavi di Stabia dal 1749 al 1782.* Naples 1881 (Ruggiero, *Stabia*).

Salmon, E. T. *Samnium and the Samnites.* Cambridge 1967.

Schefold, K. *La peinture pompéienne* (Coll. Latomus no. CVIII). Brussels 1972 (Schefold).

Schefold, K. *Pompejanische Malerei.* Basle 1952.

Schefold, K. *Vergessenes Pompeji.* Munich 1962.

Schefold, K. *Die Wände Pompejis.* Berlin 1957 (Schefold, *WP*).

Siviero, R. *Gli ori e le ambre del Museo Nazionale di Napoli.* Florence 1954 (Siviero).

Sogliano, A. "Le pitture murale campagne scoverte negli anni 1867-1879 descritte," in *Pompei e la regione sotterrata dal Vesuvio,* vol. 11 87 ff. Naples 1879 (Sogliano).

Sogliano, A. *Pompei nel suo sviluppo storico. Pompei preromana (dalle origini alle 80 av. C.).* Rome 1937.

Spano, G. "Porte e regione pompeiane e vie campane." *RAAN* n.s. XVII, 1937, 269ff.

Spinazzola, V. *Le arti decorative in Pompei e nel Museo Nazionale di Napoli.* Milan 1928 (Spinazzola).

Spinazzola, V. *Pompei alla luce degli scavi nuovi di Via dell' Abbondanza,* vols. I-III. Rome 1953 (Spinazzola-Aurigemma).

Strong, D. E. *Greek and Roman Silver Plate.* London 1966 (Strong).

Tanzer, H. H. *The Common People of Pompeii* (The Johns Hopkins University Studies in Archaeology no. 29). Baltimore 1939.

Thédenat, H. *Les villes d'art célèbres: Pompéi.* Paris 1910.

Tran tam Tinh, V. *Le culte des divinités orientales à Herculaneum* (Etudes préliminaires aux réligions orientales dans l'empire romain no. 17). Leiden 1971 (Tran tam Tinh, *Herculaneum*).

Tran tam Tinh, V. *Essai sur le culte d'Isis à Pompéi.* Paris 1964 (Tran tam Tinh, *Pompéi*).

Tran tam Tinh, V. "Les problèmes du culte de Cybèle et d'Attis à Pompéi," in *Neue Forschungen* 279-283 (Tran tam Tinh, 1975).

Van Buren, A. W. *A Companion to the Study of Pompeii and Herculaneum.* Rome 1933; 2nd ed. Rome 1938.

Venuti, M. *A Description of the Discovery of the Ancient City of Heraclea,* trs. W. Skurray. London 1750 (Venuti, *Heraclea*).

Von Rohden, H. *Die Terracotten von Pompeji.* Stuttgart 1880 (Von Rohden).

Waldstein, C., and Shoobridge, L. *Herculaneum Past, Present and Future.* London 1908.

Webster, T. B. L. *Monuments Illustrating New Comedy.* 2nd ed. (University of London, Bulletin of the Institute of Classical Studies, Supplement 24, 1969) (Webster, *New Comedy*).

Webster, T. B. L. *Monuments Illustrating Tragedy and Satyr Play.* 2nd ed. (University of London, Bulletin of the Institute of Classical Studies, Supplement 20, 1967) (Webster, *Tragedy and Satyr Play*).

Winter, F. *Die figürlichen Typen der Terracotten.* 2 vols. Leipzig 1903 (Winter).

Witt, R. E. *Isis in the Graeco-Roman World.* London 1971.

Zahn, W. *Die schönsten Ornamente und merkwürdigsten Gemälde aus Pompeji, Herkulanum und Stabiae.* 3 vols. Berlin 1827-1859.

Zevi, F. *La casa Reg. IX, 5, 18-21 a Pompei e le sue pitture.* Rome 1964.

3. Some Recent Books in English

Boethius, A., and Ward-Perkins, J. B. *Etruscan and Roman Architecture,* chs. 13 and 14 (Pelican History of Art). London 1970.

Brion, M. *Pompeii and Herculaneum: The Glory and the Grief.* London and Toronto 1960.

Bulwer-Lytton, E. *The Last Days of Pompeii,* abridged ed. London 1976.

Clay, E., and Frederiksen, M. *Sir William Gell in Italy: Letters to the Society of Dilettanti, 1831-1835.* London 1976.

Deiss, J. J. *Herculaneum, Italy's Buried Treasure.* New York 1966.

Grant, M. *Cities of Vesuvius: Pompeii and Herculaneum.* London 1971 (Grant, *Cities of Vesuvius*).

Grant, M., De Simone, A., and Merella, M. T. *Erotic Art in Pompeii.* London 1975 (Grant, De Simone, and Merella).

Leppmann, W. *Pompeii in Fact and Fiction.* London 1968.

McKay, A. G. *Houses, Villas and Palaces in the Roman World,* ch. 2. London 1975.

Trevelyan, R. *The Shadow of Vesuvius: Pompeii AD 79.* London 1976.

GLOSSARY

Acroterion (plural *acroteria*) Decorative finial at the apex or the outer angles of a gabled roof.

Aedicula A small ornamental structure projecting from a wall, usually consisting of a gable carried by a pair of colonnettes or pilasters. Often reproduced in the fantasy architecture of Pompeian wall paintings.

Aedile (Latin *aedilis*) One of the pair of junior magistrates elected annually to supervise the day-to-day administration of the city. The office already existed in Samnite Pompeii.

Ala A wing extending to right and left at the far end of the atrium of a typical Pompeian house, giving access to the rooms on either side of the *tablinum*.

Amorino A cupid.

Aphrodite, see *Venus*.

Apollo The Greek god of the arts and music, early absorbed into the Italian pantheon. The principal divinity of Samnite Pompeii.

Artemis The Roman Diana, commonly portrayed as a huntress in her role as the goddess of forests and hills and of wild creatures.

Athena, see *Minerva*.

Atrium The central hall of a traditional Italic house. The roof normally sloped inward to a rectangular central opening.

Bacchus, see *Dionysus*.

Basilica A colonnaded public hall, usually adjoining the forum, used for commercial and judicial business.

Belvedere A raised building from which to enjoy a view.

Caduceus The wand carried by Hermes (Mercury), with wings and two symmetrically entwined serpents.

Cornucopia A horn overflowing with fruits, symbol of plenty.

Cubiculum (plural *cubicula*) Bedroom.

Dionysus The Roman Bacchus, god of wine and of the theater, whose cult involved "mysteries" as well as ecstatic rites. Among his followers were satyrs, sileni, and maenads. Satyrs, originally spirits of wild life in the woods and hills, in Roman times were regularly portrayed in youthful human form but with pointed ears and tails and frequently with some of the goat-like attributes of the god Pan. Sileni, like satyrs, were originally woodland creatures part-man, part-horse, normally shown as elderly, shaggy, paunchy figures, frequently the worse for wine. Maenads were their female companions, usually portrayed in attitudes of ecstatic abandon.

Duovir (plural *duoviri*) One of the pair of senior magistrates elected annually to represent the city and to act as joint chairmen of the city council. Every fifth year these magistrates had special powers and were called *duoviri quinquennales*. The equivalent magistrates in the Samnite period were called *meddices* (singular *meddix*).

Emblema Strictly, a small panel in fine mosaic, produced separately to be inserted into a larger floor (see No. 61). Also used as the central feature of any larger decorative design.

Ephebe (Greek *ephebos*) An aristocratic Greek youth who had not yet completed his education.

Escutcheon Term used to indicate a piece of applied decoration, as commonly in metalwork.

Exedra A large rectangular or curved recess opening off a room or corridor.

Hera, see *Juno*.

Hercules Latin form of Heracles, the Greek hero who performed twelve labors for the king of Argos and was later worshiped as a god for his strength and power to repel evil. Particularly favored by merchants.

Herm The name derives from early Greek representations of the god Hermes in the form of a rectangular shaft with a carved head. Later, more elaborate versions carried heads also of other divinities and human portraits.

Hermes The Roman Mercury, the messenger of the gods and patron divinity of commerce.

Impluvium The rectangular basin in the center of the atrium of a Pompeian house, situated beneath the rectangular opening (*compluvium*) in the center of the roof.

Insula (Latin, "island") Term used conventionally to denote an ancient city block.

Intarsia (Italian *intarsio*) Shaped designs of wood, stone, or metal inlaid into a background that has been cut out to receive them. See Nos. 174-176.

Juno The Greek Hera, the consort of Jupiter and the goddess specially concerned with those aspects of life which affected women (the home, marriage, childbirth, etc.).

Jupiter God of the heavens, whose special attribute was a thunderbolt. The patron divinity of Rome (Jupiter Optimus Maximus Capitolinus) and, with Juno and Minerva, the senior member of the Capitoline triad. Generally equated with the Greek Zeus.

Lararium Household shrine, with statuettes or painted representations of the Lares, the traditional guardians of the house, and of other favored gods. See No. 210.

Lares, see *Lararium*.

Maenad, see under *Dionysus*.

Medusa A mythical female monster with snakes for hair and eyes that turned to stone those who looked upon her.

Mercury, see *Hermes*.

Minerva Goddess of wisdom, learning, and the arts and sciences. With Jupiter and Juno, the third member of the Roman Capitoline triad. Equated by the Romans with Athena.

Oecus (Greek *oikos*) A richly decorated living room.

Onkos Greek hairstyle, found commonly on theatrical masks; see Nos. 306–309.

Opus sectile Paving or wall decoration made of interlocking shaped pieces of colored marble.

Oscillum (plural *oscilla*) Originally a mask or other ritual object, hung from a sacred tree, which "oscillated" or spun in the wind. Later used in a variety of shapes in peristyle gardens, hung from the architrave between the columns.

Ovolo (from the Latin *ovum*, an egg) A convex molding of egg-shaped profile.

Palaestra Open space reserved for exercise and sport. Usually enclosed by colonnades.

Pan A Greek pastoral divinity, responsible for the fertility of flocks. Often shown as half-goat, half-man, playing on his panpipe (see Nos. 69, 114).

Peristyle The inner, colonnaded garden court of a Pompeian (or Hellenistic) house, around which the main living rooms of the later houses were grouped.

Pinax (plural *pinakes*) A panel picture painted on wood or marble and often enclosed in a frame that could be closed like a triptych. Few actual *pinakes* have survived, but there are many representations of them in wall paintings.

Priapus Rustic god of fertility, regularly portrayed displaying a huge male organ.

Satyr, see under *Dionysus*.

Silenus, see under *Dionysus*.

Siren A mythological creature, half-woman and half-bird.

Stucco A hard slow-setting plaster based on lime, used for rendering wall surfaces or for molded architectural detail.

Tablinum The central room at the far end of an atrium house, often with a window opening onto the garden beyond. It was the main reception room and could be closed off from the atrium by a screen or curtains. In the late houses it opens also onto the peristyle.

Tempietto (Italian) A small temple-shaped building, either circular or gabled, with columns.

Terra sigillata Conventional name for the red-gloss pottery first produced in Italy at Arezzo, and later in many other places both in Italy and the western provinces of the Empire. It is found both in plain forms and with molded relief decoration, in both cases closely modeled on the shapes and ornament of silverware. See Nos. 258-262.

Tesserae (*tessellae*) Small cubes or splinters of colored stone, glass, or paste used to make mosaics.

Tholos A circular columned pavilion or *tempietto*

CATALOGUE

I The Town, the Countryside, and the Volcano

1

Pair of villa landscapes
Width 53 cm, height 22 cm
Naples Museum, inv. 9406
From Pompeii

Two separate views of villa façades probably from the lateral panels of a Third
Style scheme (see illustration p. 96), now
mounted as a pair. The left-hand view
shows a straight porticoed façade upraised on a platform with a tall columnar
central porch; in front of the portico is a
garden with a large axial enclosure and at
either end, rising from a lower level, is a
double portico, of two orders, facing outward. Above and beyond the right-hand
portico is the façade of a temple-like
building facing inward; there may have
been other buildings or trees in the damaged upper left-hand part. The right-hand
view shows a central gabled porch at the
junction of two gable-ended, inward-
facing porticoes, enclosing on three sides
a trapezoidal space concentric to which is
an enclosure with posts at the angles.
Above and behind rise a number of other
buildings including a circular *tempietto*
(*tholos*) and another colonnade. The perspective of these scenes is syntactic, and
some of the detail (e.g., the half-gables of
the flanking porticoes on the left-hand
panel) is without parallel in surviving contemporary architecture, but it is generally
accepted that such façades were a feature
of the wealthy *villae marittimae*.
Peters 115f.

2

Painting of a villa beside the sea
Diameter 25 cm
Naples Museum, inv. 9511
From Stabiae

Roundel portraying the two-storied columnar façade of a *villa marittima*. The
center of the façade curves inward, toward
a tower-like circular feature. In front is a
platform with two projecting jetties,
human figures, and statues. Beyond are
other buildings, trees, and a rocky crag on
which are trees and what appears to be a
group of statuary. The roundel and its
companion pieces (Naples Museum, inv.
9408, 9409) would have occupied the
centers of large panels in a Fourth Style
scheme, comparable to those in the first
room off the peristyle in the House of
"Loreius Tiburtinus" (II, 2, 2-5; Schefold,
WP 51).
Rostowzew, "Architekturlandschaft" 75(b);
Peters 157.

1

2

3

Painting of a villa beside the sea
Length 39.5 cm, height 17 cm
Naples Museum, inv. 9480
From Stabiae

The seaward frontage of an elaborate *villa
marittima;* in the foreground is a platform
with arches and steps down to the water,
and in the background are other buildings,
gardens, and a rocky eminence crowned
by a temple. On the platform are sketched
figures, at the bottom right-hand corner
part of a boat, and behind it a statue posed
on a rock.

Probably from the center of a panel in a
Third Style wall, as in the *tablinum* of the
House of M. Lucretius Fronto (see page
96) or possibly used like the landscapes or
still lifes in the wall schemes of the courtyard of the Temple of Isis.
Rostowzew, "Architekturlandschaft" 75,
no. 3; Peters 159f.

3

Sacro-idyllic landscape
Width 30 cm, height 26 cm
Naples Museum, inv. 9447
From Herculaneum

Highly impressionistic view of a rustic sanctuary, a small, circular, tower-like structure, a rocky crag, and trees. On the left a figure is carrying a basin; on the right another figure stoops before a herm. In the center, in shadowy outline, is a statue on a pedestal.

Presumably from the field of a Fourth Style lateral panel, as in the atrium of the House of Fabius Amandio (I, 7, 2-3).

Painting of a sanctuary beside the sea
Width 62 cm, height 52 cm
Naples Museum, inv. 9482
From Pompeii

Painted in light colors on a black ground, this fragment portrays a sanctuary, set on a rocky island or promontory, and in the foreground two boats. The details of the sanctuary are conventional; a central, circular shrine, or *tholos,* flanked by porticoes and a re-entrant façade wall; in front of this, facing onto the water, is an open platform, on which are several groups of figures, including a woman and a dog. On the enclosure wall is a statue, and beyond are trees and buildings perched on rocks. In the left margin are traces of a frame and part of an ornamental column.

The scene probably formed part of a much larger panel set between columns as in the Third Style wall, found at Pompeii on 23 August 1758 (*Pitture di Ercolano* II, p. 273, pl. L), which shows above, in the background, a similar sanctuary; in the middle is a boat and below, in the foreground, another island sanctuary and a fisherman.

Rostowzew, "Architekturlandschaft" 52; Peters 117f.

Wall painting: temple in a landscape
Width 65 cm, height 40 cm
Naples Museum, inv. 9487
From Pompeii

Sacro-idyllic landscape, probably from the middle of one of the lateral panels of a Fourth Style wall. It portrays a small temple in a setting of trees. In front of the temple two figures sacrifice at an altar; behind it is a statue in a columnar setting. In the distance can be seen a portico.

4

5

6

7

8

7
Seascape with boats and buildings
Width 33 cm, height 23 cm
Naples Museum, inv. 9463
From Pompeii

A small, highly impressionistic landscape, including a central *tholos* on a rocky islet with a jetty and two fishermen, a porticoed façade with trees beyond it, and two boats. The scene is viewed as if across a palisaded fence and appears to come from one of the complex architectural framing members of a Fourth Style scheme, as Nos. 144, 145.

Rostowzew, "Architekturlandschaft" 85, note 2.

8
Landscape panel within a stucco cornice
Length 2.10 m, height 52 cm
Naples Museum, inv. 9496
From the *exedra* off the west side of the middle peristyle of the House of the Citharist (I, 4, 5)

A long, narrow, idealized landscape and seascape, set within a stucco cornice of which the left end is missing. At the left end of the field, on a fortified rocky promontory, can be seen a small temple and, at the foot of the slope, a large seated statue on a tall pedestal, accompanied by the inevitable tree. The unusual building with three receding stories is thought to represent a *belvedere*. Beyond it and at the right end are two rather similar buildings with landing stages and porticoed façades enclosing gardens and other buildings, free representations of *villae marittimae*. In the right foreground stands a large urn on a pedestal. This picture blends into a single romantic landscape elements that are derived from a variety of sources, among them some that are derived from the Hellenistic Nilotic landscapes and from the sacro-idyllic repertory and others from the contemporary architecture of the Campanian *villae marittimae*.

Rostowzew, "Architekturlandschaft" 91, no. 4; Peters 165f.

9

10

9
Inscribed slab recording the building of the colonnade round the Forum
Limestone
Height 45.5 cm, width 44 cm
Naples Museum, inv. 3825
Found in 1814 in the Forum, near the entrance to the Basilica

V[ibius] Popidius Ep[idii] f[ilius] q[uaestor] porticus faciendas coeravit.
"Vibius Popidius, son of Epidius, quaestor, had charge of the building of this portico."

The inscription, which dates from the last period before the foundation of the Sullan colony in 80 B.C., records the construction of a portico, built of tufa, around the central open area of the Forum. This Samnite portico, which marked an important step in the monumentalization of the city center, was in process of being replaced at the time of the earthquake and the eruption. The official in charge, Vibius Popidius, was at the time a *quaestor*, one of the junior magistrates of the Samnite town. He belonged to a very prominent indigenous Pompeian family, the Popidii, who are known to have provided at least two chief magistrates (*meddices*) of the pre-Roman period.
CIL x. 794; *ILS* 5538.

10
Inscribed slab recording the rebuilding of the Temple of Isis
Marble, recomposed from 37 pieces
Length 2.35 m, height 49.5 cm
Naples Museum, inv. 3765
Found in 1765 fallen from its position over the entrance from the street to the Temple

N[umerius] Popidius N[umerii] f[ilius] Celsinus aedem Isidis terrae motu conlapsam a fundamento p[ecunia] s[ua] restituit. Hunc decuriones ob liberalitatem cum esset annorum sexs ordini suo gratis adlegerunt.
"Numerius Popidius Celsinus, son of Numerius, at his own expense rebuilt from its foundations the Temple of Isis, which had been totally destroyed by earthquake. In recognition of his generosity the city council elected him to their number without any further fee, although he was only six years old."

The ostensible donor was the son of a wealthy freedman of the Popidius family, Numerius Popidius Ampliatus, who was himself debarred from election to the council of decurions because he had been born a slave. There was normally a lower age limit for the decurionate (often twenty-five years), but exceptions could be made, and in this instance the usual admission fee was also waived. Within the sanctuary the father, Ampliatus, was able to dedicate in his own name a statue of Dionysus (here, as often, identified with Osiris); and Celsinus, together with his mother, Corelia Celsa, and a brother, is named as donor of the pavement in the larger of the two rooms beyond the temple.
CIL x. 846; *ILS* 6367.

11, 12

11, 12
Plaster casts of two marble reliefs showing scenes of the earthquake of A.D. 62
Lengths 86 cm, heights 13 cm and 17 cm
Lent by Imperial Tobacco Limited
Originals from the House of L. Caecilius Jucundus (V, I, 26)

The reliefs formed part of the household shrine (*lararium*). Though carved in a strikingly "popular" style, they afford valuable evidence for the appearance of buildings that were still in ruins at the time of the eruption seventeen years later.

The first relief shows the collapse of the Capitolium at the northern end of the Forum (see plan, page 49), its steps flanked by a pair of equestrian statues. On the left is the monumental arch, of which the core still stands, and on the right an altar to Tellus (Earth), which was demolished when the Forum paving was repaired, leaving only traces of its foundations. Around the altar are shown vessels and instruments for the sacrifice of a bull.

The scene on the second relief would have been visible from Caecilius' house. It shows the Vesuvius Gate collapsing, and beside it the main distribution tower for the city's water supply (*castellum aquae*). Although the structure of the latter withstood the tremors, it was still out of action in A.D. 79. Two mules pulling a cart narrowly escape the falling gate, and on the far right, apparently just outside the walls, is a rustic altar beside a tree, presumably a familiar landmark.

Maiuri, *L'ultima fase* 10ff.

13 (not illus.)
Model of the site of Pompeii
Scale 1:250
Lent by Soprintendenza Archeologica delle Province di Napoli e Caserta

The model shows the present state of the excavations of the town, where about two-fifths remains to be uncovered. Little excavation has taken place outside the walls, and any attempts to investigate the immediate surroundings are greatly hampered by the huge mounds of debris from earlier excavations. A great deal more detailed survey work is needed before it will be possible to establish exactly where the ancient coastline and the port of Pompeii lay in relation to the town itself (see map, page 13).

14
Section through the volcanic and later debris covering the site at Pompeii

The successive layers of lava pebbles, pumice stones, ash, and dust that fell on Pompeii vary considerably in depth from point to point within the town, but the general sequence bears out the evidence of Pliny's account of the eruption (see page 37). One of the clearest, least complicated sections through the deposit was recorded on the level, open ground of the Grand Palaestra beside the Amphitheater, excavated in 1938-1939. The deposits associated with the eruption of A.D. 79 were here, on average, just under twelve feet (3.50 m) deep.

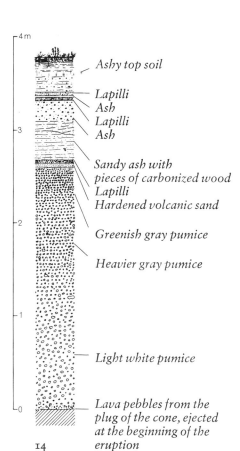

Ashy top soil

Lapilli
Ash
Lapilli
Ash

Sandy ash with pieces of carbonized wood
Lapilli
Hardened volcanic sand

Greenish gray pumice

Heavier gray pumice

Light white pumice

Lava pebbles from the plug of the cone, ejected at the beginning of the eruption

14

15

15
Plaster cast of a watchdog
Height 50 cm
Lent by Imperial Tobacco Limited
Original in Pompeii, Antiquarium
From the House of Vesonius Primus (VI, 14, 20)

The unfortunate dog, wearing his bronze-studded collar, was left chained up, and he suffocated beneath the ash and cinders. These then hardened round the corpse, forming an impression that, with the disintegration of the organic remains, became a perfect hollow mold. It was the archaeologist Fiorelli who first realized that by filling such hollow molds with plaster one could obtain faithful replicas of objects such as bodies, wooden doors, furniture, and foodstuffs.

16
Plaster cast of the body of a young woman
Length 1.50 m
Lent by Imperial Tobacco Limited
Original in Pompeii, Antiquarium

Like almost all the other human victims of the eruption, this young woman died of suffocation from the fumes of the falling ash and cinders, which she had vainly tried to keep from her nose and mouth by pulling her tunic up over her face.

II The People

17

Painted portrait of a man and his wife
Height 65 cm, width 58 cm
Naples Museum, inv. 9058
From House VII, 2, 6, on the back wall of
a small *exedra* opening off the atrium

The man, with a short curly beard and
mustache, wears a toga and carries a
papyrus scroll with a red seal. His wife
wears a red tunic and mantle, and her hair
is dressed in a fashion popular about the
middle of the first century A.D. In her right
hand she holds to her lips a *stylus* (see
No. 274) for writing on the two-leaved
wooden tablet spread with wax (*diptych,*
see also No. 243) which she holds in her
left. Although this pose might be thought
to indicate that the subject had literary
tastes, it is found in other contemporary
portraits of young women and is probably
no more than a fashionable painter's convention. Both in style and in treatment
there is a striking resemblance to the
Egyptian mummy portraits of the Roman
period (as, for example, in the National
Gallery, London, no. 2914).
     The painting belongs to the last years
of the town, when the house and the adjoining workshop area at the corner of the
insula may have belonged to a person who
was involved in baking or patisserie. The
name long but erroneously associated
with this family portrait is that of Paquius
Proculus, whose name appeared on an
election poster painted on the front of the
house. Subsequent attempts to identify
the owner of the house have been ingeni-
ous rather than convincing.

M. della Corte, *JRS* XVI (1926) 146-154;
E. Drerup, *Die Datierung der Mumienporträts*
(Paderborn 1933) pl. 4.

17

18

Wall painting: portrait of a woman in profile
Height 52 cm, width 39 cm
Naples Museum, inv. 9077
From Herculaneum or Stabiae

Framed portrait from the center of the left-hand lateral panel of a Third Style wall. Old drawings of it show bands of ribbons hanging loosely down from the hair over the shoulders, and the loss of this overpainting accounts for the seeming disproportion of the neck. The same drawings indicate that the hair-band was shown as being made of some precious metal, and that from it sprang delicate sprays of flowers probably executed in pearls and emeralds on gold wire stems. The portrait itself is obviously imitating a cameo, and it has been suggested that it represents Cleopatra.
Pitture di Ercolano IV (1765) 109f., fig. 113; R. Herbig, *Nugae Pompeianorum (Bilderhefte des D.A.I. Rom,* I, 1962) 19f.

8

19

19

Wall painting: figure of a girl
Height 56 cm, width 38.5 cm
Naples Museum, inv. 8946
From Pompeii

The girl sits beside or leans against a column, gazing down at something held in her hands, of which only part is preserved. In her hair she wears an ivy wreath. Although she is probably intended to represent a figure sacrificing or in attendance upon some religious occasion, the head has all the appearance of having been drawn from life.

The fragment comes probably from a Fourth Style architectural composition similar to those in the *cubiculum* of the House of Pinarius Cerealis or in the House of Apollo (see page 100).
Elia 215, fig. 30.

20

Bronze portrait bust of a woman
Height 37 cm
Naples Museum, inv. 4990
From the House of the Citharist (I, 4, 5)

Found in the *ala* of the atrium, together with a similar bronze bust of a man (Naples Museum, inv. 4992; see page 106, left). There is some evidence to suggest that this house, once one of the finest in Pompeii, belonged to the influential local family of the Popidii, and this pair of busts, probably of a man and wife, may well in that case represent members of that family. The analogies for both portraits, including the hairstyles, indicate a date in the early first century A.D. There is another portrait head from Pompeii representing almost certainly the same woman, in marble, slightly over life-size (Naples Museum, inv. 120424, see p. 107). The findspot of this is not recorded, but it

20

clearly comes from a public statue, confirming the suggestion that she belonged to one of the ruling families of the city.

The head was cast in two parts; the looped braid at the nape of the neck was cast separately, and all the finer detail of the hair and eyebrows was worked in with a chisel after casting. A striking and rare feature is the preservation of the original right eye (the left eye is partly restored). The eye sockets were left open in casting and were afterward filled with a very fine white cement, into which were set the lens-shaped pupils, made of a brown, semi-precious stone. The bulging of the eyes is due to the swelling of the cement under the damp conditions of burial.
Kluge-Hartleben II, 22f.; De Franciscis 49f.

21

21

Bust of a middle-aged man, perhaps a member of the Popidius family
Rather large-grained, translucent white marble, perhaps from Paros
Height 39 cm
Naples Museum, inv. 6028
Found together with No. 23 in the House of the Citharist (I, 4, 5)

The break across the left shoulder is ancient and was repaired in antiquity with a bronze dowel. The surface of the marble is weathered, suggesting that the bust may have stood originally in a tomb and have been brought to the house for safety after the earthquake of A.D. 62. There are traces of red paint on the hair at the back of the head.

As in the case of No. 23 there have been numerous attempts to identify this as the portrait of some Roman public figure (Pompey, Crassus, Horace, Agrippa, Sejanus, and others), but on balance it is far more likely to be a family portrait connected with the house in which it was found. The form of the bust and the treatment of the hair and facial details indicate a date about the middle of the first century A.D. The workmanship suggests a sculptor from the eastern Mediterranean, based presumably at Puteoli and working for local Campanian patrons.
Fiorelli, *Scavi* 164, no. 147; F. Poulsen, *RM* 29 (1914) 59; De Franciscis 49.

22

Bronze portrait of a young man on a herm shaft
Height overall 1.73 m, height of bust 37.5 cm
Naples Museum, inv. 5584
Probably one of the two bronze busts found in the Basilica at Pompeii in 1813

The surface of the bronze is heavily corroded, and a large fragment is missing from the chest. The pupils of the inlaid eyes have been lost, but the white cement of the right eyeball survives complete, while that on the left is preserved only on the inner corner. Because of the damaged surface it is difficult to assess the original qualities of the workmanship, but it appears that the modeling was rather hard and lifeless by comparison with No. 20 and that less care was taken in engraving the short strands of hair after casting. The herm shaft, which is ancient, may not belong; it is made in lava and stands on a base of tufa.

22

The head bears a marked resemblance to the other bronze bust (Naples Museum, inv. "19") considered to have been found with it and also, at least in the unusual quoif of hair over the brow, to the marble portrait of a young man (No. 23) that was found in the House of the Citharist and perhaps represents a member of the Popidius family. The special connection that the Popidii had with the Basilica (see No. 9) may be seen as further evidence to support such an identification.

Fiorelli, *PAH* 1, part 3, 225; De Franciscis 43f.

23

Head of a young man, perhaps a member of the Popidius family

Fine-grained white marble, probably from Phrygia in Asia Minor
Height 36.5 cm
Naples Museum, inv. 6025
From the House of the Citharist (1, 4, 5), found together with No. 21 on 19 October 1868 in the stable block, having perhaps fallen from an upper room.

Rough surfaces on the shoulders mark the lines of drapery folds that have been dressed off, indicating that this was probably retrieved from a statue and adapted to a bust after the earthquake of A.D. 62. When found, the nose and ears were damaged and have been restored in plaster, but the repair to the lower lip was made in antiquity, in Italian marble. The hair was probably painted a reddish brown, and the slightly roughened surfaces of the eyeballs may have had the iris and pupil rendered in red and black in the manner usual at this period. The unusually smooth, transparent quality of the flesh surfaces is due to the fine marble, which also permitted the sculptor a greater subtlety and sensitivity of modeling than usual.

The portrait is that of a young man born about the end of the first century B.C., with a quoif of hair over his brow closely resembling that found on No. 22 and in Naples Museum, inv. "19" (see page 106, right). Scholars have variously identified him with a number of Roman worthies, including the young Marcus Brutus, Agrippa Postumus, or other descendants of Agrippa, Domitius Ahenobarbus, Drusus, son of Germanicus, and there is indeed a close resemblance to a head of unknown provenance in the Capitoline Museum in Rome (Stuart Jones, *Catalogue* pl. 88). But there is also a marked family resemblance to the male bronze from the atrium of the same house (inv. 4992; see page 106, left) and to the bronze head from the Basilica, and it seems far more likely that this is a member of the local family to whom this house belonged, usually identified as the Popidii.

Fiorelli, *Scavi* 164, no. 148; F. Poulsen, *Ikonografische Miscellen* (Copenhagen 1921) 51f.; L. Curtius, *RM* 47 (1932) 228f.; De Franciscis 47.

23

24

24
Epitaph of Titus Terentius Felix, a city magistrate
Marble
Width 53 cm, height 38.5 cm
Naples Museum, inv. 3879
Found in 1763 just outside the Herculaneum Gate, where there is now a reproduction.

T[ito] Terentio T[iti] f[ilio] Men[enia tribu] Felici maiori aedil[i]. Huic public[e] locus datus et HS ∞ ∞. Fabia Probi f[ilia] Sabina uxor.

"To Titus Terentius Felix senior, son of Titus, of the tribe Menenia, aedile. The site [of this monument] was presented to him by the city together with the sum of 2000 sesterces. It was erected by his wife Fabia Sabina, daughter of Probus."

Terentius Felix may have died as a relatively young man, possibly while holding the junior magistracy of the aedileship, which would account for the contribution from public funds toward the cost of his monument. He appears as first witness to one of the documents of Lucius Caecilius Jucundus in the period preceding the earthquake of A.D. 62. The Terentii were an old Italic family long established in Campania. His wife too came from an old family, the Fabii, most of the known Pompeian representatives of which were freedmen engaged in the wine trade. Another Titus Terentius (Felix junior?), who may well have been his son, was a candidate for the aedileship in the last period of the city.
CIL X. 1019; Castrén, no. 402,9; Andreau 209, 321.

25

25
Bronze portrait bust of a young man
Height 42.5 cm
Naples Museum, inv. 5617
From Pompeii

The surface of the bronze appears severely cleaned, and the eyes have been given a modern inlay of silver and copper to replace the ancient cement and glass. Although the work is technically competent and great care went into the secondary working of detail in the hair and eyebrows after casting, the portrait lacks the character and individuality of most of the other Pompeian bronzes, having more in common with the rather cold academicism of many of the Herculaneum portrait busts (e.g., Naples Museum, inv. 5632). It has often been identified as a youthful portrait of the emperor Tiberius (born 42 B.C., died A.D. 37), but recent writers have, perhaps rightly, come to question this traditional identification. The form of the bust indicates that the portrait was executed about the middle of the first century A.D.

De Franciscis 42f., fig. 34; L. Polacco, *Il Volto di Tiberio* (Rome 1955) 184, no. 6.

26
Portrait bust of an old man
Pentelic marble
Height 37.8 cm
Naples Museum, inv. 6169
From Pompeii

The gaunt face, with its hooked nose and projecting ears, a type one can still see among Neapolitans today, is uncompromisingly realistic. It is a good example of a long-lived and popular style of Roman portrait sculpture whose origins can be sought in the various trends current in the late Republic, but which prevailed far into the first century A.D. The carving of the eyes and hair and the treatment of the flesh surfaces show that it was probably made in the first quarter of the first century A.D.

Although its original location is not recorded, the cutting of the bust shows that it was mounted on a herm shaft, perhaps to stand beside the entrance to the *tablinum* in a Pompeian house.

B. Schweitzer, *Die Bildniskunst der römischen Republik* (Leipzig 1948) 115, 119; A. N. Zadoks-Josephus Jitta, *Ancestral Portraiture in Rome* (Amsterdam 1932) 54, 7, De Franciscis 40f.

27

27
Male portrait head
Gray coarse-grained limestone
Height 24 cm
Pompeii, Antiquarium, inv. P. 76/147

The head is broken off from a life-sized statue, which has apparently not been found, but which probably stood in a tomb outside the walls of Pompeii. It is worked in a hard, linear style characteristic of the local central Italian tradition and in marked contrast to the contemporary "Roman" portraiture represented by Nos. 20, 25. The hair is treated as a formal pattern and the ears almost as abstract designs; facial details like the wrinkles on the brow and the lines in the jowls are equally reduced to a severe symmetry. The faint half-smile of the lips appears all the more expressive as a result.

28
Terracotta statuette of a tipsy old woman
Height 39.5 cm
Naples Museum, inv. 124844
From House VI, 15, 5

The subject, well known in later Hellenistic sculpture, pottery, and terracotta, may be derived from a statue by Myron that was set up at Smyrna (Izmir) in Asia Minor. The almost toothless old woman is shown seated, with hair and clothing disheveled, grumbling to herself and clutching the bottom half of a wine amphora, of which the top half lies beside her foot. The figure is hollow and is adapted to serve as a jug. On the back is a filling hole at the nape of the neck and the remains of a handle. Her mouth was the spout. Mid-first century A.D.

This piece was found in the fountain niche at the far side of the garden peristyle, together with two glazed terracotta statuettes, a marble statuette of a nymph, and another terracotta figurine of similar size representing an elephant carrying a tower (Naples Museum, inv. 124845). *NSc* 1897, 23f.; Levi 197, no. 849.

29
Terracotta doll
Height 17.5 cm
Naples Museum, inv. 123971
From Pompeii

Schematic female figure, with tall conical body and a tiny knob-like head, perhaps a simple child's toy. The details of her dress are added in red paint.
Levi no. 870.

29

28

30

31

30
Terracotta statuette of a water carrier
Height 13.1 cm
Naples Museum, inv. 20252
From Pompeii

The figure is painted red, while his eyes
and the other areas are painted white. The
load that this porter carries has been variously described as a sack or a pole with
two baskets, but in the most recent interpretation, his burden is thought to be
skins filled with water.

Some of the more prosperous private
houses of Pompeii received water, through
an elaborate system of piping, from an
aqueduct high in the nearby mountains,
which served their city as well as several
others in the area. But many other householders had to rely upon the public fountains for all their water or supplement the
supply from their own wells and cisterns.
The earthquake of A.D. 62 caused damage
to the Pompeian water supply, which had
not yet been completely repaired at the
time of the eruption, and for some households it may have put an end to the luxury
of piped-in running water. Although Pompeii probably did not have an entire class
of *aquarii*, or water carriers, such as made
up the lowest category of slaves in Rome
and Ostia, no doubt the wealthier families
each had a slave whose sole function was
to supply the needs of the household,
while in the smaller or poorer households,
carrying water was one of the duties of the
porter or kitchen slaves.
Winter II, 453, 8.

31
Slaves with sedan chair in terracotta
Height 12.5 cm, length 15 cm
Naples Museum, inv. 110340
From the House of Gavius Rufus

The porters' flesh and the carrying straps
are painted red while the rest of the piece
is painted white.

In this direct and ingenuous small-scale
work, the emphasis is on the bearers
rather than the passenger. The slaves are
characterized as old workmen bent by
their labor. In another South Italian terracotta of this type the bearers are shown
as children standing erect, hardly troubled
by their load.
Fiorelli, *Scavi* no. 209; Winter II, 453, 1;
cf. Ars Antiqua A.G., *Auction V*, Lucerne
1964, no. 90.

32
Caricature bust in terracotta
Height 11.5 cm, width of body 9.5 cm
Naples Museum, inv. 20579
Probably the piece that was found on
1 June 1755 in the Villa of Julia Felix, in
one of the small niches on the eastern side
of the garden.

It is hard to determine whether this piece
is complete as it stands or whether it was
part of a larger object, such as the jugs
in the shape of grotesque figures (see
the following, No. 33). A very similar
figure in the British Museum (inv. 1873,
5-29.10), wearing a *bulla* on a red-painted
necklace, is identified as a character from
Roman mime.
Von Rohden 53, pl. XLI, 4; Levi no. 867.

33
Terracotta jug
Height 30 cm
Naples Museum, inv. 27857
From Herculaneum, 11 May 1755

The form of the vessel is that of a grotesque old man with exaggerated physical details. He has gone back to school,
for he wears a *bulla* (an amulet of youth)
and carries his writing materials (waxed
writing tablets) in his hand. His expression of anguish is that of a pupil who has
been scolded by his teacher.
Grant, De Simone, and Merella 130-131, illus
Winter II, 455, 2.

34
Marble statuette of a sleeping slave
Length 17 cm
Pompeii, Antiquarium, inv. 93
From the Via di Mercurio

This tiny sculpture, made for a fountain
is carved with a light touch but has a
rather sour, ironic humor. A slave boy
lies on the ground in an exhausted sleep.
The childish appearance of his hooded
garment contrasts with the expression o
his face, which is hard and careworn. In
his obliviousness he pulls up his clothing
around his shoulders, displaying bony
thighs and conspicuous genitals. Water
spills from his flask; a mouse gnaws at h
wicker basket. The malicious delight in
such images is Hellenistic, as is the compositional type, but the sculptor improvised freely on his model.

Kapossy, *Brunnenfiguren* 45; Grant, *Cities
Vesuvius* 162-163, illus.

2

34

35
Bronze lamp with the head of a Negro
Length II cm
Naples Museum, inv. 72269
From Pompeii

Bronze lamps of this type are fairly common, but in this example a refreshing precision of observation can be discerned both in the individuality of the head and in the puffed-out cheeks, which suggest that the boy is blowing the lamp's flame out of his mouth.

36
Wall painting: boys playing
Width 63 cm, height 29.6 cm
Naples Museum, inv. 9103
From the House of Marcus Lucretius
(Pompeii IX, 3, 5)

A boy at the center holds a cord tied to a peg in the earth. Flanking him are three boys with upraised sticks or switches. Another boy with a rope or cord advances at the left. A sixth boy advances somewhat apprehensively at the right. The peg might also be interpreted as a top that is being spun with a cord.

S. Reinach, *Répertoire de peintures grecques et romaines* (Paris 1922) 76, no. 3, cf. 76, no. 1.

35

36

37
Small bronze bust of the emperor Augustus
Height (excluding the modern base)
13.4 cm
Naples Museum, inv. 5473
From Herculaneum, 26 October 1752

The first Roman emperor is portrayed in a variant of his most popular official portrait type, best known from the statue found in the Villa of Livia at Prima Porta (Vatican, Braccio Nuovo 14). The little bust, which is hollow cast, was made after his death, probably in the reign of Tiberius or Claudius, and was possibly dedicated in a shrine of the Imperial cult somewhere near the Theater.
P. Zanker, *Studien zu den Augustus-Porträts.* 1. *Der Actium-Typus* (Göttingen 1973) 32, no. 20.

39

37

38
Bronze statue of Lucius Mammius Maximus
Height 2.12 m
Naples Museum, inv. 5591
From Herculaneum, found in the Theater on 24 December 1743.

The statue, which honors a wealthy benefactor of Herculaneum (see No. 39) was found, together with its marble pedestal and bronze dedicatory inscription, on the highest level of the auditorium of the Theater. It is hollow cast in a rich copper bronze. The head and neck, the left hand, the right forearm, part of the drapery, and the two feet were cast separately. The casting is technically accomplished, and the surfaces have been very carefully worked over to remove traces of the processes of casting and assembly and to cor-

rect minor blemishes. The head is a portrait and was certainly modeled by a different sculptor, probably from a different
workshop and working to order.

Bronze public statuary was common in
antiquity, but the vast majority has since
disappeared into the melting pot. Large
bronze statues such as this are very rare
survivals, and it is in marble sculpture that
one has to look for parallels. Stylistically
the head of Mammius closely resembles
the portrait statue of Fundilius, an actor,
found at Nemi and now in Copenhagen.
The arrangement of the toga, too, closely
resembles that on the Fundilius statue and
on another piece found in the theater at
Caere (Cerveteri), a mode that appears
to date from the years immediately following the middle of the first century.
This fits well with the likely date of Mammius himself.

Venuti, *Heraclea* 75; Kluge-Hartleben II 65ff.;
Goethert, *RM* 54 (1939) 240f.

38

39

Bronze dedicatory inscription
Height 70 cm, width 45 cm
Naples Museum, inv. 3748
Found at Herculaneum, attached to the
marble base of No. 38.

*L. Mammio Maximo Augustali municipes
et incolae aere conlato.*

"To Lucius Mammius Maximus, Augustalis, [this statue is erected] by the
citizens and other residents, by public
subscription."

The name of L. Mammius Maximus
figures on a number of other inscriptions
at Herculaneum, three of which (*CIL* x.
1, 1413, 1417, 1418) record dedications to
Livia, who was deified by the emperor
Claudius, to Antonia, his mother, and to
Agrippina, his niece and the mother of
Nero; a fourth (*CIL* x. 1. 1451), recording an unspecified donation to the city,
and a fifth (*CIL* x. 1, 1450), his construction or restoration of a market building
(macellum) and his giving of a public banquet on the occasion of its dedication. The
Mammii (sometimes spelled Mamii) were
an old Samnite family, represented also at
Pompeii, where they were one of the first
non-colonist families to achieve public
office after 80 B.C., at Capua, at Aquinum,
and in the mountains of Samnium. It was
a relative or connection of this family,
L. Annius Mammianus Rufus, who built
the Theater at Herculaneum, probably
under Augustus (*CIL* x. 1, 1443-1445). As
an Augustalis, Mammius Maximus was
almost certainly a freedman, which would
accord with his failure to mention his
father's name. Born the slave of a powerful, land-owning family, it was doubtless
with the family's support that as a freedman, like Petronius' Trimalchio, he
achieved great wealth and, by his lavish
use of it, achieved high civic honor.

CIL x. 1, 1452; *ILS* 6352. For the Mammii,
see Castrén 188, no. 237.

40
Gold bulla
Length 6.5 cm, weight 14.08 grams
Naples Museum, inv. 145490
From the House of the Menander (I, 10, 4)

The *bulla,* a small bag-shaped amulet, was
worn around the neck, a practice the
Romans derived from the Etruscans,
among whom it seems to have been worn
as an ornament by both sexes. Among the
Romans the gold *bulla* (sometimes known
as *Etruscum aureum*) took on a more restricted significance, being worn from infancy by the sons of citizens as a visible
token of free birth. On coming of age and
formally assuming the dress of manhood
(the *toga virilis*), it was customary to lay
the *bulla* ceremoniously aside in the
household *lararium* (see No. 210). At a
later date its use was permitted also to
the sons of freedmen.

This example is shaped in the form of a
miniature pouch, with a lens-shaped body
made of two plain convex discs, riveted to
an elaborately ornamented flap, through
which passed the small suspension ring of
beaded gold wire. The decoration of the
flap is symmetrical about a central braid
made up of two ribbons, each of three
strands of gold wire plaited and framed
between two pairs of counter-twisted
wire, which are arranged so as to convey
the impression of a minute chain of heart-
shaped links. This frame is continued
round the plain fields to right and left of
the central braid. Along the junction of
the flap and the body are pendant triangles of gold beading.

This handsome piece was found in the
House of the Menander, together with
several other pieces of fine jewelry, in the
same wooden chest as the famous set of
silver plate (see page 109).

Maiuri, *Menandro* 381, no. 127; Breglia
no. 918; Siviero no. 340.

41 (withdrawn from exhibition)
Gold finger ring with sardonyx cameo
Naples Museum, inv. 25181

42
Gold ring with sardonyx intaglio
Diameter 1.8 cm
Naples Museum, inv. 111775
From Pompeii

The heavy gold ring with an inset stone
is of a very common Roman form. The
finely cut intaglio shows the profile of a
curly-haired, Hermes-like youth in a
courtly classicistic style. The head is cut
through from a light into a dark-colored
layer of the stone, with strikingly decorative effect.

Breglia no. 532, pl. XXIX, 7; Siviero no. 410,
pl. 228 a.

40

42

43

43
Gold serpent ring
Diameter 2.1 cm
Naples Museum, inv. 25041
From Herculaneum

This ring, in the form of a serpent wound
around the finger, is a reduced version of
armbands like No. 48, where a simple spi-
raling body with incised scales terminates
in a powerfully modeled head.

Breglia no. 678; Siviero no. 220, pl. 169 e.

44
Pair of cluster earrings
Gold, pearls, and green plasma
Length 2.8 cm and 3.0 cm
Naples Museum, inv. 25266 and 25267
From one of the sites in the Vesuvius area

The center of each flower-like cluster consists of an oval cabouchon of green plasma
set in a gold frame edged with gold beads.
Radiating from it are sixteen petals, consisting alternately of shaped gold sheet
and of irregularly shaped pearls set on
pegs of gold wire. A globule of mother-of-
pearl hangs from the bottom-most gold
petal. A large gold hook is soldered to the
back. First century B.C. to first century A.D.
Breglia nos. 226, 227; Siviero no. 307.

44

45
Gold and pearl earrings
Length 3.3 cm
Naples Museum, inv. 145482
From the House of the Menander

The pearls are threaded onto a gold wire armature; six rows, with a transverse reinforcement, form a dome-like cluster. This type of earring, sometimes made with stones or glass paste beads, is common at Pompeii and Herculaneum. Its shape varies from the rigidly geometrical to more irregular forms suggesting bunches of grapes.

Maiuri, *Menandro* 380, no. 119, pl. LXV; A. Morassi, *Antica oreficeria italiana* (1936) 22, nos. 32, 33; Breglia 59, nos. 236, 237, pl. XXXIII, 7, 8; Siviero no. 283, pl. 190, color pl. 189.

46
Gold earrings
Length 2.7 cm and 2.5 cm
Naples Museum, inv. 116077
From Pompeii or Herculaneum

Numerous variants of this neat, elegant form of earring come from the cities destroyed by Vesuvius. The fashion apparently ran from the first century B.C. through the first century A.D. The simple dome shape with a much smaller disc (or in other versions, a bead) attached to its edge is here enhanced by granulated decoration.

Breglia 59-60, no. 278, pl. XXX; Siviero no. 278, pl. 186 a.

47

48

47
Gold armband in the form of a snake
Diameter 8 cm, length 11 cm
Naples Museum, inv. 24824
Probably found at Pompeii

One of a pair of armbands, each shaped from a flat ribbon of gold on which the scales were indicated with a V-shaped punch. The head was cast separately, and the eyes were originally set with green vitreous paste. First century B.C. to first century A.D.

MB 7 (Rome 1831) pl. XLVI; Breglia no. 827; Siviero no. 202.

48
Gold snake armband
Diameter 8.1 cm
Naples Museum, inv. 24772
From Pompeii

This snake armband is one of a pair, as such pieces usually were. The body has been schematized into a simple, regular spiral with a circular cross-section. The incised scales have been omitted in the central part of the two turns. The powerfully modeled and incised head with its gaping jaws has, however, a striking reptilian vitality. The eyes were originally filled with green glass paste.

Breglia no. 831; Siviero no. 203, pl. 160.

49
Gold pin with head in the form of a cantharus
Length 13 cm
Naples Museum, inv. 145488
From the House of the Menander

This hair ornament is a pin topped with a miniature cantharus (drinking cup) of Hellenistic form. It is enriched with beaded decoration and topped by a light-colored glass paste "jewel."

Maiuri, *Menandro* 381, no. 126, pl. LXV; Breglia no. 924, pl. XXXIII, 21; Siviero no. 135, pl. 126.

50
Gold bracelet
Diameter 8.3 cm
Naples Museum, inv. 109587
From House I, 2, 3

Two lengths of thick gold wire loosely intertwined to form eight large loops, soldered together at the crossings; over one of these is an applied gold ornament. First century B.C. to first century A.D.

Breglia no. 868; Siviero no. 238.

49

50

51

51

Gold bracelet
Length 25.2 cm
Naples Museum, inv. 136792
From Pompeii

The bracelet was found with the skeleton
of a person who was attempting to flee,
carrying a casket of jewelry. Looter or
owner, he or she had waited too long,
until the ash had accumulated some ten
feet deep, then climbed out of the building
from an upper-story window and after a
few steps dropped dead, scattering the
precious objects. The bracelet is made up
of links, each consisting of two gold
domes joined by a double row of beaded
ornament and connected with the next
link by two loops. A leaf-shaped clasp
fastens the bracelet, which was one of a
pair and belongs to a type often found
at Pompeii.
V. Spinazzola, "Rinvenimenti di due scheletri
e di oggetti preziosi," in *NSc* 1914, 207,
fig. 2; Breglia no. 860; Siviero no. 250, pl. 179 b

52

Part of a necklace of gold ivy leaves
Length 53 cm
Naples Museum, inv. 111114
From Pompeii, 9 June 1877

The necklace consisted originally of two
concentric bands of ivy leaves stamped out
of sheet gold and linked to each other by
tiny loops of gold wire; the loops are
masked by small gold bosses. The 48
leaves of this piece converge symmetrically
upon a large convex gold disc. Its companion piece (Naples, inv. 111113) contained
46 leaves but was otherwise identical. The
clasp that joined the two bands behind
the neck is missing. The form, rare in
Roman jewelry, probably derives from the
Hellenistic world. First century B.C. to
first century A.D.
Breglia no. 478; Siviero no. 166.

53

Gold necklace
Length 2.52 m
Naples Museum, inv. 25260
Probably from Pompeii

The long chain of delicately interwoven
links is interrupted only by two wheel-like
ornaments, one of which functions as a
clasp. From the chain hangs a small crescent-shaped pendant. Both the wheel and
the lunar crescent, though primarily
decorative here, can have implications of
love-magic and so are especially suited to
feminine adornment.
Spinazzola 226; Breglia no. 483; Siviero
no. 168, pls. 138, 139.

52

54
Gold pendant
Height of figure 2 cm, length with chain
5.5 cm
Naples Museum, inv. 24673
From Herculaneum

The nude baby pours from a vessel in his
raised left hand to the bowl in his right.
This is the gesture of the little household
god, the Lar, but also of a festive cup
bearer. His hair is dressed in bunches of
ringlets over his ears.

Spinazzola 226; Breglia no. 183, pl. XXII, 1;
Siviero no. 142, pl. 129 b.

55
Gold mesh necklace set with emeralds
and pearls
Length 34.5 cm
Naples Museum, inv. 113576
From the seaside suburb of Pompeii
(contrada Bottaro)

Large, irregular stones, alternately emeralds and baroque pearls, are superimposed
on an exquisitely made gold mesh, reinforced with larger dots of gold where the
links cross. This taste for openwork and
for light, abstract, bubbly forms characterizes much jewelry found at Pompeii and
amounts to a fashion trend of Imperial
times, away from the modeled, often representational elements of Greek jewelry.
Since the mesh and the clasp are obviously
the work of a superb craftsman, the use of
the stones with large simple shapes must
have been deliberate and carefully
thought out.

NSc 1881, 27; Spinazzola 226; Breglia 62,
no. 473, pl. 31, 2; Siviero no. 164, pl. 133.

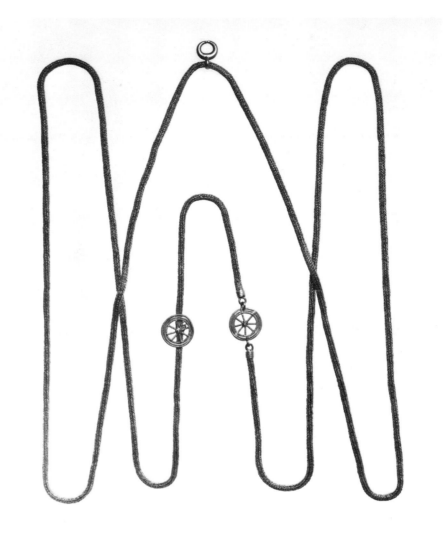

53

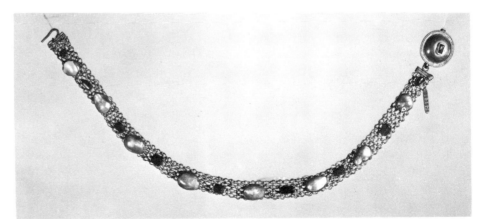

55

56

57

56
Silver hand mirror
Diameter 10.5 cm, length of handle 11 cm
Naples Museum, inv. 76/243
From one of the sites in the Vesuvius area

The reflecting disc of the mirror has a
cusped border. The back bears a simple
decoration of engraved concentric circles.
The looped form of the handle is unusual.
For similar forms, see Mau-Kelsey 372-373,
fig. 205; Strong 157.

57
Silver hand mirror
Diameter 11 cm, length of handle 9.3 cm
Naples Museum, inv. 25716
From Pompeii

A very common form of hand mirror. The
back is decorated with concentric circles
and a border of palmettes edged with two
rows of beaded dots. The baluster handle
is one of the two most usual types, the
other being in the shape of a club of
Hercules.

Strong 157.

58
Silver hand mirror
Height 34 cm
Naples Museum, inv. 145524
From the House of the Menander

This silver hand mirror is decorated on
the back with a separately made *emblema*
of a profile female head in repoussé. The
idea of the profile head goes back to those
in high relief on the outside of Greek
mirror covers. The head shown here, however, with its delicate technique, its extremely refined and precise beauty, seems
more influenced by Greek coins or, as has
been suggested, by the gem cutter's work,
which reached such perfection in late
Republican and early Imperial times. Like
many *emblemata*, it was probably copied
by the silversmith from a plaster cast of a
famous model; a number of these casts
have come down to us. The form and
ornament of the mirror are completely
Roman, with bold and, in its way, very
pure use of flat, cutout shapes, piercing,
and turned elements.

Maiuri, *Menandro* 350ff., no. 15, pls. XLVII,
XLVIII.

59
Fragment of a bone hair comb
Width 6.1 cm, surviving length 8 cm
Naples Museum, inv. 119990
From a *cubiculum* off the atrium in House
IX, 6, 5

Combs in antiquity, made of ivory or
bone, were normally of this shape, with
teeth down both long sides. As in many
modern combs, the teeth are spaced dif-
ferently, about seven to the centimeter on
one side and about fourteen on the other.
Similar combs have been found in some
numbers at Pompeii, among them one that
is painted with a design of two ducks in
red, black, and white.

Mau-Kelsey 371.

9

58

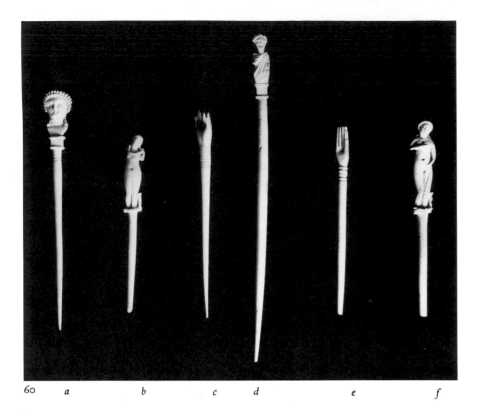

60   *a*   *b*   *c*   *d*   *e*   *f*

61

60

Six hairpins with variously decorated finials

a. Bust of a female divinity. Ivory
Length 13.2 cm
Naples Museum, inv. 77441
From Pompeii

b. Aphrodite (Venus) tying her hair. Ivory
Length 9.8 cm
Naples Museum, inv. 121730
From the corridor beside the *tablinum* in the House of the Cenaculum (v, 2, Mau D).

c. Hand with fingers spread. Ivory
Length 11.6 cm
Naples Museum, old inv. 9326
From Pompeii

d. Male herm wearing a mantle (*himation*) Bone
Length 18.2 cm
Naples Museum, old inv. 9272
From Pompeii

e. Hand with fingers together. Ivory
Length 10.3 cm
Naples Museum, old inv. 9327
From Pompeii

f. Pudicitia, personification of modesty and chastity. Bone
Length 10.8 cm
Naples Museum, old inv. 9270
From Pompeii

Many Roman hairstyles involved the use of tight curls made with hot tongs, and some of these pins would have been toilet instruments, used for arranging the hair rather than as ornaments or for fastening the hair in place.
Mau-Kelsey 372, fig. 203.

61 (cover illus.)

Mosaic portrait of a woman
Height 25.5 cm, width 20.5 cm
Naples Museum, inv. 124666
From a small *cubiculum* in House VI, 15, 14

Portrait, probably from life, of a young woman. Her hair is parted centrally and tied behind with a ribbon. She wears earrings of pearls set in gold, a pearl necklace with a gold clasp set with precious stones, and a dark, low-necked dress, which shows through a gold-embroidered transparent veil. Dress and jewelry suggest a woman of rank.

This is a studio piece (*emblema*) made with very small tesserae, shaped and toned, set within a shallow, tray-like limestone frame. It was found in the center of an *opus sectile* pavement made up of hexagons, lozenges, and triangles of blue-gray, white, and red marble, dating from the last period before A.D. 79. In this context it was almost certainly reused. The mosaic itself can hardly be later than the end of the first century B.C.
A. Sogliano, *NSc* 1898, 171ff.; A. Mau, *RM* 16 (1901) 283f.; Pernice VI, 88 and 178-179.

III The Garden

62.

6778.

63

62

Large Neo-Attic vase (crater)
Pentelic marble
Height 82 cm, diameter at the rim 65 cm
Naples Museum, inv. 6778
From Stabiae

Both the form and much of the decoration
of this vase derive closely from metalwork
prototypes, commonly reproduced also in
South Italian bronzeware and in the fine
South Italian pottery. The figured decoration is Dionysiac in inspiration. On one
side is Dionysus himself, portrayed in the
Archaic manner, holding a jug and a
thyrsus and leading personifications of
Summer and Autumn; on the other side
are Spring and Winter with a satyr. At the
junctions of the tall volute handles with
the body are Silenus heads.

   Some of the best Athenian craftsmen of
the later first century B.C. were engaged in
producing large marble vases of this sort.
They were normally used as garden
ornaments.

63

Dionysiac herm in colored marbles
Height 87 cm
Naples Museum, inv. 126252
From Pompeii

The head is that of an elderly Silenus, one
of the drinking companions of Dionysus,
shown wreathed with ivy berries. The
slightly tapering shaft stands on two bare
human feet, carved out of the same block
of white Italian marble as the base, which
in its turn is veneered with profiled moldings and a deeply cusped facing slab. A
narrow rectangular pillar runs up the back
of the herm. The head, shaft, and pillar
are of colored marbles imported from
Imperial quarries overseas: the head, of
yellow Numidian marble, *giallo antico,*
from Simitthu (the modern Chemtou) in
northwestern Tunisia; the shaft and base
moldings, of purple and cream variegated
marble from Skyros, an island in the north
Aegean; the pillar, of green and white
marble, *cipollino,* from Euboea off the
eastern coast of Greece.

   A herm of this sort was probably used
as a table support (cf. No. 113) in a peristyle or garden.

64

65

66

64
Oscillum in the form of a theater mask
Italian marble
Height 36 cm
Naples Museum, inv. 6613
From Pompeii

Oscilla hung between the columns of a peristyle garden; see also Nos. 65, 69, 75, 78. The mask, that of a heroine in Greek tragedy, is distinguished by sloping brows, wavy hair, and a low *onkos*. First century A.D.

MB 7 (Rome 1843) pl. VIII; Bieber, *Theater,* fig. 567; Webster, *Tragedy and Satyr Play* 85, NS 5.

65
Theater mask in high relief
Italian marble
Height 31 cm
Naples Museum, inv. 6611
From Pompeii

Though possibly made to be hung as an *oscillum,* this mask was probably set in a wall, as in the garden of the House of Neptune and Amphitrite at Herculaneum. With its tall, rounded peak and hair falling in corkscrew curls, this would appear to be a mask from Tragedy. The fillet (ribbon) across the brow, with two dangling ends, and the wreath of ivy leaves and berries suggest specifically Dionysiac associations.

MB 7 (Rome 1843) pl. VIII.

66
Rectangular panel with theater masks in relief
Pentelic marble
Height 25.5 cm, width 33 cm
Naples Museum, inv. 6619
From Pompeii

The panel, which is carved on both faces, probably stood on a small column in a Pompeian garden similar to that of the House of the Gilded Cupids, or Amorini (see page 55). In high relief on one side are masks belonging to stock characters in Greek New Comedy: on the right, the scheming, impudent, leading slave; and on the left, the delicately brought-up youth *(hapalos),* suitor for the hand of the daughter of the old man whose mask lies below. Beyond the youth, in low relief, is the mask of a satyr, and on the other face of the panel, again in low relief, those of an elderly Silenus *(papposilenos)* and of a young satyr.

Bieber, *Theater* 155; Webster, *New Comedy* 194, NS 17.

67

67

68

67
Rectangular panel with theater masks in relief
Pentelic marble
Height 29.5 cm, width 40 cm
Naples Museum, inv. 6633
From Pompeii

The panel is carved on both sides and, like No. 66, was probably mounted on a low column. In high relief on the front are masks from Greek New Comedy: a delicate youth, a curly-bearded old man (top right), and a leading slave (bottom left). In the background is a temple front in low relief. A large fragment missing from the bottom right-hand corner may have contained a fourth mask, of an angry youth, as on a similar relief from Ostia. On the reverse of the panel, facing one another in low relief, are two masks of Tragedy, laid on rocks, both with high *onkoi*. One is accompanied by a sword and probably represents a hero, the other is a woman with a large kerchief covering her hairpiece and side-locks.

MB 8 (Naples 1844) pl. XLVII; Bieber, *Theater* 155f.; Webster, *New Comedy* 195, NS 22; idem, *Tragedy and Satyr Play* 92, NS 8.

68
Bronze fountain figure of a raven
Height 26 cm, length 58 cm
Naples Museum, inv. 4891
From a villa at Stabiae, not found in position

Hollow cast, the wings cast separately and added. The water pipe led in under the tail and out through the mouth. The raven was one of the attributes of Apollo, many of whose sanctuaries were built around springs.

Kapossy, *Brunnenfiguren* 52; Ruggiero, *Stabia*, p. viii, villa no. 1; *MB* 8 (Rome 1844) pl. LIII.

69
Circular oscillum
Italian marble
Diameter 34 cm
Naples Museum, inv. 6647
From the peristyle garden of the House of the Black Wall (VII, 4, 59)

An *oscillum* was an ornament freely suspended by a chain from the architrave between the columns of a peristyle. On one side of this example is carved in low relief a figure of the youthful Hercules, a lion skin about his shoulders and carrying a club and bow; in front of him runs a boar, the sacrificial animal proper to his cult. On the other side an elderly Pan plays his pipes beside a tree, from which hangs a goatskin bag of fruit.

F. G. Welcker, *Alte Denkmäler* II (Göttingen 1848), 132, no. 40; *MemErc* III (1843) 238.

70

70

Bronze fountain group: two hounds attacking a boar
Height 50 cm, maximum width 1.22 m
Naples Museum, inv. 4899, 4900, 4901
From the House of the Citharist (1, 4, 5)

The group, which derives from Hellenistic animal sculpture, stood between bronze figures of a snake, a deer, and a lion on the semi-circular fountain basin in the middle peristyle. Water gushed into the pool from a pipe in the boar's mouth and also, it seems, from the mouth of the hound on the right, which is trying to bite the boar's leg. The front paws of the hound on the left were fixed to the side of the boar by rivets. Tails and ears were cast separately, and great care went into the working of such secondary details as the boar's hide. The group is among the liveliest pieces of sculpture found at Pompeii.
Kapossy, *Brunnenfiguren* 48.

71

Rectangular panel with theater masks in relief
White Italian marble
Height 29.5 cm, width 39.5 cm
Naples Museum, inv. 6631
From Pompeii

The panel, carved on both sides, was probably set up in a garden (as No. 65). In relief on the front, and resting on a rocky shelf, are masks that derive from those used in the Greek Satyr Play: on the left Dionysus and on the right a maenad. Both are treated in the Archaic style. An unusual feature is that, instead of the large drill holes normally used for the pupils of such masks, the eyes are blank and were presumably painted. On the reverse, in very low relief, are the masks of a Silenus and a satyr.
Bieber, *Theater* 158.

72

Fountain figure: boy with dolphin
Italian marble
Height 49 cm
Naples Museum, inv. 6112
From the peristyle of House IX, 2, 27

The boy sits on a small base, his right hand on the dolphin's head, his left holding the tail, watching the water pouring from the dolphin's mouth. The hair and eyebrows were painted red, and red paint was used also to indicate the eyelashes and the iris, with the pupil marked by a black dot. The figure belongs to a large series of small children and Erotes riding dolphins or clutching amphorae, shells, dolphins, frogs, hares, ducks, or doves, variously adapted as fountain jets. It was made in Campania, about the middle of the first century A.D.
Fiorelli, *Scavi* 165, no. 159; Kapossy, *Brunnenfiguren* 42.

73

Fountain figure: Cupid on dolphin
Marble
Height 40.5 cm
Pompeii, Antiquarium, inv. 2084/4
From the House of Ceres (1, 9, 13)

An agile, diminutive Cupid perches side-saddle on a plunging dolphin and with his right hand holds an octopus by one tentacle. The workmanship is dainty, lively, playful, with an interesting rendering of the waves splashing around the dolphin's head. The group is one of four such pieces from the House of Ceres.

Kapossy, *Brunnenfiguren* 39.

73

61 12

74

74
Herm of Hercules
Yellow marble *(giallo antico),* from
Tunisia
Height 80 cm
Naples Museum, inv. 6383
From Herculaneum

Hercules is portrayed as bearded and
wearing a large lion skin wrapped around
him like a cloak, a type that seems to date
back to Greek sculpture of the fourth century B.C. The head, body, and base are
carved separately in three different qualities of the same stone. Close parallels are
found in other colored stones: one from
Sparta in red Laconian marble *(rosso
antico)* and another, also from Herculaneum but adapted as a table support, in a
black and red marble *(africano)* from
western Turkey.
Cf. Daremberg and Saglio, s. v. *Hercules*
fig. 3802.

75
Pelta-shaped oscillum
Italian marble
Height 22.5 cm, width 37 cm
Naples Museum, inv. 6664
From Pompeii

An angular version of the *pelta,* the traditional shield of the Amazons. The central
projection from which it hung is carved as
a palmette, and the outer ends of the crescent as griffins' heads. Rather simply
carved in low relief within the field are a
bird eating cherries and, on the opposite
face, a basket of fruit.

76
Bronze fountain figure of a bull
Length 51 cm, height 39 cm
Naples Museum, inv. 4890
From the atrium of the House of the
Bull (v, 1, 7)

Hollow cast, with the short horns, ears and
tail added separately, the bull is shown as
a young and powerful animal. Though
perhaps a purely ornamental piece, it
would have had associations with several
well-known divinities, including Zeus (see
No. 129), Poseidon, and Dionysus. The
figure stood on the edge of the *impluvium*
basin in the center of the atrium, water ·
spouting from the jet in his mouth. Although interior fountains had been a feature of the large Campanian country villas
since the first century B.C. (e.g., the Villa
of the Papyri at Herculaneum), their appearance in the town houses of Pompeii
is a late phenomenon.
Niccolini III, pl. 21; Kapossy, *Brunnenfiguren*
53.

75

76

77
Archaising female herm
White Italian marble
Height 96 cm
Naples Museum, inv. 126251
From Pompeii

The figure of a woman, possibly a Muse, in the Archaic Greek manner, has been adapted to the form of a herm. She wears a fillet in her hair, and her long tunic, tied with a knotted girdle below her breasts, is carved in shallow relief on the three flat sides of the herm shaft. The eyes are hollowed out for inlay.

The shaft is socketed into a heavy block of lava, and a pillar of travertine runs up the back of the herm to a point slightly above the head. The herm was probably used as a table support in a garden or in a peristyle corridor.

78

77

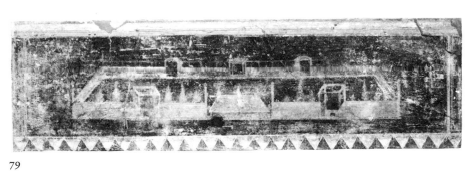

79

78
Oscillum in the form of a theater mask
Italian marble
Height 29 cm
Naples Museum, inv. 6618
From Pompeii

The *oscillum*, one of a pair, is in the form of a theatrical mask of a youth from Greek New Comedy, distinguished by a roll of corkscrew curls and hanging corkscrew locks. At the top are the remains of the bronze rod by which it was hung from the architrave of the peristyle. First century A.D.

MB 7 (Rome 1843) pl. VIII; Webster, *New Comedy* (1969) 194, NS 16.

79
Wall painting of a garden
Length 1.25 m, height 35.5 cm
Pompeii, Antiquarium, inv. 1200-4
From the western portico of the Villa Imperiale, near the Porta Marina

Part of the dado of the Third Style decoration of the back wall of the portico. The garden, a rectangular enclosure with low trelliswork walls, is shown as if viewed obliquely from above. The façade is symmetrical around a wide central opening flanked by a pair of tall pillars bearing vases. These frame a square pool with a central fountain figure set on a pedestal. Two identical pillars mark the outer corners of the façade, and midway between the right-hand and left-hand pairs of pillars are two square, openwork pavilions. The side walls of the enclosure are plain. The rear wall echoes the scheme of the façade, with a central *aedicula* flanked by two trellis-vaulted arbors. The vegetation within the garden is indicated schematically by a line of trees immediately behind the front wall.

Cf. P. Grimal, *Les jardins romains* (Paris 1969) 265f.

80

80
Wall painting of a garden
Length 1.37 m, height 32 cm
Naples Museum, inv. 9964
From Herculaneum

This scene, probably from the dado of a
wall of the late Third or Fourth Style,
shows one side of a garden enclosure, the
trellised fence of which is laid out symmetrically around three semi-circular
exedrae. Midway between the latter are
two passageways arched over with trelliswork, while at the two ends of the composition there are two rectangular openwork arbors planted with vines. Fountain
basins set on pedestals stand at the entrances to the passages, and at four points
along the fence taller, trellised posts support large, slender, bronze-colored vases.
Five long-legged, stork-like birds complete the scene.

Most of the elements of this sort of
fenced garden are already present in the
Garden Room paintings from the Villa of
Livia at Prima Porta (see page 96), and
they recur in varying combinations in
many Pompeian paintings (see No. 79).
The type was evidently firmly established
in painting. This does not, of course, pre-
clude the use of similarly fenced formal
gardens in the *villae marittimae* of Campania. Real gardening and painted representations of gardens are two aspects of a
common tradition.

Pitture di Ercolano I, 239; *MB* 9 (Rome 1845)
576, pl. LXXXVI; P. Grimal, *Les jardins
romains* (Paris 1969) 267.

81
Wall painting: part of a garden
Height 80 cm, width 80 cm
Naples Museum, inv. 9705
From Pompeii

This painting and its companion pieces
(Naples Museum, inv. 8723, 8762, and
"9710") come probably from the walls of
a small garden enclosure *(viridarium)* or
covered garden room. A large fluted fountain bowl stands in the re-entrant recess
of a wooden fence, on the rail of which a
bird is perched, trying to drink from the
fountain jet. Beyond the fence is dark
foliage of trees or bushes, and in the foreground are the faded traces of low, iris-
like plants.

H. Roux Aîné, *Herculanum et Pompéi* V
(Paris 1870) 98, pl. 52.

81

82
Statue of Artemis in the Archaic manner
Pentelic marble
Height 1.08 m
Naples Museum, inv. 6808
Found 19 July 1760 in one of the houses
of VIII, 2 or 3 (VIII, 3, 14?)

The goddess is represented striding pur-
posefully forward, bow in hand (the bow
itself being of bronze or wood); she may
also have held some object in her left hand.
The manner of the face and drapery is
consciously derived from Archaic Greek
sculpture, but such features as the movement of the body (involving liberal use of
marble struts), the carving of the hair, the
smoothly polished flesh surfaces, and the
execution of the drapery (with considerable use of the drill and with the surfaces
left as worked with a fine, flat chisel) — all
point to it being the work of Athenian
workshops at the turn of the first centuries
B.C./A.D., or slightly later. Such archaizing
work was in great demand in Rome (see
also No. 83), and there were many copyist
workshops both in Greece and in Italy
busy turning out work of this sort.

The statue was found in the garden of
the same house as Nos. 199, 301, 302. It
stood on a base veneered with colored
marbles, within a shrine that was approached by steps and preceded by a pair
of herm shafts in *cipollino* marble. When
found, it still retained many traces of
color: yellow (gilded?) hair; eyes with red-
brown irises and black pupils; black eyelashes and eyebrows; diadem, pink with
yellow rosettes; quiver, pink with white
decoration; pink and yellow, finely detailed border on the drapery; sandals with
pink, yellow, and blue straps; and on the
plinth, traces of black.

PAH I, 114; F. Studniczka, "Die archaische
Artemisstatue aus Pompeji," *RM* 3 (1888)
277-302; Reuterswaard, *Polychromie* 184,
note 518; W. Fuchs, *Die Skulpturen der
Griechen* (1969) 241f.

82

83
Statue of the youthful Apollo in the Archaic style
Pentelic marble
Height 1.05 m
Naples Museum, inv. 146103
Found in the House of the Menander
(I, 10, 4) in the northern corridor of the peristyle, near the *tablinum*

The figure of the god, supported by a tree stump and socketed into a rectangular plinth, is accompanied by a griffin. His right hand appears to hold a *plectrum,* which strongly suggests that the left arm (carved in a separate piece of marble and attached with an iron dowel) held a lyre. The front part of the left foot, where it overlaps the plinth, is another added piece, the sculptor having slightly miscalculated the size of the statue in relation to the block of marble. There are clear traces of original coloring: on the eyeballs a faint circle of black for the iris and a large black dot spotted with white for the pupil; reddish brown for the eyebrows; and carmine red for the corners of the mouth. The dirty brown color on the hair is the decayed remains of the substance used as a base for a golden yellow coloring, possibly gilding. The tree stump was bluish gray.

Both the treatment of the head and the rigidly frontal pose derive directly from the conventions of Archaic statuary, but the generally more naturalistic treatment of the body, with the weight resting firmly on the right leg, betrays a knowledge of later, more sophisticated Greek sculptural traditions. Apollo holding or accompanied by a griffin is in any case uncommon in Greek statuary; there does not seem to be any close parallel. This is evidently the eclectic work of Athenian sculptors, producing for the Roman market around the beginning of the first century A.D. and adding the figure of a griffin from the familiar repertory of late Hellenistic decorative motifs. The same workshop may well have produced the Apollo in the Vatican Museums (Chiaramonti 285), of which the dimensions and basic pose are almost identical, but the position of the arms is reversed and the griffin is omitted.

No suitable base was found within the House of the Menander. It has been suggested that the statue originally stood in the Temple of Apollo, and that it was removed temporarily for safe custody during the restorations after the earthquake of A.D. 62.

Maiuri, *Menandro* 410ff.

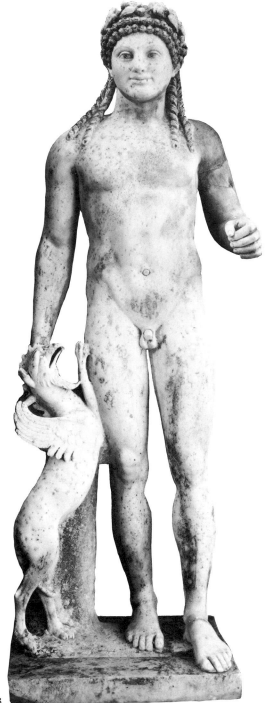

83

84

Head of a youth in the Archaic style
Pentelic marble
Height 28 cm
Naples Museum, inv. 109621
From Pompeii, House VII, 3, 40

The head is that of a youth with his hair dressed in a style favored by the Greek aristocracy about 500 B.C. The sharpness of the detail and the smooth finish on the face, however, indicate a date around the beginning of the first century A.D. The base of the neck is carved for insertion into a body, perhaps a herm.

The closest parallels to this head are found on double herms, in association with the head of a bearded old man with a similar hairstyle (the forerunner of the theatrical *onkos*), e.g., Louvre inv. 198.
M. Bieber, *JdAI* 32, 1917, 85; idem, *Theater* 24.

85

Garden painting: a white stork and lizard and a pet dog
Length 1.90 m, height 55 cm
Naples Museum, inv. 110877
From the House of the Epigrams (V, 1, 18)

The painting, on a black ground and divided into two panels by red lines, stood in the southeast corner of the peristyle, where it occupied a position closely resembling that of the very similar paintings in the peristyle of the House of the Menander, except that in this instance the green wall continued upward, occupying the entire space between the two columns. On the left is a white stork picking at a lizard, and on the right a large green plant; between them, painted over the vertical red framing line, is the figure of a small, terrier-like dog, above the head of which is painted in white, A. SYNCLETVS. The adjoining panel to the left (Naples inv. 110876) shows a white stork grappling with a snake.
Bull Inst XLIX (1877) 30.

85

86

Wall painting of a cat
Height 33 cm, width 42 cm
Naples Museum, inv. 8648
From Pompeii

A fragment probably cut from the upper zone of a late Third Style wall, which contained Egyptianizing elements. The cat, painted in silhouette, is shown curled up on a low upholstered stool.

86

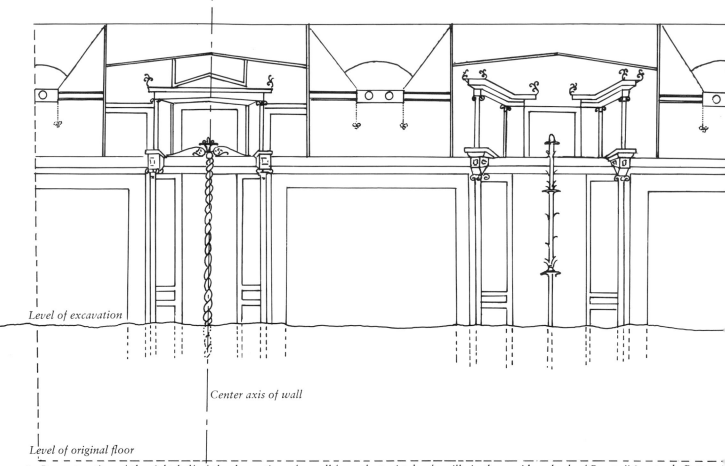

Level of excavation

Center axis of wall

Level of original floor

87 *Reconstruction of the right half of the decoration of a wall from the peristyle of a villa in the seaside suburb of Pompeii (contrada Bottaro)*

87 *Museum of Fine Arts, 33.497*

87 *Museum of Fine Arts, 33.506*

87 *Museum of Fine Arts, 33.496*

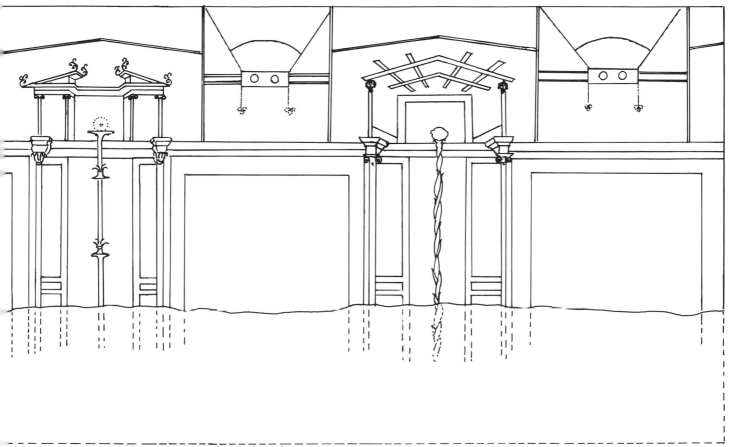

The left half of the wall was symmetrical with the right.

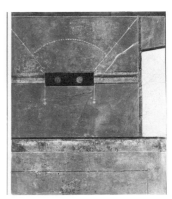

87 *Museum of Fine Arts, 33.501*

87 *Museum of Fine Arts, 33.500*

87 *Museum of Fine Arts, 33.498*

87

Decorative wall paintings
Museum of Fine Arts, Boston
Inv. 33.496: height 1.907 m, width 1.465 m
Inv. 33.497: height 2.01 m, width 1.445 m
Inv. 33.498: height 2.052 m, width 1.365 m
Inv. 33.500: height 1.938 m, width 1.393 m
Inv. 33.501: height 1.35 m, width 97.8 cm
Inv. 33.506: height 1.37 m, width 75.2 cm
From the colonnaded courtyard (peristyle)
of a villa in the seaside suburb of Pompeii
(contrada Bottaro)

The paintings come from the decoration
of one side of the courtyard. Simple panels, which were largely destroyed when the
paintings were removed from the wall in
the first years of this century, alternated
with column-framed "niches," which have
been almost completely preserved. Another unit from the wall is in the Field
Museum in Chicago. The ensemble forms
a flat, continuous surface; the niches act
as shallow frames for the candelabra
that give a decorative focus to each unit.
The window-like panels above give the
only suggestion of deep space. The paintings may have been executed after the
earthquake of A.D. 62, but the designer
was still in sympathy with the flat, severe
Third Style decoration of the earlier part
of the century. His restrained approach
may have been influenced by the architectural setting: a long corridor-like space
whose main feature was the view out into
a garden filled with elegantly made sculpture. A seated bronze Hercules, now in
the Naples Museum, and several small,
decorative marble sculptures were found
in the excavation.

NSc 1902, 572ff.; L. D. Caskey, *BMFA* XXXVII
(1939) 9-16; cf. H. F. De Cou, *Antiquities from
Boscoreale in Field Museum of Natural
History* (Chicago 1912) pl. CXXVIII, no. 24672.

88

Wall painting: the Judgment of Solomon
Width 1.60 m, height 65 cm
Naples Museum, inv. 113197
From the House of the Doctor (VIII, 5, 24)

Pygmies enact what appears to be the well-
known story of King Solomon giving judgment in a case where two women disputed
the ownership of a child. Solomon is
shown bearded, seated on a raised dais
(*tribunal*) between two counselors, with a
bodyguard of armed soldiers. Before him
the true mother kneels and pleads for her
child's life, while the false mother watches
with apparent indifference as a soldier
prepares to cut it in half. The scene is one
of three matching panels that were painted
on the parapet wall surrounding a miniature garden peristyle, the other two being
Egyptianizing landscapes, one with pygmies fighting off crocodiles and hippo-
potami, the other with pygmies banqueting beneath a large awning slung from
trees (No. 89).

Pygmies portrayed in Egyptianizing
settings are one of the commonplaces of
Roman Imperial art. Because of the strong
element of caricature, this picture can
hardly be ascribed to direct Jewish influence in Pompeii, although there were
unquestionably many Jews settled in
Campania. If correctly identified, it is,
rather, evidence at second hand of the
strong influence of the very large Jewish
community in Alexandria. An alternative
possibility is that the picture represents an
older, native Egyptian version of some
traditional story of royal wisdom, such as
that attributed to King Bocchoris.

NSc 1882, 322-323; G. Gatti, "Il Giudizio di
Salomone in un dipinto pompeiano," in
Rivista Antimassonica IV, 1898; Lumbroso,
RendLinc ser. III, 11, 1882-83, 303-305; J. Gut-
mann, *Antike Kunst* 15, 1972, 122-124.

89

**Wall painting: pygmies in a Nilotic
landscape**
Height 60 cm, width 220 cm
Naples Museum, inv. 113196
From the House of the Doctor (VIII, 5, 24)

Pygmies are shown engaging in the ridic-
ulous activities normally attributed to
them in ancient art. A pygmy attacks an
ibis and is restrained. Another pygmy is
being swallowed by a hippopotamus in
spite of the efforts of two friends to save
him. Banqueting pygmies watch indecent
entertainment.

Such scenes provide evidence for contact between the ancient Mediterranean
and central Africa, but they also show
how indirect that contact was. Already in
Archaic Greek art, pygmies were shown
in battle with birds (cranes), and subsequent embellishments are dictated more
by humorous fantasy than by any direct
experience. In Hellenistic times the pygmies were thought of as localized in the
Nile valley since the Nile formed the principal line of contact between central
Africa and the Mediterranean.

NSc 1882, 322-323; J. Marcadé, *Roma Amor*
(New York 1961) 46; cf. *EAA*, s. v. *Pigmei*;
J. Leclant, in *The Image of the Black in
Western Art* I (New York 1976) 269-273;
Schefold, *Vergessenes Pompeii* 77f., 151,
154-155, pl. 144,2

88

89

IV The House

The poet Menander

90

Model of the House of the Menander
(1, 10, 4)
Scale 1:25
Lent by Imperial Tobacco Limited

The House of the Menander, which takes its name from a portrait of the poet painted on the walls of an *exedra* opening off the peristyle, occupies the greater part of an insula situated in the heart of the residential quarter that lies to the east of the Via Stabiana and to the south of the Via dell' Abbondanza. A seal found in the quarters of the steward bearing the name of Eros, the freedman or trusted slave of a certain Quintus Poppaeus, tells us that at the time of the eruption the house belonged to a member of the prosperous local family of the Poppaei, the family of which Nero's wife, Poppaea Sabina, was a member and to which the Villa at Oplontis probably belonged. It was excavated by Maiuri from 1927 to 1932.

The site had a long and varied history. At this point the ground slopes quite sharply southward toward the river Sarno, and although only further excavation could determine its earlier history in any detail, the plan and the masonry still upstanding tell us quite a bit of the story. The earliest visible remains date from the second half of the third century B.C., at which time the insula was subdivided into a number of small houses, of which five faced north along the northern frontage. The rest seem to have followed the line of the slope, at least three facing east and two more facing west, of which one, the House of the Lovers at the southwest angle, still retained its separate identity in A.D. 79. Three rooms of one of these early houses, with remains of First Style wall painting, were found by Maiuri when relaying the floor of the large *triclinium* (Room 18) off the east wing of the later peristyle. The early floors were about six feet deeper than those of the later building, and the walls several degrees out of alignment with it. At this early period the House of the Menander probably consisted simply of the atrium with, probably, a garden plot behind it.

Some time in the second century B.C., this nucleus was modernized and enlarged, with a handsome new façade and the insertion of the Corinthian columns flanking the entrance to the *tablinum*, together with a formalization of the garden area beyond, to which belonged the three central columns of the north wing of the later peristyle. Then, shortly after the middle of the first century B.C., came another and more radical development. The old buildings around the atrium were again partly modernized, but the main living quarters were transferred to a new setting around a large rectangular peristyle. To create this, several of the adjoining properties were bought up, and place was made for the peristyle by terracing upward and outward across the middle of the insula, leaving only the servants' quarters at the old level. A series of handsome living rooms (14-18) was added along the east side and a bath suite along the southern part of the west side. The old *tablinum* and the rooms to right and left of it now opened southward onto the north side of the peristyle. The south side, where the terracing did not allow for rooms, was modeled into a series of decorative *exedrae*. With the subsequent purchase of the property at the southeast corner of the insula for conversion into farm quarters, the house occupied the whole insula except for the House of the Lovers and the buildings at the northeast and northwest corners.

As everywhere else in Pompeii, the earthquake of A.D. 62 did serious damage here. In A.D. 79 the atrium area, which had been redecorated in the early Fourth Style manner shortly before the earthquake, was still awaiting restoration, and many of the rooms were found unfurnished; and although work was in progress in the peristyle area and by A.D. 79 had been nearly completed (only the baths still retain their Second Style ornament), the family had not yet resumed residence. As in the Villa of the Mysteries and at Oplontis, the property was left in the charge of the steward, Eros, who continued to operate the agricultural side of the estate, which may very well have consisted of vineyards and market gardens situated in the belt of substantially open ground that lay immediately to the south, inside the walls between the Stabian Gate and the Palaestra. Except for their positions inside and outside the walls respectively, the House of the Menander and the Villa of the Mysteries in this respect had a great deal in common.

Space does not permit a room-by-room account of the decoration of the house. The wall painting offers a fine range of Fourth Style work, some of it (in the atrium area) painted before the earthquake of A.D. 62, most of it (in the peristyle and the rooms opening off it) in the later post-earthquake phase. Of the Second Style paintings, which once adorned the whole of the peristyle area, one can now catch some tantalizing glimpses in the bath suite, notably in the apse of the hot room *(caldarium)* with its frieze of black and white figured panels simulating stuccoed niches and, above it, a second frieze with three polychrome scenes of women bathing; but most of this earlier work had been ruthlessly stripped off by the Fourth Style decorators. They were, on the other hand, glad to retain the fine mosaic pavements of the earlier period. These include a splendid polychrome Nilotic panel in the "Green Room" (11) with pygmies and boats in a landscape of river birds, plants, and architectural scenery (see page 109) set in a severely simple black and white surround; a sadly damaged panel of a satyr and nymph in a double *cubiculum* (Room 21), which in the last period appears to have been converted into a library; and the fine series of pavements in the bath suite. The last-named in particular illustrate the art of decorative paving at a turning point in its Roman development: those of the *caldarium* and of the *apodyterium* still strongly influenced by the sort of Hellenistic work one finds on Delos, whereas that of the corridor between them, portraying four strigils, an oil flask, and a Negro slave bearing two *askoi,* clearly foreshadows the "popular" Italic style of the skeleton mosaic (No. 109). The floor of the atrium vestibule is a fine example of a pavement made entirely of fragments of colored marble set in a ground of black tesserae.

Of the individual rooms we can only mention Room 4, a symmetrical early Fourth Style scheme incorporating three lively panel pictures with scenes from the Trojan War; the "Green Room" (11) at the northwest corner of the peristyle, a fine example of the sort of late Fourth Style work that tends to refer back to earlier styles and motifs, including a frieze, 25 cm high, portraying in white on red the rape of the Lapith women by the Centaurs, a rare survival of a type of figured frieze that was common in the late Hellenistic world; and the large *triclinium* (Room 18), which exemplifies another trend in late Fourth Style painting, one that relied for its effect on the contraposition and repetition of broad sheets of color, picked out with dainty decorative detail and small, isolated figures. Along the south side of the peristyle the two semi-circular *exedrae* (22 and 24) illustrated Diana hunting (22) and a rustic shrine with an image of Venus (24), both displayed within spacious landscape settings; while the central, rectangular *exedra* (23), the focus of the whole architectural scheme, contained figures of three of the great dramatic poets of the past, or of two of them flanking a central figure of Dionysus. Sadly, two figures are now unrecognizable, but the third, on the right-hand wall, is the seated Menander from whom the house takes its name.

Other features of note are the traces of a wooden screen, 2.10 m high, set across the opening between the *tablinum* and the atrium, and of a curtain across the entrance to Room 4; the terracotta surround of the *compluvium* (the opening in the roof); the gabled *lararium* in the atrium, on the right-hand side on entering; and a second household shrine at the southwest corner of the peristyle. This last, in a room decorated with Second Style paintings that may have been retained in the last period as a mark of respect for tradition, consists of a rectangular altar of masonry set in front of a recess, in which were displayed one small seated figure and four small heads or busts, made of wood or of wax, the *imagines maiorum,* symbolic images of the family ancestors (see page 108). Of more specifically architectural interest are the extreme irregularity of the peristyle colonnades, with the columns spaced so as

to give the maximum visibility outward from the principal living rooms, regardless of the architectural proprieties; the lighting of the great *triclinium* (Room 18) by means of a window set high in the walls, above the adjoining roofs (remains of a window frame were found among the masonry fallen from the gable); and the traces of a wooden, open-air *triclinium* beneath a wooden pavilion in the center of the peristyle garden, as in the House of P. Paquius Proculus (II, 7, 1).

At its greatest extent the residence occupied the whole of the center of the insula, terraced out at a level corresponding to that of the atrium and of the main entrance in the middle of the north side. Built around and up against this terraced area were the service quarters. To the west of the peristyle, beyond the baths at the end of a long corridor, lay the kitchen, a small vegetable garden, and some storerooms. On this side there was no access from the street. To the east, along the street frontage, there were more storerooms, and at an upper level, the quarters of the domestic staff. Alongside this block, at the north end of it, was the steward's lodging, and at the south end, occupying the southeast corner of the insula, were the stables and farm buildings.

The kitchen block (Rooms 26-28) was by any modern standards impossibly remote from the *triclinium* where the food was served, but this does not seem to have worried a Roman householder—what were slaves for, after all? From the corridor, steps led down into an enclosed courtyard at the old ground level, which was used as a vegetable garden. Along the east side of it lay four basement rooms, which constituted the substructures of the bath building. In one of them, under the *caldarium* (and helping to heat it) there was a large bread oven, and the other three were used as storerooms. It was here, securely protected from recovery after the eruption, that the excavators found the remains of two large chests and their contents. One of these had contained jewelry and the family store of ready cash, forty-six gold and silver coins to a total value of 1,432 sestertii together with a collection of family silver, 118 pieces in all, weighing a total of just under 53 lb (24 kg). Many of them were handsomely decorated and included a number of antique pieces. The only comparable find from the Vesuvius area is the Boscoreale treasure (see page 108).

The slaves' quarters, which were accessible from the residence only by a narrow, sloping corridor at the southeast corner of the peristyle, call for little special comment. They had a small independent kitchen and a lavatory. A group of bodies found at the foot of the stairs to the upper story (between Rooms 19 and 21), one of them carrying a lantern identical to No. 163, are now thought to be those of workmen overcome while engaged in a salvage

operation after the eruption. Most of the staff, it seems, got away in time. The steward Eros, on the other hand, died at his post, stretched out on his bedstead in Room 43. This was the living room of a small separate house, with its own entrance leading into a substantial atrium (41) and, beyond it, a tiny garden courtyard (44) with a private kitchen and lavatory. In the steward's room were found his signet ring; a leather purse containing his savings, ninety coins totaling 527 sestertii; some fine bronze vessels; and a large number of iron tools (including fifteen vine-pruning knives) for issue to the farmworkers.

The farm quarters were built around three sides of a courtyard (34) with a wide entrance from the street. Along the north side there was an open lean-to gallery, in which were found the remains of a two-wheeled cart. The far end was occupied by stabling for four animals, together with a cistern and a drinking trough (29, 30), and along the south side were storerooms, a lavatory, and a wooden stair up to the farmworkers' quarters (31, 32). The corner of the block, always a valuable property, was let out independently as a bar (*thermopolium*), as was also a single-roomed shop facing onto the street to the south. Although the farm property evidently included vines, it did not press its own wine (as did the Villa of the Mysteries). There was no press, and a stack of forty-three amphoras were all empties awaiting disposal.

The two houses at the northwest corner of the insula both date back to the third century B.C., one of them still retaining traces of its First Style painting. Both ceased to be residences after A.D. 62. One became a weaving establishment, the other the workshop of a smith who also practiced carpentry. The miniature two-story apartment in the angle between the latter and the House of the Menander was, as the *graffiti* make very clear, the lodging of a group of popular call-girls. The houses at the northeast corner, too, seem to have been taken over in this last period for commercial or industrial use, including a cookshop (*caupona*). Thanks to a lively exchange of *graffiti*, we even know the name of the barmaid, Iris, one of whose boyfriends was a weaver from down the street. In the last period before the eruption this was evidently still a lively quarter, but socially it had come down in the world.

One final *graffito* was found just outside the front door of the steward's quarters. It tells the traveler where to find company at Nuceria: *Nucerea quaeres ad porta[m] Romana[m] in vico venerio Novelliam Primigeniam* ("At Nuceria ask for Novellia Primigenia, in the street of Venus near the Rome Gate").

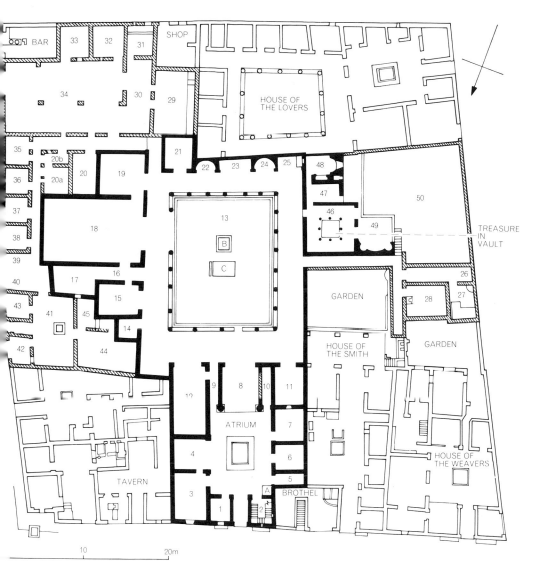

1. Door keeper's lodge
2. Staircase to upper floor
3. Bedroom later used as workshop
4. "Ala"
5. Storeroom
6-7. Bedrooms
8. Tablinum
9. Corridor
10. Cupboard
11. Green oecus
12. Large exedra
13. Peristyle garden
14. Store
15. Red oecus
16. Corridor
17. Bedroom
18. Dining room (triclinium)
19. Yellow oecus
20. 35-40. Servants' quarters
21. Day bedroom/library
22-24. Exedrae
25. Exedra with imagines maiorum
26-28. Kitchens
29. Stable
30-34. Farm quarters
41-45. Steward's lodging
43. Bedroom
44. Garden
46. Vestibule to bath suite
47. Warm undressing room
    (apodyterium)
48. Hot room (caldarium)
49. Sun terrace
50. Kitchen garden
A. Household shrine (lararium)
B. Fountain basin
C. Wooden dining area
    (triclinium)

10   20m

91

93

92

91
Bronze figure of an old donkey
Length 12 cm, height 9 cm
Naples Museum, inv. 4955
From one of the sites in the Vesuvius area

Hollow cast and carefully worked over after casting to give the effect of coarse hair. A square hole in the belly suggests that the figure was attached to some larger object as a handle or decorative finial.

92
Bronze figurine of a deer
Length 28 cm, height 30 cm
Naples Museum, old inv. 2134 (base, 109992)
From one of the sites in the Vesuvius area

Hollow cast in two halves, the body is engraved with a delicate flower design that serves to mask the joint. Although the alabaster on which it stands is ancient, it does not belong; but the figure does seem, rather unusually, to have been a purely decorative piece.

Cf. De Ridder, *Bronzes antiques du Louvre* (1913), no. 196.

93
Statuette of a Placentarius in gilded bronze and silver
Height 25.4 cm
Naples Museum, inv. 143759
From the House of the Ephebe (1, 7, 10-12)

One of a group of four identical figures found together in a wooden box in a room off the atrium. The figure is bronze and the tray and base silver. They are usually thought to represent *placentarii* (sellers of *placentae;* see Cato, *De Re Rustica,* 76), itinerant piemen crying their wares. The element of caricature is typical of late Hellenistic art. Equally typical of Roman taste is the adaptation of a *genre* type to a functional purpose. These were probably pieces for the service of some special delicacy.

Maiuri, *BdA* 1925, 268-275.

94 (withdrawn from exhibition)
Terracotta toad with traces of blue-green glaze
Naples Museum, inv. 76/166

95
One-handled glass cup
Height 14.3 cm, upper diameter 13.8 cm
Naples Museum, inv. 11961
From Pompeii

The glass is yellowish green. Five lines have been incised below the handle. This kind of cup imitates prototypes in metalwork like the silver cup decorated with ivy leaves, No. 324.

Isings 52, form 37.

96
Tall glass beaker with molded decoration
Height 14.4 cm
Naples Museum, inv. 12279
From Pompeii

The greenish glass is densely ornamented with bands of relief decoration. The bands comprise, from top to bottom, a row of bosses, an ivy vine, a maeander separating scallop shells, "tear drops" and ovoids, and a laurel wreath. Faint vertical ridges reflect the join between the two halves of the mold.

Isings 45, form 31.

95

99

97

101

96

100

98

7

mall bulbous glass jug

Height 12.2 cm, diameter of body 7.8 cm
Naples Museum, inv. 109423
From the atrium of House VII, 7, 13 (?),
January 1872

In imitation of a fine metal form, free-
blown, with short raised ribs running up
from the base. The attachment of the
handle to the rim is decorated with im-
pressed ridges.
Isings 76, form 57.

8

emmed goblet in cobalt blue glass

Height 14 cm, diameter of rim 15.4 cm
Naples Museum, inv. 76/215
From one of the sites in the Vesuvius area

The body was blown into a mold; two
horizontal wheel-cut lines decorate the
outside. The stem is formed from two
large beads of glass and the foot added
separately. Such drinking cups were used
table; for a silver version see No. 246.
Isings 50, form 36a.

99
Ribbed blue glass bowl
Height 8.9 cm, diameter 18.9 cm
Naples Museum, inv. 13810
From Pompeii

These bowls were made by pressing soft
glass into a mold; the interior was polished on a wheel, the exterior by a second,
brief exposure to fire. Bowls of this form,
in multi-colored as well as in monochrome glass, were popular in the first
century A.D.
Harden, *Camulodunum* 301ff.

100
Small blue glass jug (askos)
Height 11 cm, length 21.1 cm
Naples Museum, inv. 109433
From Pompeii, House IX, 2, 26

The glass-blower has imitated a shape
long familiar in Greek pottery and in
Campanian bronze ware. These *askoi* are
commonly found in pairs and were evidently so used; they are often very finely
worked, being blown into a mold rather
than free-blown, as is this example. Mid-
first century A.D.
Isings 77, form 59.

101
Small jug (askos) in black and white marbled glass
Height 9.5 cm, length 13.4 cm
Naples Museum, inv. 118143
From Pompeii, in IX, 7, 6

Like No. 100 this is free-blown, but it is
squatter in shape and made in thicker,
opaque glass. It was found in 1888, together with three other *askoi* in an
aedicula opposite the entrance to IX, 7, 6;
altogether 23 pieces of glass, some of
them colored, were found in this building.
Brightly variegated glass in strong colors
was very popular in the early stages of
Roman glass production. Late first century B.C. to early first century A.D.
Isings 77, form 59.

102
Shallow two-handled glass cup
Height 3.8 cm, diameter 12.6 cm
Naples Museum, inv. 133273
From Pompeii, from the *tablinum* of VI,
16, 28

One of a pair of identical cups, mold-
blown with formal decoration in relief.
Second half of the first century A.D.
NSc 1908, 277.

103
Long-necked glass flask
Height 15 cm
Naples Museum, inv. 12435
From Pompeii

The form is free-blown, decorated with
thin threads of glass trailed over the bulbous body as ribs. Such flasks are very
common at Pompeii, though usually un-
decorated, and were used for serving
liquids or for oils used in bathing, as was
the bronze example, No. 221. Inside the
flask is a quantity of black powder, the
decayed remains of its contents. Early first
century A.D.
Isings 34, form 16.

104
Dark blue glass jug
Height 18 cm
Naples Museum, inv. 13539
From Pompeii

Fine-quality work, free-blown with a
drawn-out spout and an applied handle.
The form clearly imitates that of a bronze
vessel.
Isings 71, form 54.

102

103

104

105

105
Large glass dish
Height 3.5 cm, diameter 22.3 cm
Naples Museum, inv. 11588
From Pompeii

Blown into a mold. A large dish of the
same kind, filled with fruit, is shown in a
Fourth Style still life painting from Pompeii (Naples Museum, inv. 8645). The
form is copied from *terra sigillata* pottery.
Isings 39, form 23; cf. Beyen pl. VIII.

106
Fragment of a Second Style wall painting
Height 1.18 m, width 60 cm
Naples Museum, inv. 9847
From the Villa of Diomedes, Pompeii,
1772

The scheme to which this fragment belonged was divided into three main panels
by four fluted columns. Between the outer
pairs of columns ran a tall screen wall,
over the top of which could be glimpsed
a receding architectural perspective. A
tholos occupied the middle of the central
intercolumniation. The fragment formed
part of the right-hand panel and shows
part of one column and of the red screen
wall. Hanging against the latter is shown
a dead hare and, placed on top of it, the
mask of an old father in Greek New
Comedy. To the right of it is part of a
column shown in perspective beyond the
screen wall. Naples Museum, inv. 8594
comes from a similar wall in the same
room (see drawing).
Curtius, figs. 74-76; Webster, *New Comedy*
185, NP 3.

107
**Wall painting of a silver wine bucket
(situla)**
Height 77 cm, width 41 cm
Naples Museum, inv. 9965
From the peristyle wall in the Villa of
Publius Fannius Synistor at Boscoreale

This *situla* is one of several objects, mostly
prizes for athletics, shown as if placed on
a dado in front of the painted screen wall
of a Second Style scheme. It stands on
three low feet in the form of animal's legs,
and from the rim spring two tall, ornate
handle mounts. Placed diagonally behind
it is a trident entwined with a snake.
P. W. Lehmann, *Roman Wall Paintings from
Boscoreale* (Cambridge, Mass. 1953) 11f.

106

107

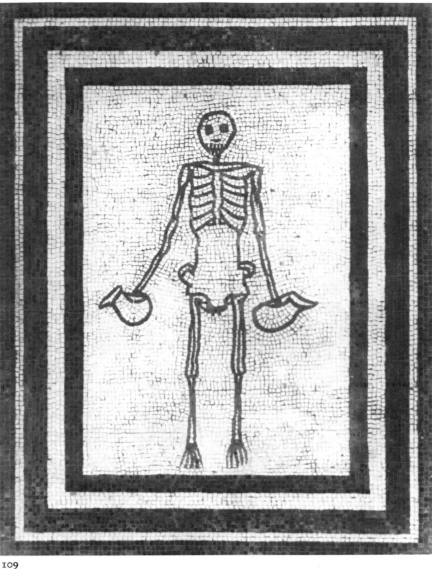

109

108
Mosaic representing a crab or spider
Width 41 cm, height 45 cm
Pompeii, Storerooms, inv. 13933
From House VI, 15, 3

This naive portrayal of some indetermi-
nate crustacean or spider-like creature
represents the opposite extreme of competence and artistic intent to the sophisticated late Hellenistic school of craftsmanship exemplified by Nos. 238, 305. The
work of some local craftsman used to
laying simple black and white geometrical
patterns, it would have been displayed in
the middle of a much larger area of white
tesserae. Like similar mosaics portraying
animals and other symbolic figures, it
would have been placed near the entrance
to avert ill luck.

109
**Mosaic representing a skeleton carrying
two askoi**
Height 91 cm, width 70 cm
Naples Museum, inv. 9978
From one of the sites in the Vesuvius area

The skeleton, set within a rectangular
frame and carried out in black and white
mosaic, holds a pair of wine jugs (*askoi*).
A product of the *memento mori* conventions fostered by Epicurean philosophy,
it probably adorned the center of a *triclinium*. Unlike the colored floor mosaics,
which derive from Hellenistic models,
these black and white mosaics were a specifically Italian creation. Often naive, but
always direct and lively, they are the
artistic equivalent of the "popular" strain
in contemporary painting.

159

110

111

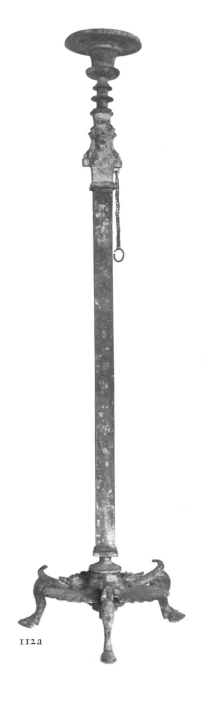

110
Tall bronze bowl
Height 33.7 cm, diameter of rim 31 cm
Naples Museum, inv. 73146
From Herculaneum

The bowl, which has a molded foot and a frieze of molded ornament below the rim, has two identical applied handles. Early publications show it as standing on a graceful molded pedestal, about 23 cm high, with three animal's-paw feet, but this has become separated and appears now to be lost. The handles portray two trousered barbarians, molded in the round, fighting, with their lozenge-shaped shields locked between them. They stand upon and are attached to the body of the bowl by a calyx-shaped escutcheon, on which are displayed a pair of crossed spears and two similar shields. At the base of the calyx is an ox-skull (*bukranion*), a common decorative motif in late Hellenistic work of all sorts. Barbarian shields, in this case oval, are the principal motif also of the frieze on the body of the bowl.

The same earlier publications speak of this piece as a trophy awarded for victory in gladiatorial combat, and the pedestal, to which it appears to have been fastened by a rivet, would indeed suggest some form of ceremonial use. But if these are gladiatorial combatants, they represent an earlier stage of gladiatorial history than the sophisticated, stylized gladiatorial combat of Imperial times, to which alone such trophies would have been appropriate. Barbarians, and in particular Gauls, were one of the commonplaces of Hellenistic art, and pairs of figures fighting were one of the stock themes of Capuan bronzework. From its shape this piece could well be as early as the second century B.C.

MB VIII (Naples 1832) pl. XV; Ceci VI, no. 37.

111
Landscape panel of a rustic sanctuary
Height 34 cm, length 61 cm
Naples Museum, inv. 9419
From Herculaneum

Against the white ground of a lateral panel in a Third Style scheme is a picture framed in red, mounted on a slender support. On a rocky outcrop is a small shrine, behind which is a walled garden with two columns capped with urns and a large tree. In front of the sanctuary is another column, tied with a garland and supporting a tripod. In the distance are two figures carrying bundles, and the faint outline of another building.

Rostowzew, "Architekturlandschaft" 84, fig. 50.

112a
Bronze adjustable candelabrum
(lamp stand)
Height from 87.2 cm minimum to 138.4 cm maximum
Naples Museum, inv. 111228
From Herculaneum

This lamp stand is made in three pieces. The base, which can be removed, has three legs, ending in bull's feet, which arch outward from beneath a plate decorated with three projecting scallop shells and sea monsters in the form of dogs' heads with pectoral fins. On the base rests a hollow shaft, square in section, topped with a small double herm of a satyr and maenad supporting a *calathus*. The upper part consists of a square rod that fits into and is free to move within the shaft, and that carries the actual lamp support, in the form of a vase. The height of the stand could be adjusted by fitting a small bronze pin, chained to the underside of the satyr's left "arm," into one of a series of holes spaced down the length of the movable rod.

This piece is one of a group, of which the detail of the little herms and of the bases varies considerably, but of which the technical features are so closely related throughout that they are almost certainly the product of a single workshop. About the end of the first century B.C.

Chiurazzi no. 469.

112a

112b

12b

ronze oil lamp

iameter 9.7 cm, length 14.1 cm
Iaples Museum, inv. 72435
robably from Pompeii or Herculaneum

he lamp bears a striking similarity to
rracotta lamps with plain nozzles of the
ter first century A.D. The higher-quality
etal piece, however, has the added fea
res of a leaf-decorated handle and a lid to
ose the filler hole. The chain is fastened
the lid and handle with modern wire
ops.

f. H. Menzel, *Antike Lampen* (Mainz 1969)
ff., nos. 303, 307, 308.

13

able support (trapezophorus) with a ǧure of Attis

ray and white Italian marble
eight 83 cm
aples Museum, inv. 120425
om the atrium of House no. 78 on the
ia Stabiana, found 3 March 1866

ables of bronze or marble, set against a
all and supported on a single leg, are a
mmon feature of Pompeian house fur
ture. To the column of marble, which
nstitutes the actual support, is often
lded carved decoration, and colored
arbles were popular. Although the com
onest motifs are Dionysiac, the use of a
ǧure of Attis, as here, is by no means
common. Identical pieces have been
und at Herculaneum and Capua.
Attis, beloved by Cybele, the Great
oddess of Asia Minor, was a beautiful
uth whose self-castration, death, and
ansformation into a pine tree was the
bject of the wild rites of annual mourn-
; associated with her cult. He is here
rtrayed as a shepherd boy, in oriental
ess and wearing a Phrygian cap.

an tam Tinh (1975) 283; M. J. Vermaseren,
e Legend of Attis in Greek and Roman Art
iden 1966) 14.

114

Wall painting: Pan and the nymphs

Height 1.22 m, width 93 cm
Naples Museum, inv. 111473
From the left-hand wall of the same
cubiculum in the House of Jason as
No. 129

Third Style panel showing Pan, pipes in
hand, seated on a rock with a goat at his
feet. To the left are seated two nymphs,
one of them holding two reed pipes in her
hand, while to the right another stands
playing a lyre (*cithara*). Beyond the left-
hand nymphs is a building set in a rocky
landscape, central to which is a pine tree,
sacred to Pan.

Schefold, *WP* 265; Peters 97.

115-126

Decorative wall paintings

From Room 15 (*cubiculum*) in the Villa
of Agrippa Postumus at Boscotrecase

115-116 Naples Museum, inv. 138992,
138993: height 2.00 m, width 44 cm

117-126 Metropolitan Museum of Art
(withdrawn from exhibition)

117, inv. 20.192.1: height 2.441 m,
width 1.251 m
118, inv. 20.192.2: height 2.445 m,
width 0.591 m
119, inv. 20.192.3: height 2.435 m,
width 0.606 m
120, inv. 20.192.4: height 2.041 m,
width 0.390 m
121, inv. 20.192.5: height 1.861 m,
width 0.559 m

113

114

122, inv. 20.192.6: height 1.994 m,
width 0.567 m
123, inv. 20.192.7: height 1.854 m,
width 0.581 m
124, inv. 20.192.8: height 1.032 m,
width 0.302 m
125, inv. 20.192.10: height 0.371 m,
width 0.375 m
126, inv. 20.192.11: height 0.390 m,
width 0.832 m

The country villa of Boscotrecase, near
Pompeii, was discovered in 1902 during
the building of a railway. Paintings from
four of its *cubicula* were salvaged in the
excavations of 1903-1905. In 1906 a new
eruption of Vesuvius covered the site.

The brilliant, innovative wall paintings
were done for a patron from the highest
level of Roman society. Epigraphical evidence from Boscotrecase indicates that
the villa belonged to Agrippa Postumus,
grandson of Augustus and son of Augustus' most trusted advisor, Agrippa. The
villa was probably begun for the elder
Agrippa, but the paintings were part of a
project carried out around 11 B.C., after
Agrippa Postumus had inherited it.

Room 15 has a red dado and walls of
polished carbon black. Elongated decorative elements—tripods, candelabra, reed-
like colonnettes—divide the walls into
panels, on which tiny, unframed landscapes float in what seems to be a noctur-
nal blackness. The ornamental details are
minute, fanciful, exquisite. Many evoke
the fabled world of Pharaonic Egypt.
There are lotus buds, falcons, and miniature vignettes of exotic pseudo-Egyptian
cult ceremonies. Other elements, the
paired swans and the griffins, have nothing to do with the Nile. On the North
Wall, a roof of the central *aedicula* rests
on disc-shaped supports painted with
portrait-like profile heads.

Blanckenhagen and Alexander, *Boscotrecase*
pls. 1-9, color pls. A, B.

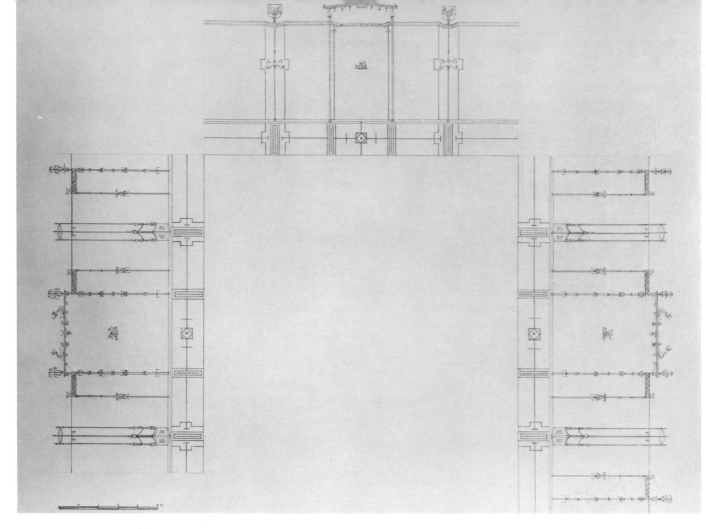

117–126 Reconstruction of decorative scheme of west, north, and east walls of Room 15 in the Villa of Agrippa Postumus

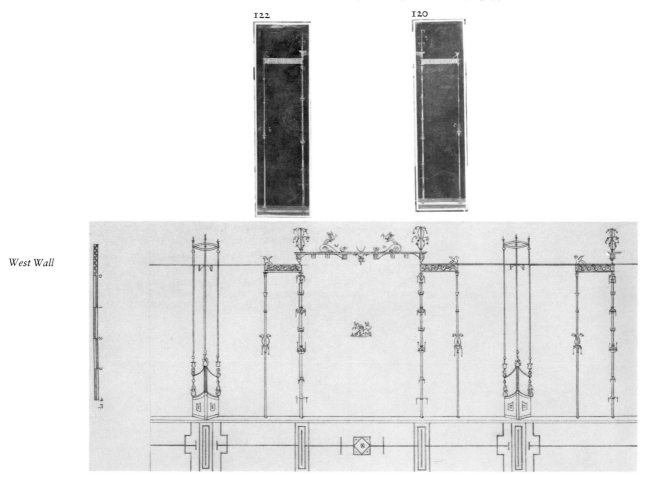

West Wall

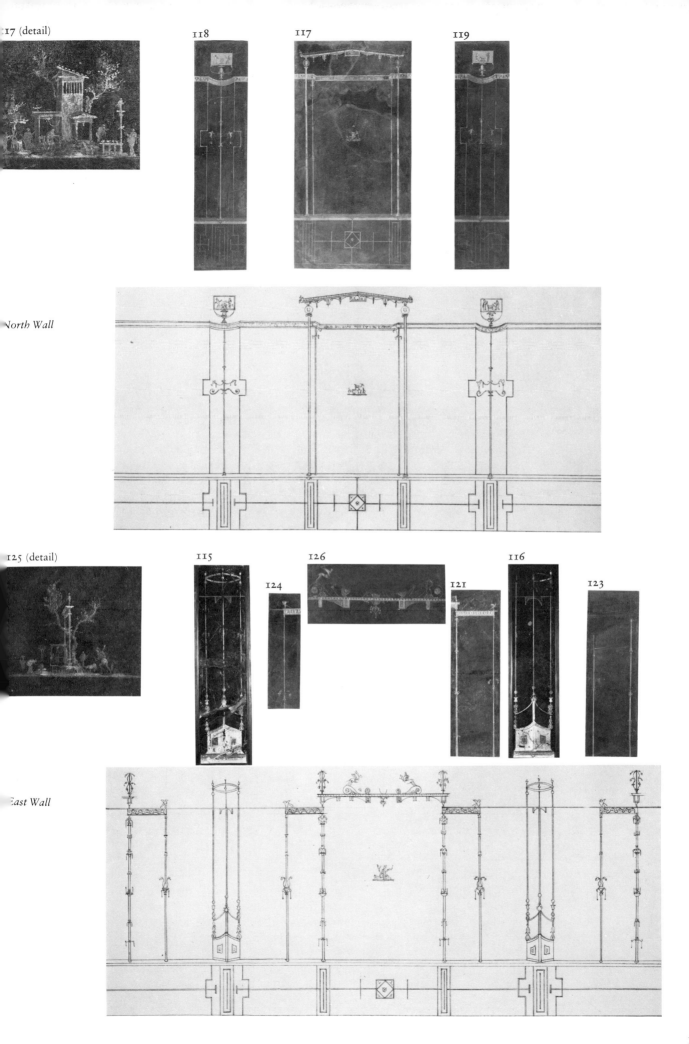

117 (detail)

118 117 119

North Wall

125 (detail)

115 124 126 121 116 123

East Wall

128 *Reconstruction of the East Wall of Room 19 in the Villa of Agrippa Postumus*

127

128

127, 128 (withdrawn from exhibition)
Wall painting: Polyphemus and Galatea
Height 198.12 cm, width 130.81 cm
Metropolitan Museum of Art, inv.
20.192.17
From the West Wall of Room 19 (cubiculum) in the Villa of Agrippa Postumus at Boscotrecase

Wall painting: Perseus and Andromeda
Height 198.12 cm, width 129.54 cm
Metropolitan Museum of Art, inv.
20.192.16
From the East Wall of Room 19 (cubiculum) in the Villa of Agrippa Postumus at Boscotrecase

Two mythological panels come from facing walls of a room that had Third Style architectural decoration, surviving in fragments, on a red ground. Each myth is set in a landscape whose axis is a craggy, improbably vertical pinnacle of rock. Sea laps about its base, merging in a horizonless unity with the misty sky beyond. Figures are dotted about without regard to consistencies of distance and scale. Polyphemus is the central figure of one panel; the outsize lover gazes longingly with his single eye at Galatea, the sea nymph with whom he is infatuated. His flock of goats grazes near a statue on a tall pedestal. Far away, another figure of Polyphemus acts out a later part of the brute's sad history, hurling a rock after the departing ship of Odysseus, who has blinded him.

The complementary panel illustrates the virtuous, happy love of Perseus and Andromeda. The princess is chained to the cliff; in the foreground the sea monster, come to devour her, lifts his terrifying head from the water. A little Perseus flies in on winged sandals to rescue the girl, attacking from high above, while a female figure, perhaps a personification, perhaps Andromeda's mother, sits mournfully at the side. A second Perseus participates in a sequel episode shown at the upper right. Returning triumphant, the hero is welcomed by Andromeda's father, King Cepheus, and his retinue in front of palatial buildings.

Blanckenhagen and Alexander, *Boscotrecase* pls. 40-46, color pl. D.

129
Wall painting: Europa riding the bull
Width 99 cm, height 1.25 m
Naples Museum, inv. 111475
From the back wall of a *cubiculum* in the House of Jason (IX, 5, 18)

Third Style central panel portraying Europa, daughter of the king of Phoenicia, who, while playing on the seashore with her handmaidens, was approached by Zeus in the form of a white bull, which lured her into seating herself on its back and thereupon carried her off, across the sea to Crete. There, after bearing Zeus three sons, she married the King of Crete, who adopted her sons, one of whom, Minos, became his heir. Europa is shown seated on the bull in a rocky landscape painted in tones of gray on a white ground, against which the figures, which were painted first, stand out in sharp relief. The landscape, with its central oak tree (the tree sacred to Zeus), echoes the central scene.

On the left-hand wall of the same bedroom *(cubiculum)*, by the same hand, was the painting of Pan and the nymphs (No. 114) and on the right-hand wall a painting of Hercules, Deianira, and the centaur Nessus. Common to all three paintings was the symbolic use of trees within the landscape.
Schefold, *WP* 263-264; Peters 96f.

130
Wall painting: Nile landscape
Width 1.41 m, height 38 cm
Naples Museum, inv. 8561
From Herculaneum, 1748

A typical combination of Nilotic flora and fauna with elements of Egyptianizing architecture, from the dado (lower zone) of a Third Style wall. Within a setting of marsh and river, with date palms and lotus flowers are, on the left, a crocodile; in the center, an island enclosure with buildings made of reeds, including a tower similar to that shown in No. 190; on the right, an Egyptian goose and a hippopotamus on a rocky island.
Pitture di Ercolano I, 50, 263.

129

131

132

131
Three-sided base for a candelabrum
Pentelic marble
Height 56 cm
Naples Museum, inv. 6857
From one of the sites in the Vesuvius area

The base, which is carried on the backs of three crouching rams, is topped with an inverted capital, in the center of which is the socket for a bronze candelabrum. The three faces are carved in low relief; on one side two rams reach up to nibble grapes on the top of a candelabrum with a similarly three-sided base; on the second side two birds (ravens?) drinking from a fluted vase (*crater*) hung with garlands; and on the third a doe suckling a fawn in the shade of an oak tree. Large numbers of such ornate pieces of marble furniture were being produced in the later first century B.C. and the first century A.D. by Athenian workshops operating within the academic traditions of late Hellenistic decorative sculpture. There is a piece probably from the same workshop in the Museo Nazionale Romano (inv. 371; *Annali dell'Inst.* XXII [1850] 60ff.).

132
Bronze candelabrum (lamp stand) and three hanging bronze lamps
Height 56.7 cm
Naples Museum, inv. 72226
From Pompeii

The shaft of this candelabrum takes the form of a growing, twisted vine with leaves and tendrils; the largest of the tendrils become the supports for the hanging lamps, two of which are in the form of snail shells. Palmettes and tendrils inlaid in silver decorate the top of the flat base. A pair of bulls' skulls draped with ribbons, a *thyrsus*, and laurel wreaths are inlaid with silver on the front of the round drum from which the shaft springs. Since a splendid example of this type of vegetable-form lamp stand was found at Pergamum, it is very likely the Romans inherited a taste for such works of decorative art from the cities of western Asia Minor.

Chiurazzi 227, no. 494; Spinazzola pl. 292.

133
Relief with scenes from the myth of Telephos
Pentelic marble
Length 1.20 m, height 52 cm
Naples Museum, inv. 76/128
From Herculaneum, House of the Telephos Relief

Originally set into the wall plaster of a small anteroom to a *triclinium*, the relief shows two episodes in the history of the Trojan Wars. Achilles, on his way to Troy, had landed by mistake on the territory of Telephos, king of Mysia, who received from Achilles' spear a wound in the thigh that refused to heal. Achilles consulted an oracle, which told him he

would only reach Troy if Telephos would
consent to guide him. Telephos too consulted an oracle and was told that only
he that wounded could cure." In the
left-hand scene Achilles is consulting the
oracle. In the right-hand scene he is
scraping rust from his spearhead ("he that
wounded") onto Telephos' wound, effect-
ing a rapid cure.

The relief belongs to a large series
showing mythological scenes, produced
by Athenian workshops in the later first
century B.C. for Roman patrons, who had
them set into decorative painted or
marble-veneered wall schemes in both
public and private buildings. Wall paintings of the Second Style (e.g., the House
of the Lararium, I, 6, 4, *cubiculum*) sometimes incorporated painted imitations.

There are indications that the relief was
originally brightly colored.

JdI V (1952) 147; C. Bauchhenss-Thüriedl,
*Der Mythos von Telephos in der antiken
Bildkunst* (Würzburg 1971) 91; Maiuri,
Ercolano 355.

34
Wall painting: satyr and maenad
Width 37 cm, height 37 cm
Naples Museum, inv. 9135
From the *tablinum* of the House of the
Dioscuri

This painting, like so many found in the
early days of Pompeian excavation, had
been chopped out of a larger wall composition. The dancing couple would have
been the center of a panel of a Fourth
Style wall, sailing on its empty light blue
expanse as though through the upper air.
A muscular, sunburned young satyr,

crowned with leaves and carrying a cloth
weighted down with the land's produce,
embraces a white-skinned maenad. She
brandishes the *thyrsus*, symbol of sacred
revelry; the wind of their flight blows the
drapery back from her nude torso. Flick-
ering highlights add to the feeling of
motion; black, decisive shadows lend
weight to the strong little bodies.

Spinazzola pl. 145; Schefold, *WP* 117.

135
Fragment of Fourth Style wall painting
Width 98 cm, height 90 cm
Naples Museum, inv. 8514
From Pompeii

Fragment from the upper zone of an early
Fourth Style wall, including the upper
border and an *aedicula* set in a formal
quasi-architectural scheme of delicate
garlands and slender rods entwined with
tendrils, reminiscent of fine late Third
Style work (as in the White Triclinium in
the House of M. Lucretius, IX, 3, 5).
Within the *aedicula* is the figure of a
woman with flowing draperies, poised as
if flying.

134

135

137

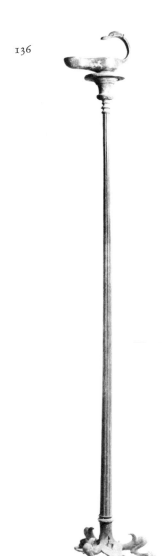

136

136a
Bronze candelabrum (lamp stand)
Height 1.12 m
Naples Museum, inv. 78537

The tall, gently tapering, fluted stem springs from a three-legged base and carries a lamp stand in the form of a vase (*crater*). Each leg consists of the hind leg of a lion, resting on a low drum and springing from beneath an upward-curling leaf. Ivy leaves fill the angles between the legs. Early first century A.D.
Pernice IV, 47f., fig. 60.

136b
Bronze lamp
Height 11 cm, length 20 cm
Naples Museum, inv. 72483
From Pompeii

The reservoir and nozzle of this lamp are drawn out into an elongated tear-drop shape, which is emphasized by a gentle molding similar to that on No. 161. The handle is arched over the filling hole and is decorated with a dolphin's head holding a cockle shell in its mouth. This motif is also found on the feet of bronze candelabra.

137
Wall painting: Pyramus and Thisbe
Height 1.05 m, width 80 cm
Naples Museum, inv. 111483
From the *triclinium* on the left of the northern *ala* of House IX, 5, 14

This artless painting, the central panel of a Fourth Style wall, represents the final scene of the story of the unhappy Babylonian lovers, Pyramus and Thisbe, "the most lamentable comedy, and most cruel death of Pyramus and Thisby," which Bottom the Weaver and his company presented at the court of King Theseus in Shakespeare's *Midsummer Night's Dream*. Pyramus, believing Thisbe dead, has killed himself beneath a mulberry tree; she, finding him dead, is stabbing herself with his sword. The pillar supporting an urn represents the tomb where they were to have met. There is a Third Style version of the same composition in the garden *triclinium* of the House of "Loreius Tiburtinus" (II, 2, 2-5) and another in a Fourth Style *triclinium* in the House of M. Lucretius Fronto (IV, II, 1).
Schefold, WP 260.

139

140

141

38

138
Bronze folding tripod
Height 58.2 cm
Naples Museum, old inv. 1452
From Pompeii

The uprights of this tripod consist of three rods, which rest on animal's-paw feet; they are punctuated by three sheath leaves, and at the top each terminates in a decorative finial in the form of an *uraeus*, crowned with a lotus bud and springing from two small birds' heads. Hinged to the inner face just below the finial are two transverse struts, each of

which is pivoted at the center to one of its neighbors and linked to another at the bottom by means of a ring that is free to slide up and down the length of a rectangular loop on the inner face of the upright. Although the mechanism closely resembles that of adjustable stands that could accommodate bowls of various sizes, in this case there were only two possible positions: closed, with the uprights and transverse rods all folded together, or open, with some circular object, probably a flanged bowl, resting on the top of the finials and locking the legs in a fully splayed position.
Ceci pl. IV, no. 4; *MB* 5 (Naples 1829) pl. LX.

139
Wall painting: basket
Height 24 cm, width 20 cm
Naples Museum, inv. 8689
From one of the sites in the Vesuvius area

The basket, on a white ground, occupied the center of one of the lateral panels of a Third Style wall. The most plausible identification is that it represents a work basket containing spindles of colored wool, one of which is shown resting against the rim of the basket.
Beyen, *Stilleben* 23f.; Croisille 44.

140
Wall painting: head of Pan
Height 19 cm, width 11 cm
Naples Museum, inv. 9126
From Herculaneum

The head has been cut from an ornamental frieze in a Fourth Style wall.

141
Wall painting: medallion with busts of Dionysus and a maenad
Diameter 44.5 cm
Naples Museum, inv. 9284
From Herculaneum

Dionysus, god of wine and of ecstatic liberation, is shown with a wreath of grapes and vine leaves; in his right hand he holds a drinking cup (*cantharus*) and in his left, resting against his shoulder, the characteristic Dionysiac staff, or *thyrsus*. Behind him, her hand on his shoulder, is one of his attendant devotees, a maenad; she wears a mantle and earrings, with flowers in her hair.

Medallions such as this, containing real or mythological portraits, were placed in the middle of the lateral panels of many Fourth Style compositions (e.g., in the *tablinum* of the House of the Bicentenary at Herculaneum). This one, from its subject matter, may have adorned a *triclinium;* its companion piece (inv. 9283) showed Dionysus and a satyr.
Elia no. 304.

169

142

143

142
Bronze stool
Height 27 cm, length 29.4 cm, width
(side with curve) 26 cm
Pompeii, Storerooms, inv. 13355

Metal was widely used in fine Roman
furniture; large pieces were ornamented
or sheathed with bronze, while a small
accessory like this could be made entirely
of metal. The material makes possible
airy, attenuated supports and fine openwork ornament. The struts between the
legs are made up of tendrils, which
enframe blossoms in the finely detailed
panels under the seat. The simple panels
on the long sides are almost entirely reconstruction. The concave upper surface
shows that this piece was a stool, not a
table, and probably held a cushion. There
are similar seats in Naples, London, and
Berlin.

Cf. G. M. A. Richter, *The Furniture of the
Greeks, Etruscans and Romans* (London
1966) 111, fig. 564.

143
Wall painting: Pan and Hermaphroditus
Width 1.25 m, height 74 cm
Naples Museum, inv. 27700
From the atrium of the House of the
Dioscuri (VI, 9, 6)

Part of the upper zone of a Fourth Style
scheme, from above the doorway leading
from the *fauces* into the atrium. Hermaphroditus, one of the most curious
by-products of Greek mythology, was a
minor divinity of bisexual form, with
female breasts and male genitals. In this
picture he is seated by a pool, and Pan,
aroused by his apparently female charms,
has just discovered his mistake. Beyond
Pan is a tower within a square enclosure,
set in a rocky landscape. On the right is a
statue of Priapus, standing on a pedestal
and holding a cornucopia.

Richardson pl. 23.1; Schefold, *WP* 116;
Peters 138; Kraus and von Matt no. 276.

144, 145
Wall paintings: fantasy architecture from a Fourth Style wall
Height 1.88 m, width 52 cm
Naples Museum, inv. 9710, 9707
From Pompeii, May 1760

Narrow vertical panels depicting slender
fantasy architecture in receding perspective are commonly used to frame the
central panel in one type of Fourth Style
wall. On the broad plane surface of the
central panel in the scheme from which
these elements came was painted a small
framed picture of Perseus and Andromeda
(Naples Museum, inv. 8995), and in the
middle of each lateral panel were roundels
(see also Nos. 2, 141). One of these was
the famous "Sappho" (Naples Museum,
inv. 9084).

A. Allroggen-Bedel, "Herkunft und
ursprünglicher Dekorationszusammen-
hang einiger in Essen ausgestellter
Fragmente von Wandmalereien," *Neue
Forschungen in Pompeji* 118f., fig. 95b.

146
Wall painting: Theseus, slayer of the Minotaur
Width 88 cm, height 97 cm
Naples Museum, inv. 9043
From the *exedra* off the peristyle in the
House of Gavius Rufus (VII, 2, 16)

The central panel of the left-hand wall of
a Fourth Style scheme. It shows Theseus
victorious from his battle with the Minotaur, the bull-headed monster of Crete to
whom the Athenians had each year to
send a tribute of youths and maidens. The
Minotaur lies dead in the entrance to his
lair, the Labyrinth, and his destined victims press round Theseus in gratitude. A
finer version of the same Greek original
(Naples Museum, inv. 9049) was found in
the Basilica at Herculaneum. The companion pieces of the picture at Pompeii
were (on the opposite wall, inv. 9044)
Pirithous, the companion of Theseus, re-
ceiving the centaurs and (on the rear wall,
inv. 9449) Dionysus, Aphrodite, and the
sun god, Helios.

Schefold, *WP* 136; Bianchi Bandinelli 110f.,
illustrating both this piece (fig. 116) and the
piece from Herculaneum (fig. 115).

147
Panel from a painted ceiling
Width 88 cm, height 82 cm
Naples Museum, inv. 9973
From Pompeii

The design, here reduced to a formal
pattern, is reminiscent of a ceiling coffer.
A small head of Medusa occupies the
center.

44

146

147

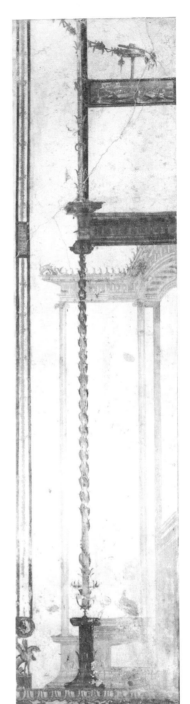

145

149

148

150

148, 149
Wall painting: pair of sea centaurs
Height 34 cm, width 24 cm
Height 30 cm, width 18 cm
Naples Museum, inv. 8888, 8887
From one of the sites in the Vesuvius area

Acroteria from a pair of panels of Fourth Style fantasy architecture similar to those flanking the panel of the Infant Hercules in the House of the Vettii (see page 100). They are shown blowing horns and holding tambourines.

150
Wall painting: woman giving water to a traveler
Width 44 cm, height 38 cm
Naples Museum, inv. 9106
From the *tablinum* of the House of the Dioscuri (VI, 9, 6)

The picture formed part of a longer landscape frieze, with painted moldings top and bottom, over the side panels of a Fourth Style wall (as in the atrium of the House of the Menander). In front of a rustic shelter made of canes, a woman, seated on a circular platform and wearing a conical hat, dips a beaker from a jar and hands it to a traveler, whose dog sits waiting for him.
Spinazzola-Aurigemma 580; Richardson 124f.; Schefold, *WP* 118; Peters 164.

151
Portable pottery brazier
Height 17 cm, width 32 cm, depth 24 cm
Naples Museum, inv. 76/198
From one of the sites in the Vesuvius area

The brazier is a simple box, with a series of holes pierced through the top to allow the heat to escape and provided with two lug handles for carrying.

152
Wall painting: Phaedra and Hippolytus
Width 1.03 m, height 1.04 m
Naples Museum, inv. 9041
From Herculaneum

Phaedra, wife of Theseus, King of Athens, had conceived a guilty passion for her stepson, Hippolytus, a passion that he rejected; whereupon Phaedra accused him of trying to seduce her. He was subsequently killed while out hunting, and she hanged herself. In this painting Phaedra's old nurse tells Hippolytus of her mistress' love, as he is setting out for the hunt. The scene, of which there were several variant copies at Pompeii, is based on a Hellenistic original, which in turn was inspired by Euripides' tragedy *Hippolytus*. In this version, from a Fourth Style wall, Phaedra has been given a Flavian court hairstyle; it must have been painted very shortly before A.D. 79.
Schefold, *WP* 335.

153
Wall painting: the Three Graces
Width 53 cm, height 56 cm
Naples Museum, inv. 9236
From the *tablinum* of the House of Titus Dentatus Panthera (IX, 2, 16)

Panel cut from the middle of a Fourth Style wall. The Three Graces, or *Charites*, daughters of Zeus by various mothers, personified beauty, grace, and intellectual and moral wisdom. There are innumerable examples of this group both in painting and in sculpture, all obviously copied from the same original, presumably a well-known Hellenistic sculpture. The Graces are commonly portrayed, as here, holding or wreathed with spring flowers. This explains the presence of flowers in the landscape setting, a feature not represented elsewhere in Pompeian mythological scenes.
Schefold, *WP* 242; Peters 139.

154
Bronze apparatus for heating liquids
Height 51 cm, base 43 cm square
Naples Museum, inv. 72986
From a villa near Stabiae

Rather like a samovar, this apparatus was designed to maintain a continuous supply of hot wine or any other hot fluid. The liquid was poured into a gently tapering, churn-shaped container (A) with a hinged lid; from this it was free to pass through a tall, narrow duct (B) into the hollow walls of a cylindrical fire-box (C), from which it could be drawn off as required through a tap (D) in the shape of a lion's head. The source of heat was a charcoal fire in the middle of the fire-box. Fuel could be stored in the square, four-legged tray, which also served to contain the ashes. As long as the level of the liquid within the main container was kept above that of the tap, a constant supply was assured, piping hot. In addition to the tap there are a number of applied bronze fittings: on the main container a comic actor's mask (see No. 167) and a handle in the form of a miniature bust of Mercury; on the rim of the fire-box three swans poised for flight; and on the tray four legs in the form of sirens, and four drop handles.
MB 4 (Rome 1841) pl. xx.

152

153

51

154

173

156

openwork heart. The nozzle is plain except for the rosettes at the point of junction. The filling hole is fitted with a small plug, which is attached to the base of the handle by means of a chain of twisted loops of bronze wire.

156
Dionysiac scene in marble intarsia
Slate and colored marbles
Length 67 cm, height 23 cm
Naples Museum, inv. 9977
From the House of the Colored Capitals
(VII, 4, 31-51)

One of a pair of Dionysiac scenes found in the *tablinum,* where they were probably used on the walls as panel pictures *(pinakes).* On the left a maenad dances in ecstasy, with torch and *tympanon;* on the right a satyr clutches a *thyrsus* and is waving a goatskin; and in the center is a small shrine. The companion piece portrays a maenad dancing toward a Priapus herm; a statue on a pedestal; a nude youth with a panther; and a tree beside a sacred pillar monument or baetyl (as in the sacro-idyllic landscapes).

The technique is that of intarsia, a sophisticated variant of *opus sectile,* composed of shaped and inscribed pieces of colored marble (*giallo antico* from Africa, *fior di persico* from Euboea, and *paesina verde* and *palombino* from Italy) cut out and fitted into a slate panel. Third quarter of the first century A.D.

Mau, *Bull Inst* XLVI (1874), 98; Elia, *BdA* IX (1929) 265ff.; Dohrn, *RM* 72 (1965) 131; Kraus and von Matt no. 272.

157
Crescent-shaped terracotta lamp with three nozzles
Height 4 cm (with reflector, 9 cm)
length 14 cm, width 13 cm
Pompeii, Storerooms, inv. 14040
Found in the house of Fabius Rufus
(Insula occidentalis)

Fashioned of lustrous red-brown clay, this richly decorated lamp is of an unusual shape and is also exceptional in having three heart-shaped nozzles rather than the usual one or two. The characteristic form of the nozzle indicates a date in the third quarter of the first century A.D. Both the date and the relative rarity of this type of

lamp at Pompeii suggest that it may have been a new fashion in lamps whose production was cut short by the eruption.

An eagle, symbol of Jupiter, perches on the outer curve of the crescent to act as a reflector. In low relief on the well of the lamp, a thin crescent moon curves around the filling hole, with a star on either side to carry out the celestial motif.

Roman lamps burned low-grade olive oil with a fiber wick. The two small holes at each point of the inner crescent allowed air to circulate within the body of the lamp for better burning.

Andreae, *Pompeji* 96, no. 58.

157

158

155a
Bronze candelabrum (lamp stand)
Height 1.265 m
Naples Museum, inv. 78485
From one of the sites in the Vesuvius area

The slender shaft is made in the form of a bamboo cane, which divides into three at the top to carry the round plate on which the lamp stood. The three feet arch outward from the base of the stem, with long, tongue-shaped leaves between them. Such candelabra appear commonly in Pompeian wall paintings of the Second and Third Style.

155b
Bronze oil lamp
Height 13 cm, length 20 cm
Naples Museum, inv. 72490
From Pompeii

The two stems of the handle support a vertical escutcheon in the shape of an

155

160

161

159

161

8

[T]erracotta lamp
[H]eight 10 cm, length 17 cm
[Po]mpeii, Antiquarium, inv. 12836

[Th]is lamp solves the problem of a multi-
[pl]e light source in a novel way. Instead of
[sim]ply increasing the number of nozzles,
[as] in Nos. 159-162, the potter has joined
[tog]ether a number of independent lamps
[of] standard forms: a large round-nozzled
[lam]p as base for two small "factory
[lam]ps," a type introduced in the last years
[of] Pompeii. The hemispherical cup with
[ser]rated edge mounted on the large lamp's
[ha]ndle may have been intended for in-
[ce]nse. The cup is surrounded with four
[fig]hting cocks with victory palms.
[Sta]mped circles decorate the background.
[An] oak wreath fills the central disc of the
[lar]ge lamp. The lamp represents an
[att]empt by an artisan trained in mass-
[pr]oduction techniques to create a sculp-
[tur]ally interesting as well as functionally
[spe]cialized object.

[9]

[Gl]azed terracotta lamp with two nozzles
[He]ight 22 cm, length 37.8 cm
[Na]ples Museum, inv. 76/165
[Fro]m Pompeii

[Th]e vine leaf is a simplified version of that
[fou]nd on bronze lamps (No. 160). The
[noz]zles are joined to the body by large
[vol]utes, of which the outer pair end in

horses' heads. The well in the middle is
decorated with an ovolo border and scalloped fluting radiating from the filling
hole.

The blue-green glaze, colored with copper oxide, is characteristic of a substantial
group of fine terracotta objects, including
small statuettes and fountain figures, as
well as lamps and pottery vessels. There
were several centers of production em-
ploying this technique, but it has been
suggested that these large lamps with
horse's-head volutes were imported from
Cnidos in southwestern Asia Minor,
where large numbers of them have been
found, and that the glaze was applied by
a local potter.

160
Two-nozzled oil lamp on a low stand
Bronze
Lamp: height 26.5 cm, length 40.5 cm
Stand: height 10.3 cm, diameter 11.5 cm
Naples Museum, inv. 72284 and 72270
From Pompeii

In both the shape of the body and the vine-
leaf handle, the lamp resembles the example copied in glazed terracotta, No. 159,
except that the volutes linking the nozzles
to the body are plain. The vine leaf is also
found used decoratively between the legs
of lamp stands (e.g., Naples Museum, inv.
72251; Pernice IV, fig. 78).

The stand is of a common three-legged
type, enriched with oak leaves springing
between three lion's-paw feet. Such lamps
stood on side tables, and they are also
found on the counters of shops and bars.
Pernice IV, fig. 81; Chiurazzi no. 523.

161
Two-nozzled oil lamp on a low stand
Bronze
Lamp: height 20.3 cm, length 28 cm
Stand: height 15.6 cm, diameter 13 cm
Naples Museum, inv. 72331 and 72212
From Pompeii

The lamp is cast in bronze, its ring foot
and the ornate handle added as separate
castings. The handle consists of a bat-like
creature, with a panther's head and spread
wings, perched on the volutes of an acanthus palmette. The small circular stand
consists of a molded top and, below it,
twelve equally spaced, arched projections,
three of which are prolonged downward
and end in lion's paws. First century A.D.
Pernice IV, 58, fig. 79 (the stand).

162
Gold lamp with two nozzles
Height 15.1 cm, length 23.2 cm
Naples Museum, inv. 25000
From Pompeii

The body bears a design of lotus leaves similar to that found on late Hellenistic bowls in precious metals or their pottery equivalents; it was worked in relief from the outside with a punch, after filling the interior with pitch. The leaf-shaped reflector in front of the handle is similarly worked with a palmette design. The plain spouts and base were cast separately and soldered into place. The lid, now missing, would normally have been the most highly decorated part.

The discovery of this lamp was one of the sensations of the excavations of 1863.
Breglia no. 1025; Siviero no. 341; *Bull Inst* XXXV (1863) 90-91.

162

163

163
Bronze lantern
Height of lantern 19 cm, total height (excluding modern brass hook) 39 cm
Naples Museum, inv. 72078
From Pompeii

The wick holder, with a cap that could be removed for cleaning and refilling, is set in the middle of a circular base plate, which stands on three small feet. The flame was originally protected by semitransparent sheets of horn slotted between the double ring of bronze mounted on the base plate and a similar ring above, which is soldered onto the backs of two vertical rods in the form of pilasters with Doric capitals. To the tops of the latter were attached the rings and chains, linked to the ends of a yoke-shaped cross bar, by which the lantern was held. The lid, a shallow inverted bowl, is pierced with a pattern of holes for ventilation when closed. The lantern could also be carried with the lid raised. A chain attached to the top, ends in a short rod slotted through the main carrying bar, with a ring to stop it slipping too far, and has its own yoke handle. Rings on either side of the lid loop around the main chains to keep the lid centered over the lantern body.
Cf. *BMC Lamps* no. 1495.

164
Bronze plaque with a lion's-head ring handle
Width 19.5 cm, height 12.8 cm
Naples Museum, inv. 72738
From Pompeii

One of a pair. The four holes show that it was attached to some large wooden object, probably a door. Although appearing also on other large objects such as chests or vats, handles of this form are very common in representations of doors in classical art.

164

165

165
Bronze drop handle
Mounting plate: width 19 cm, height 3.3 cm
Handle: width 17.5 cm, drop 7.7 cm
Naples Museum, inv. 72980
From Pompeii

The ends of the handle are in the form of elongated animal's heads, perhaps intended to portray hounds with their ears pressed flat against their necks. The absence of nail-holes shows that this piece was probably soldered onto some portable bronze object, such as a brazier or a heating apparatus (see No. 154).

166
Bronze door handle
Length 31.3 cm, width 4.8 cm
Naples Museum, inv. 70277
From the Vesuvius area, possibly from the Villa of Publius Fannius Synistor at Boscoreale

The handle was mounted as shown in the diagram, with the grip fixed through the thin bronze base plate, and through slots in the thicker door plate, to two levers on springs that it could raise or drop by slid-

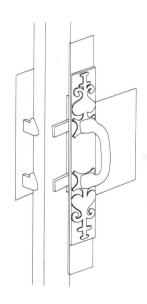

166

167   168   169   171

ng up or down. On the face of the base plate, developing from cusped rectangles below the feet of the grip, are heart-shaped motifs turning into volutes and ending in motifs like the hilt of a sword with a strongly marked rib down the central axis. This combination of motifs is found in Campanian bronzeware as early as the second century B.C. It was used on door handles certainly by the early first century B.C. and enjoyed a long popularity.

Cf. Pernice IV, 63; *JdAI* XIX (1904) 15f.

167
Bronze ornament in the form of a theater mask
Height 5.3 cm
Naples Museum, inv. "94"
From one of the sites in the Vesuvius area

The mask, cast solid, represents a slave in New Comedy. It was probably applied to an elaborate piece of domestic bronze equipment such as the heating apparatus, No. 154.

168
Miniature herm in bronze
Height 19.5 cm
Naples Museum, inv. 5343
Found in Herculaneum, October 1764

The herm, in the form of a child, is hollow, with an iron rod running down the back of it. It was evidently the foot of some large piece of iron furniture.

Bronzi di Ercolano 2, 356f., pl. LXXXIX; K. A. Neugebauer, *Die griechischen Bronzen der klassischen Zeit und des Hellenismus* (Berlin 1951) 27, no. 18.

170

169
Bronze bust of a satyr in high relief
Height 16 cm
Naples Museum, unnumbered
Probably from Herculaneum or Pompeii

This wild companion of Bacchus has a snake twisted around his shoulders. Horns sprout through his bushy hair, and tufts of hair swirl on his chest and forehead.

Busts or plaques of this type were fashioned to be applied to the heavy chests in which the householders of Pompeii kept their valuables. The dramatic turn of the figure's head, shoulders, and arm indicates the prototype was created in western Asia Minor, probably near Pergamum, after about 200 B.C.

Chiurazzi 251, no. 574; Ruesch 367, no. 1608.

170
Bronze ring with a Medusa head
Diameter 11.2 cm
Naples Museum, inv. 72969
From Pompeii

This handle, from the door of a cupboard or a wooden coffer, consists of a grooved ring hinged at the top to a circular base plate, upon which is portrayed in relief the head of Medusa, the snake-haired female monster whose glance turned all who looked upon her to stone and who was slain by Perseus (see No. 307). By an easy extension of ideas a Medusa head was thought to protect the object it adorned. Its shape is well suited to filling circular spaces, and it is used commonly in handles of this sort. The eyes are inlaid with silver, in the center of which is a hole for the pupil, which may have been made of colored glass.

Pernice IV, 19.

171
Ivory panel from a piece of wooden furniture
Height 10.5 cm, width 6 cm
Naples Museum, inv. 10158
From one of the sites in the Vesuvius area

The panel probably formed part of the veneer on an elaborately turned leg of a wooden couch or stool. Its dimensions and slightly tapering convex shape are closely paralleled by ivory plaques in the Field Museum of Natural History, Chicago, thought to have come from a funerary couch.

Carved in relief is the figure of the Muse Terpsichore, patron of the dance, holding a plectrum in her right hand and a lyre beside her left shoulder.

Cf. C. L. Ransom, *Studies in Ancient Furniture*, 1 (Chicago 1905) 56f. and 102f.

172

172
Bronze couch ornament (fulcrum)
Length 44 cm
Naples Museum, inv. 78/98
From the Vesuvius area

The type of couch from which this bronze
ornament comes was, like most at Pompeii, an invention of Hellenistic times,
reproduced with only subtle variations of
detail and proportion. It stood on high
turned legs; a frame with stretched
webbing carried the mattress. There was a
low headboard, contoured to support
cushions on which a diner could lean.
The ornament here was a bracket decorating and reinforcing the edge of the headboard. It combines a graceful duck's head,
a favorite motif of Greek metalwork and
furniture, with sinuous moldings and a
face of Medusa. The organic, irregular
form of the support has been broken
down into representational components.
The workmanship of this example is particularly bold, stiff, and definite, far from
the sketchy vitality of Hellenistic examples. Details like the duck's feathers are
engraved after casting.
Cf. G. M. A. Richter, *The Furniture of the
Greeks, Etruscans and Romans* (London 1966)
figs. 532, 533.

173

173
Small bronze bust of a goddess of plenty
Height 10 cm
Naples Museum, inv. 5150
Found in Herculaneum

Cast bronze fitting, probably from the
lower end of the curved support (*fulcrum*)
on a couch. The figure wears a short veil
over the head, covering a high hair-piece,
and round her neck is a silver necklace of
beads from which hang large, lozenge-
shaped silver pendants. Her eyes too are
inlaid with silver. In the folds of her loose
tunic she carries a selection of fruit, identifying her as Pomona, the Italian goddess
of orchards and gardens, or possibly as
Fortuna, goddess of plenty.
Bronzi di Ercolano, I, 47, pl. X; MB 9 (Rome
1845) 352, pl. XXXVII.

174, 175
**Decorative intarsia strips, from a
banqueting couch**
Length 56 cm, height 3.9 cm
Length 56.7 cm, height 4.4 cm
Naples Museum, old inv. 5451, 70995
From Pompeii

Two almost identical panels of bronze,
delicately ornamented with inlaid silver-
work in the long, narrow recessed panel
and in the shorter, flat panels at the two
ends. Comparison with another, longer
piece in the Naples Museum (inv. 70992)
shows that the designs on the end panels,
meaningless as they stand, are abbreviated
versions of a scheme with acanthus leaves
and sprays of tiny leaves set symmetrically
about a central palmette. The craftsman
was using repertory motifs fitted as best
they might be within the space available.

Panels of this sort were used to decorate
and strengthen the long horizontal members of couches, also sometimes on foot-
stools. They were recessed into the wood
with the flange uppermost.
Mau-Kelsey 361f., fig. 180.

176
**Decorative intarsia strip, from a piece of
furniture**
Silver on bronze
Length 61.7 cm, height 3.8 cm
Naples Museum, inv. 70990
From Pompeii

Despite the obvious resemblance of this
piece to Nos. 174 and 175, the absence of
any flange along the upper edge suggests
that it was let into some other piece of
wooden furniture, such as a table. The
vine scroll of the two long recessed panels
would have been appropriate to a table or
stool used in a dining room. The central
panel contains an elaborate formal rosette, the two end panels a section of a
latticework design with simpler, eight-
petaled rosettes.

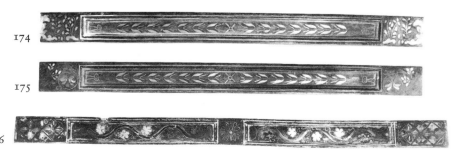

174

175

176

V Cults and Beliefs

Hall of the Mysteries, Pompeii

177

Wall painting: the arrival of Io at Canopus

Height 80 cm, width 66 cm

Naples Museum, inv. 9555

From the room north of the atrium in the House of the Duke of Aumale (VI, 9, 1)

From the center panel of a late Third Style scheme, the painting illustrates a scene from the story of Io, the virgin priestess of Hera at Argos, who had the misfortune to attract the amorous eye of Zeus. Transformed by Hera into a white heifer, she was watched over by the hundred-eyed herdsman Argus, until the latter was slain and Io released by Hermes. After interminable wanderings she found haven in Egypt, where she was kindly received by Isis and resumed human form, giving birth to Epaphos, legendary ancestor of, among others, the royal house of Argos. Within the Isiac cult she tended to be assimilated with the cow goddess Hathor.

In this painting Io is borne by the river god of the Nile into the presence of Isis, who is shown enthroned in her great sanctuary at Canopus, near Alexandria. Isis holds the royal cobra of Egypt in her left hand; her feet rest on a crocodile, and, facing her, a small sphinx symbolizes the land of Egypt. Behind her are two white-robed attendants who hold *sistra* (see Nos. 186, 187) and the messenger's staff (*caduceus*) of Hermes; and at her side, finger to his lips, stands the child god Harpocrates (see Nos. 182, 183). Io's past wanderings are symbolized by the pair of horns on her forehead. Another painting of this scene, larger and of superior quality, clearly derived from the same Hellenistic original, was found in the Temple of Isis (Elia, *Mon Pitt* 27–30).

Curtius fig. 129.

177

178

180

178
Section of a painted frieze
Length 2.18 m, height 82 cm
Naples Museum, inv. 8546
From the portico wall of the Temple
of Isis

The frieze, on a black ground, represents
an ornate acanthus plant scroll, in the
spirals of which are lotus-flower heads alternating with pygmies and with animals
and birds associated with Isis: from left to
right, a pygmy running, a cobra, a hippopotamus, and an eagle. Below the frieze is
part of the central zone of the wall, including the top of the frame of one of the
panels, which contained a landscape
similar to No. 190. In the frame is a small
panel containing a theater mask.

179
Wall painting: seated figure of Bes
Width 66 cm, height 1.14 m
Naples Museum, inv. 8916
From the Temple of Isis, from the west
wall of the smaller of the two rooms at
the west end of the sanctuary (see also
No. 180)

179

This inner room, possibly used for initia-
tions, was decorated on the west, north,
and east walls with figures relating to the
cult of Isis, all very broadly executed on a
white ground with little or no attempt at
relative scale.

The Egyptian god of the dance, char-
acteristically portrayed as a squat, obese
figure, is seated nude on a throne, with his
hands on his knees and a large flower on
his head.
Tran tam Tinh, *Pompéi* 145, no. 52; Elia,
Mon Pitt III. 4, 21.

180
Wall painting of an ibis
Width 56 cm, height 82 cm
Naples Museum, inv. 8562
From the Temple of Isis, from the north
wall of the same room as No. 179

This large Egyptian ibis occupied the
center of the north wall between representations of the discovery of Osiris and a
lion. On the west wall Isis, Serapis, and
Bes (No. 179) sat enthroned, and facing
them were the bull Apis and a number of
other sacred animals: monkey, sheep,
mole, jackal, sparrowhawk, vulture,
cobra, and mongoose (ichneumon). The
ibis has a lotus flower on the top of its
head and a stalk of wheat in its beak.
Tran tam Tinh, *Pompéi* 144, no. 48; Elia,
Mon Pitt III. 4, 22.

181
Bronze statuette of Isis-Fortuna
Height 33.5 cm (43 cm with base)
Naples Museum, inv. 5313
From Herculaneum

The richly draped and adorned goddess
wears an Egyptian headdress with the
solar disc and the horns of Hathor. She
holds a rudder and a horn of plenty out
of which emerge fruits and a pyramidal
object usually interpreted as a kind of
sacrificial cake. These attributes form an
allegory of navigation through the seas of
life to the land of plenty and also symbolize the link between the grain of Egypt
and the ports of Italy. An ivy garland, a
bull's skull, and two eight-pointed stars
are inlaid in silver on the base.
Chiurazzi 81, no. 131.

181

182
Bronze statuette of Harpocrates
Height 8 cm
Naples Museum, inv. 5329
From the *lararium* in the House of the
emperor Joseph II (VIII, 2, 38-39)

Harpocrates, in origin the Egyptian child-
god Harpa-Khruti, son of Isis and Serapis,
is shown in the conventional attitude of
childhood, with his finger on his lips, later
misinterpreted by the Romans as a gesture
of silence. His curly hair is crowned with
ivy leaves and a top-knot. A *bulla* (see
No. 40) hangs round his neck. On his back
he has little wings, a quiver, and a ring for
suspension. He rests his left arm, holding
a cornucopia (horn of plenty) entwined by
a snake, on a knobbly tree trunk.
PAH I, i, 233; *MB* 12 (Naples 1850) pl. xxx. 2;
RM 2 (1887) 119; Boyce no. 349 note; Tran
tam Tinh, *Pompéi* 162, no. 107.

183
Bronze statuette of Harpocrates
Height 8.3 cm (12.2 cm with base)
Naples Museum, inv. 5368
From one of the sites in the Vesuvius area

Similar to No. 182, but the snake is coiled
round his left thigh, and he holds the
cornucopia unsupported. Probably from a
lararium.
Tran tam Tinh, *Pompéi* 164, no. 111.

184
Terracotta figurine of a priest
Height 18 cm
Naples Museum, inv. 20477
From Pompeii(?)

The figure, dressed in long robes edged
with a richly embroidered border, holds
some object, perhaps a key, in his left hand
and is thought to represent a priest. Which
particular cult he served is uncertain.
Levi no. 865.

185
Two figures of ibises
Marble and bronze
Length 39 cm, height 25 cm
Length 41 cm, height 25.5 cm

182   183   184

Naples Museum, Egyptian Collection,
inv. 765 and 766
Possibly from the Temple of Isis

The heads, necks, and legs of the birds are
in bronze, while the bodies are made of
white marble, following their natural
coloring. The technique of combining
such materials at this date is most unusual.
Tran tam Tinh, *Pompéi* 175, nos. 145 and
146; *Pitture di Ercolano* 5, 119.

186
Bronze rattle (sistrum)
Length 22.3 cm
Naples Museum, inv. 109669
Found in the atrium of House I, 2, 10

The head consists of a broad strip of
bronze shaped into a loop and, strung
across it, four bronze rods, which are
looped over at the ends to hold them in
but are otherwise free to move to and fro,
giving a tinkling sound when shaken. On
the top of the loop is a figure of a cat with
a pine cone on her head and suckling two
kittens. The handle is plain. Though normally of bronze, silver *sistra* are known
(e.g., Naples, inv. 111770).

The *sistrum*, an instrument of Egyptian
origin, is one of the commonest symbols
of the worship of Isis, who took it over
from Hathor, the Egyptian goddess of
music. In sculpture and painting Isis normally holds a *sistrum* in her right hand
(see No. 191), and *sistra* were carried and
shaken by worshipers as part of the standard rituals of the cult, to repel the forces
of evil or to express joy or mourning.
Apuleius describes their use vividly in his
Metamorphoses (XI, 4).
Daremberg and Saglio, s.v. *Sistrum*.

187
Bronze rattle (sistrum)
Height 19 cm
Naples Museum, old inv. 2386
From Pompeii

A smaller version of No. 186. On the top
of the loop is the cat with kittens, and near
the base two small jackals; the ends of the
rods are shaped as ducks' heads. The
ornate handle incorporates two sacred
cobras and figures of Bes, Egyptian god of
the dance (cf. No. 179), and of Hathor,
goddess of music.

185

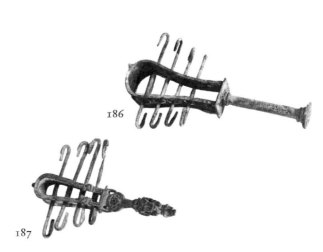

186

187

188
Pair of small bronze cymbals (cymbalum)
Diameter 11 cm
Naples Museum, inv. 76943
From Pompeii

Two circular sheets of bronze, each concave internally and surrounded by a broad flange, linked from the centers by a loose chain. Cymbals, usually portrayed in conjunction with tambourines *(tympana)* and pipes (see No. 310), were commonly played both at religious and at social functions (see also No. 193, group IX).

Daremberg and Saglio, s.v. *Cymbalum;*
H. Hickmann, *Annales du Service des Antiquités de l'Egypte* 49 (1949) 451-545.

188

189
Bronze votive hand of Sabazius
Height 18 cm, width of base 8 cm
Naples Museum, inv. 5506
From Herculaneum, 8 February 1746

Sabazius was originally a Thracian or Phrygian divinity of vegetation, and in particular of barley and wheat. Known in Greece as early as the fifth century B.C., during the Roman Empire he was worshiped increasingly in a variety of syncretistic forms, most commonly as Zeus Sabazius or as Dionysus Sabazius, but also (just like Isis, see page 83) taking on the attributes of many other divinities.

One of the most striking features of his cult is a series of votive hands, of which the fingers form the gesture of benediction still familiar from the Latin Christian rite. Sabazius himself, bearded and wearing a tunic, trousers, and a Phrygian cap, is seated in the palm of the hand, his feet on a ram's head and his hands raised in the same characteristic gesture. Around him are his major attributes: on his right, curling up the back of the hand, his own serpent; on his left, the pine cone of Dionysus; and above him, the eagle of Zeus (of which only the claws now survive) grasping a thunderbolt. On the wrist is a curious, grotto-like frame enclosing the figures of a mother and child. Elsewhere on the hand are shown a scarab, two cymbals, a double flute (Phrygian pipes), a winged staff of Mercury *(caduceus)*, a pair of scales, an owl, a lizard, a frog, a tortoise, a wine bowl *(crater)*, a flaming altar, a whip, and a little table with another pine cone.

Two very similar hands were found at Pompeii in 1954, in a shop (II, 1, 12) identified by the excavators as that of a dealer in small religious and magical objects.

C. Blinkenberg, *Archaeologische Studien* (Copenhagen & Leipzig 1904) 75, no. E13;

189

O. Elia "Vasi magici e mani pantee a Pompei," *RAAN* XXXV (1960) 7ff.; E. Lane, "Two Votive Hands in Missouri," *Muse* 4 (1970) 43-48.

190
Architectural landscape with figures
Length 36 cm, height 37 cm
Naples Museum, inv. 9475
Found in the Temple of Isis, 1776

One of a series of idealized landscapes, found on the walls of the portico enclosing the main precinct. The landscapes occupied the centers of large monochrome panels within the composition, alternating in this position with representations of priests and of other ceremonial attendants of the goddess (see also No. 178). They follow the familiar "sacro-idyllic" conventions, but most of them include elements that would have been recognizably Egyptian in intention: in this instance the tall tower with curving "horns," which may be compared with an altar, and which may represent a tomb.

Elia, *Mon Pitt* 12; Rostowzew, "Architekturlandschaft" 79, no. 3.

190

191
Statue of Isis in Archaic style
Pentelic marble
Height of statue 1.06 m, height of base 95 cm
Naples Museum, inv. 976
From the northwest corner of the colonnade in the Temple of Isis

The goddess' hair is dressed in an elaborate Archaic Greek style, with a garland of five rosettes. She wears a long, clinging tunic in fine material, held tight under her breasts with a belt the clasp of which is formed of two snakes' heads. Over her shoulders, making sleeves, is an equally thin shawl, tucked into the belt. In her right hand she held a *sistrum,* of which only the handle remains; from her left dangles an *ankh,* the Egyptian symbol of life. When found, the statue was rich in traces of its original coloring, with remains of gilding on the hair, rosettes, the collar and hem of her tunic, and the snake bracelets on her wrists. She has heavy red eyebrows and pupils, and there are traces of red also on the tree stump beside her left leg and among the folds around the hem of her tunic.

She stands on her original base, which bears the dedicatory inscription: *L. Caecilius Phoebus posuit l[oco] d[ato] d[ecurionum] d[ecreto].* "Lucius Caecilius Phoebus set [this statue] up in a place granted by decree of the town council"; it is one of many indications that this temple was official municipal property. L. Caecilius Phoebus was a freedman of the rich Pompeian banking family. The statue is the only complete figure of Isis found in the temple. Of two others, composite works in wood and marble, only fragments of the marble part survive.

Mau-Kelsey 170; Tran tam Tinh, *Pompéi* 156, no. 81; Reuterswaard, *Polychromie* 186f.; *CIL* X, 849.

192
Wall painting: Dionysiac cult objects
Height 46 cm, width 46 cm
Naples Museum, inv. 8795
From Pompeii

Along a narrow ledge at the top of a small flight of steps are, from left to right: a tambourine; a wicker basket, on which are a drinking horn draped with a panther skin, a drinking cup, and a *thyrsus;* and a second, taller drinking cup decorated with vine leaves. On the steps are a spray of bay, a pair of cymbals, and a small panther grappling with a snake. All these objects are associated with the cult of Dionysus. The picture, which appears to come from the middle zone of a Fourth Style monumental composition, is one of several in the Naples Museum portraying attributes of various gods, all of which may have come from the same decorative scheme.

MB 5 (Rome 1841) pl. LVIII.

192

193 (see illus. p. 179)
Painted frieze from the Hall of the Mysteries (reproduction)
Lent by Imperial Tobacco Limited
Original at Pompeii, Villa of the Mysteries

The Villa of the Mysteries was a wealthy suburban residence (*villa urbana*), built toward the middle of the second century B.C. a short distance outside the walls, between the two roads that converge on the Herculaneum Gate. It was extensively remodeled, modernized, and redecorated about 60 B.C. During the last years of the town, after the earthquake, parts of it continued to be used as the center of a farming property under the charge of a steward, who was a freedman of the old Samnite family of the Istacidii, but (just as at Oplontis, see No. 327) the residence, with its magnificent series of early Second Style paintings lay empty. Who the owner responsible for these paintings was we do not know.

The so-called Hall of the Mysteries lay near the southwest corner of the building, entered by a large door in the west wall and with a large window in the middle of the south wall, looking out across a portico toward the Bay of Naples. The walls were covered with nearly lifesize figures, arranged like a frieze against the background of what was still in effect a First Style wall scheme. This background was already in place when the figures were painted, though whether this means that the figures were an afterthought, added at a slightly later date, or whether this sequence merely represents the way the artist chose to lay out and execute his composition, we have no means of telling.

Ever since the discovery of these paintings in 1929-30, their significance has been the subject of lively debate. The suggestion that this was a hall in which the Dionysiac Mysteries were actually celebrated can certainly be excluded. The essence of the Mysteries was that they were secrets, to be guarded jealously from profane eyes, not openly displayed where any passer-by could see them. On the other hand, the paintings are shot through and through with Dionysiac imagery; they reflect in intimate detail the world of ideas to which an initiate of the Mysteries belonged. Side by side with the gods and their attendant train of satyrs, maenads, and other Dionysiac followers, there is also a continuous thread of strictly human action, and it is a striking fact that at this human level the small boy reading from a scroll is the only male figure present. This is a women's world, and according to one widely held interpretation the whole cycle portrays and symbolizes the ceremonies and rituals prior to the wedding of a human bride. There is room for discussion how far one can distinguish the actual physical ceremonials of marriage from portrayals of the symbolic rituals of mystic marriage with the godhead—if indeed the two were clearly distinguishable. But, on this interpretation, the overall intent seems to be clear enough.

191

There seems to be fairly general agreement that both in its broad conception and in much of its detail the frieze derives from a Hellenistic model or models and is thus at one remove a unique representation of the lost world of Greek lifesize figured painting (*megalographia*). How closely it followed its sources is open to discussion. It would be pressing coincidence too far to imagine that the available wall space was exactly the same in both cases; and the fact the frieze falls into a number of distinct compositional groups (some of which, such as that of Dionysus and Ariadne [VI], are known from other replicas) would have allowed for a measure of rearrangement, omission, or addition. The fact that, despite the unifying hand of the Campanian copyist, one can detect models that were ultimately of different styles and dates, is not in itself significant. Some such assimilation could well have taken place already in the Hellenistic sources. On balance, it seems likely that the relationship between model and copy was a close one but that, as was customary in ancient copying, the process was one of adjustment and adaptation rather than of slavish imitation.

The interpretation that follows, though not free from problems and uncertainties, does offer a plausible and consistent account of these remarkable paintings. It reads from left to right round the room, starting from the small doorway at the northwest corner.

I. Entry of the bride for her initiation. A nude boy reads out a sacred text under the guidance of a woman with a scroll and a writing stylus in her hand. A wreathed attendant, bearing an olive branch, carries in a silver platter of cakes.

II. Preparations for sacrifice. A seated priestess removes a cloth from a basket carried by an attendant, while another attendant pours purifying water on her right hand.

III. The scene shifts to a supranatural level dominated by the figures of Dionysus and Ariadne in the middle of the east wall. An elderly Silenus plays his lyre, resting it on a column. A youthful satyr and his female counterpart are seated on a rock, he playing the panpipes, she suckling a she-goat.

IV. A woman in an attitude of startled alarm, left hand raised as if to ward off the influence of the scenes that follow on the east wall. This figure cleverly links the two walls, gazing across the corner of the room to bind the two together.

V. A young satyr gazes into a bowl held up before him by an elderly Silenus, while a second young satyr holds up a theatrical mask. The precise meaning is doubtful, but gazing into bowls was a well-known form of divination.

VI. Central to the east wall, dominating the room, Dionysus reclines in the lap of an enthroned Ariadne.

VII. A kneeling woman, with a long torch over her shoulder, reaches out to unveil an object that is almost certainly to be identified as a huge ritual phallus. On the ground lies a winnowing basket. Two women look on.

VIII. A female figure, with dark wings spread, holds up her left hand as if to shut out the previous scene and raises her right, to strike with a whip the kneeling figure of scene IX. Like figure IV, this winged figure, though compositionally part of the previous group of scenes, really belongs with the next group, linking the two walls across the angle of the room.

IX. A half-naked girl kneels, burying her face in the lap of a seated woman, who helps to bare her back to the ritual flagellation inflicted by the winged figure. On their right are two women. One, fully clothed, brings forward a *thyrsus,* the wand of Dionysus and his followers; the other, naked, dances in ecstasy, clashing a pair of cymbals.

X. The bride's toilet. An attendant helps her to dress her hair. A winged Eros holds up a mirror.

XI. Once again the scene is completed across the corner of the room. A second Eros leans on a pillar gazing up at the bride.

XII. The bride, robed and veiled, sits on the marriage couch. On her fourth finger she displays her wedding ring.

A. Maiuri, *La Villa dei Misteri* (Rome, 1931); O. Brendel, *JdAI* 81 (1966) 206ff.; Kraus and von Matt, 93-96, whose interpretation we follow. For a totally different interpretation see *Guida Archeologica di Pompei*, ed. F. Coarelli (Verona 1976) 340-346.

Inscribed marble slab recording a dedication by the Ministri Fortunae Augustae
Height 70 cm, length 47 cm
Naples Museum, inv. 76/248
Found loose in the Basilica, 1884

L[ucius] Numisius Primus L[ucius] Numisius Optatus L[ucius] Melissaeus Plocamus ministr[i] Fortun[ae] Aug[ustae] ex d[ecreto] d[ecurionum] iussu L[ucii] Iuli[i] Pontici [et] P[ublii] Gavi[i] Pastoris d[uo] v[iri] i[ure] d[icundo et] Q[uinti] Poppaei [et] C[aii] Vibi[i] aedil[um] Q[uinto] Futio [et] P[ublio] Calvisio co[n] s[ulibus].
"Lucius Numisius Primus, Lucius Numisius Optatus and Lucius Melissaeus Plocamus, ministers of the cult of Fortuna Augusta, [made this dedication] in accordance with the decree of the decurions, on the instruction of Lucius Julius Ponticus and Publius Gavius Pastor, chief magistrates, and of Quintus Poppaeus and Caius Vibius, aediles, during the consulship of Quintus Futius and Publius Calvisius."

The cult of Fortuna Augusta, i.e., of the prosperity of the emperor, was established at Pompeii by Marcus Tullius, a prominent citizen who had been a chief magistrate *(duovir)* and who built a temple of this dedication shortly before A.D. 3. Although the dedicators named in this inscription were all freedmen of wealthy Pompeian families, the body of *ministri* might also include slaves. It seems to have been the practice of this body to dedicate a new statue shortly after the accession of each new emperor. The pair of Roman consuls named here is not recorded elsewhere, but the inscription is probably to be dated to the reign of Caligula, *c.* A.D. 39-40.

CIL X. 187; *ILS* 6384; Castrén 76-78.

Inscribed slab recording a dedication by the Ministri Augusti
Marble, restored from four pieces
Length 37.5 cm, height 31 cm
Naples Museum, inv. 3794
Pompeii, find-spot not known

Narcissus Popidi Moschi [servus et] Nymphodotus Capras[ii] Iucundi [servus] min[istri] Aug[usti] d[ecurionum] d[ecreto] iussu P[ublii] Vetti[i] Celeris D[ecimi] Alfidi[i].
"Narcissus, slave of Popidius Moschus, and Nymphodotus, slave of Caprasius Jucundus, ministers of the cult of Augustus, [made this dedication] by decree of the decurions, on the instructions of Publius Vettius Celer and Decimus Alfidius."

Members of the college of *ministri Augusti* held office for one year, and membership was open to slaves as well as freedmen. Dedications such as this one seem to have marked important events within the Imperial family. The first

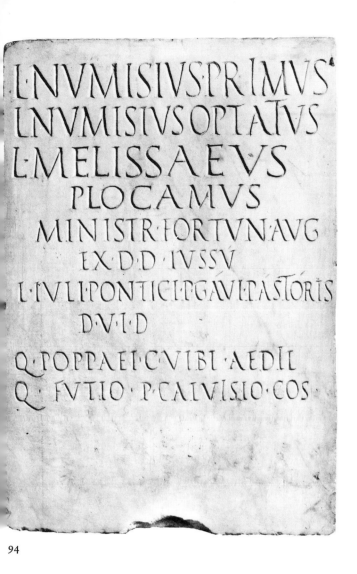

94

196

95

record of the college dates from 2 B.C.
(*CIL* x. 890), when one of the *ministri*
was Numisius Popidius Moschus, a freedman of the influential Popidius family.
The subsequent election to the college
of one of his own slaves, Narcissus,
illustrates very clearly the network of
patronage to which the service of the
Imperial cult gave rise. This inscription
must date from the early years of the first
century A.D.
CIL x. 908; Castrén 75.

196
Wall painting: figure of a priestess
Height 95 cm, width 43 cm
Naples Museum, inv. 8903
From Herculaneum

The fragment, and its companion piece
showing a youth carrying a stool (Naples
Museum, inv. 9374), were probably cut
from the architectural framework of a
Fourth Style scheme. The woman is veiled
and carries an incense box on a tray in
her left hand.
Helbig no. 1795; cf. *Pitture di Ercolano* IV,
5, pl. I.

197
Wall painting of Mercury
Height 73 cm, width 49 cm
Naples Museum, inv. 9452
From Pompeii

The youthful god, who was patron of
commerce as well as messenger of the
gods, is shown with wings at his temples
and his ankles and bearing his symbolic
staff, or *caduceus* (see No. 216) in his left
hand. In his right hand, instead of the
usual money bag, he carries what may be
a fish trap, and beside his right foot is a
small tortoise (or turtle). The most likely
position for such a painting would be in a
household shrine or on the outer wall of
a shop, belonging to somebody who was
connected with fishing or the sale of fish
products.

Helbig 358; *Pitture di Ercolano* v, 89, pl. xix.

199

197

198
Bronze brazier on three legs
Height 78 cm
Naples Museum, inv. 1572
From one of the sites in the Vesuvius area

The bowl, which is removable for
emptying, rests on a three-legged stand
on animal's-paw feet and is strengthened
with bronze hoops, a rigid version of the
collapsible tripods such as No. 138. The
distinctive shape, in a more ornate
version, the so-called Delphic tripod,
appears frequently in the late Second Style
paintings, as on the wall at Oplontis
(No. 327).

198

199
**Wall painting from a household shrine
(lararium)**
Width 1.83 m, height 1.28 m
Naples Museum, inv. 8905
Found in viii, insula 2 or 3, 6 June 1761

The painting is divided into two registers.
In the upper register, below three garlands, is a scene of sacrifice. The *genius*,
or presiding divinity of the household,
with head veiled and bearing a cornucopia, symbolic of plenty, holds out a
dish *(patera)* over a marble altar. He is
attended by a small boy carrying a fillet
(a wreath, with ribbons for tying) and a
platter; opposite him a musician plays the
double pipes, beating time with a wooden
clapper beneath his left foot, while a slave
brings forward a pig for sacrifice (see No.
200). On either side stand the two Lares
of the household, pouring wine from a
drinking horn, or *rhyton*, into a small
wine bucket, or *situla*. In the lower
register two serpents approach the offerings (of fruit?) upon an altar. Together
with the setting of rich vegetation, they
symbolize the fertility of nature and the
bounty of the earth beneath.

PAH 1, 133; *MB* 9 (Rome 1845) 161, pl. xxvii.

00

Small bronze pig on a rectangular stand
Length 13.5 cm, height 11.5 cm
Naples Museum, inv. 4905
From Herculaneum

Hollow cast, the details sharpened with a chisel after casting. It is mounted on its original base, which stands on four splayed cloven hooves springing from formal, palmette designs. On the pig's left flank are inscribed the letters *HER. VOE. M.L.* No satisfactory interpretation of this abbreviated text has been proposed. The prominent position of the letters *HER* suggests the possibility of a dedication to Hercules, to whom a pig was the customary animal of sacrifice. The figure would in that case have been placed in a household shrine *(lararium)*.
Bronzi di Ercolano 1, 83 and 279.

201

202

0

204

tural character. It stands on three lion's-paw feet, the shafts of which splay out into forms that are based on the elements of an Ionic capital. Like No. 201, this altar is a miniature version of a shape used also for braziers (e.g., Naples Museum, inv. 73012) and would have been made for use in a *lararium*.
MB 3 (Rome 1839) pl. XXXII.

203

01

Miniature bronze altar
Height 11 cm, length 19 cm, width 15 cm
Naples Museum, inv. 74001
From Pompeii

The rectangular box in which the offering was burnt is decorated with simple profiled moldings and with crenellations. It stands on four legs, with wings at the junction with the body and ending in animal's cloven hooves. The form is also found on a much larger scale used as a brazier (e.g., Naples Museum, inv. 73005). Little altars were part of the equipment of a household shrine *(lararium)*. They were normally built in or made of terracotta, only rarely of bronze.
Boyce 16; Gusman 134.

2

Miniature bronze altar
Height 13 cm, diameter 15 cm
Naples Museum, inv. 73997
From Pompeii

Beneath a line of tiny crenellations, engraved with a T-shaped design, alternately upright and inverted, the circular drum is ornamented with moldings of an architec-

203
Bronze statuette of Bacchus
Height 34.8 cm (40 cm with base)
Naples Museum, inv. 5009
From Herculaneum

The god of wine, with upswept hair, holds a pine-cone-topped staff *(thyrsus)* in his left hand and once tipped up a drinking cup *(cantharus)* in his raised right. The slender forms of the figure suggest that the original of this bronze goes back through the age of Julius Caesar and Sulla ultimately to the tradition of Praxiteles in the late fourth century B.C. Such household gods gave Romans around the Bay of Naples a very distant view of the great epochs of Greek art.

Chiurazzi 65, no. 98.

204
Bronze statuette of Hercules
Height 21 cm
Naples Museum, inv. 5780
From Herculaneum

The drunken Hercules is shown nude, with a beard, his club over his right shoulder and his left hand probably holding a drinking cup, now lost. The statuette is of good workmanship, and the molded base, which does not belong to the statuette, is finely decorated.

205

206
Bronze tintinnabulum in the form of a gladiator; four of the five original bells preserved
Height of figure 21 cm
Naples Museum, inv. 27853
Found in Herculaneum, 8 February 1740

These fanciful combinations of bells and phallus, intended to ward off evil spirits, at times take on a remarkable complexity. Here a gladiator armed with a knife and with a protective leather strap wrapped around his left arm attacks his own phallus, which turns into the foreparts of a panther.
Grant, De Simone, and Merella 138, 143.

207
Pottery lamp in the form of a figure of Priapus
Height 14 cm, length 11.5 cm
Naples Museum, inv. 27869
From Pompeii

The little rustic god of fruitfulness, protector of flocks, bees, vineyards, and market gardens, son of Dionysus and Aphrodite, is modeled as a lamp, provided with a ring for suspension, and probably hung from the lintel of an entrance doorway to bring good luck and to ward off evil spirits.
Fiorelli, *Raccolta pornografica* no. 201.

206

205
Bronze tintinnabulum with three hanging bells
Length 11.5 cm
Naples Museum, inv. 27837
From Herculaneum

Tintinnabula (tinkling bells of the type used also in some forms of dancing) were hung in the doorways of houses and shops, often together with a lamp, as a protection against evil spirits. This elaborately and aggressively male object, equipped with wings and the hind legs of a lion, was a symbol of plenty as well as a deterrent to evil spirits, and as such it was a favorite component of such bells. It is also found, used with the same intent, on terracotta plaques let into the outer walls of buildings, particularly at street corners (see page 64).
Grant, De Simone, and Merella 140, illus.; cf. Col. Famin, *Musée Royal de Naples: peintures, bronzes et statues erotiques du cabinet secret* (Paris 1857) 29f., pls. XXIV, XXVII, and XXVIII.

207

208
Statuette of Aphrodite with Priapus
Fine white, translucent marble, possibly
from Paros
Height 62 cm
Naples Museum, inv. 152798
Found on a table in the *tablinum* of House
II, 4, 6

The group represents Aphrodite preparing to bathe (see No. 209), raising her left
foot to remove her sandal and resting her
left forearm on the head of a small figure
of the god Priapus; a tiny Eros sits below
her foot. Aphrodite's left hand, now missing, was carved in a separate piece of
marble. The group is remarkable for the
extensive remains of gilding as well as
some traces of paint. In addition to her
necklace, armbands, a bracelet, and gilded
sandals, Aphrodite wears an exiguous,
bikini-like harness. Her eyes are inlaid

209

with cement and glass paste. The hair and
pubic hair of both main figures were once
gilded (the dark red paint now visible was
the underlay), and there are traces of red
paint on the lips of the goddess and on the
tree stump that supports the group; of
green on Priapus' pedestal; and of black
on the base.

The statuette was found in the large
complex of rented accommodation, including a bath-house and tavern, known
as the villa of Julia Felix. *Graffiti* and
other finds suggest that this part of the
complex may have served as a brothel in
the last years of the town's history.
Reuterswaard, *Polychromie* 184f.; *BJb* 170
(1970) 142, M50.

209
Bronze statuette of Aphrodite
Height 17.5 cm
Naples Museum, inv. 5133
Found in Herculaneum, 22 February 1757

The figure belongs to a large series of representations of Aphrodite (Venus) preparing to bathe (cf. No. 208). She is taking off
her left sandal, supporting herself against
a narrow tree trunk, around which is
curled a dolphin, one of her many characteristic attributes. Her armbands and
anklets are made of gold, and the palmette-
and-scrollwork decoration on the base is
inlaid in silver.
Bronzi di Ercolano 2, 53f., pl. xiv.

208

152798

210
Replica of the household shrine (lararium) in the House of the Gilded Amorini (vi, 16, 7) (not illustrated)
Lent by Imperial Tobacco Limited
Height 2.07 m, width 1.25 m, depth 74 cm

This *lararium*, the lower part of which
was built of rubble faced with plaster and
painted to represent colored marble veneer, and the upper part constructed of
wood and painted stucco and supported
on two fluted colonnettes of greenish *cipollino* marble, stood against the north
wall of the peristyle. A *lararium* was essentially the shrine of the Lares, the
protecting divinities of the house (see
No. 199), who figured in it in association
with whatever other divinities the family
held in special honor. Within it the master
of the house would make small daily offerings, and it was the scene of ceremonial
offerings on important family occasions.

The group here displayed (Jupiter,
Minerva, Mercury, two Lares, and a
lamp), with the exception of the figure of
Jupiter, is not that actually found in this
particular *lararium*; though absolutely
characteristic, it is a composite group,
made up from other *lararia*. The *lararium*
in the House of the Gilded Amorini contained (along the upper ledge) Jupiter
(No. 215) flanked by the other members of
the Capitoline triad, Juno and Minerva,
and accompanied by Mercury (Hermes;
cf. No. 197), the patron god of commerce,
who was very popular in this context, and
(on the lower ledge) two Lares and a
bronze vessel.
NSc 1907, 565-571; Boyce 57, no. 221.

211

211
Bronze lamp in the shape of a duck
Height 8 cm, length 13.5 cm
Naples Museum, inv. 110674
From Pompeii, 3 March 1875

The body of the duck is hollow, forming
the reservoir, with a hole for filling in the
middle of the back. The tail constitutes
the nozzle, and the head looks backward
to form the handle. The legs are indicated
in shallow relief, tucked up below the
wings.

212
Bronze statuette of Minerva
Height 20 cm (25 cm with base)
Naples Museum, inv. 5288
From Herculaneum

With her crested helmet, *aegis* (goatskin
mantle with Medusa's head and snaky
locks), libation dish, and spear, the goddess of wisdom and industry is based on
famous cult-statues of the fifth century
B.C. The style is designed to recall the
Athenian statues of about 460 B.C., the
generation before Pheidias, but the mixture of elements in dress and secondary
details indicates the model for this statuette belonged to the eclectic age of Julius
Caesar or Augustus. The Minerva was
doubtless one of a group of Olympians
and other divinities (like Isis-Fortuna,
No. 181, or Bacchus, No. 203) in a household shrine *(lararium)* or on the sideboard
of a private room. Alternate rows of
scales in her *aegis* are gilded.
Chiurazzi 78, no. 123.

213
Bronze statuette of a Lar
Height 29 cm
Naples Museum, inv. 5424
Found at Herculaneum in April 1762, near
the theater

The Lares, originally Etruscan divinities
of locality, in Roman times were worshiped as protectors of the house, usually
placed in pairs within the household
shrine *(lararium;* see No. 210) on either
side of the figures of whatever other gods
were specially favored by the family. They
are regularly portrayed as youthful figures, wearing short-sleeved tunics and
mantles, often with skirts swirling in the
dance. This example carries a sacrificial
dish and a cornucopia, or horn of plenty.
Bronzi di Ercolano 2, 197, pl. LII; cf. *Antike
Welt* 6 no. 4 (1975) 26f.

214
Bronze statuette of a Lar
Height 27 cm
Naples Museum, inv. 5427
Found in the earliest excavations at
Herculaneum

Figure similar to No. 213 but in a more
restrained pose. He carries a wine bucket
(situla) and waves a sheaf of wheat.
Bronzi di Ercolano 2, 213, pl. LVI; *MB* 8
(Rome 1844) pl. LXXIII.

215
Bronze statuette of Jupiter
Height 16.5 cm
Naples Museum, inv. 133323
From the *lararium* in the peristyle of the
House of the Gilded Amorini (VI, 16, 7)

This figure of Jupiter sat, enthroned, on
the upper shelf of the *lararium* (see
No. 210) together with the other members
of the Capitoline triad, Juno and Minerva,
and with Mercury, the patron of commerce. Jupiter is bearded, the upper part
of his body naked, the lower half wrapped
in a mantle. In his right hand is a thunderbolt, and the left probably held a scepter,
now missing.
Boyce 57, no. 221; *NSc* 1907, 565-571.

213

212

214

216
Bronze statuette of Mercury
Height 19 cm
Naples Museum, inv. 115553
From Pompeii, 15 January 1887

Mercury, the Greek Hermes, messenger of the gods and patron god of commerce, stands on a circular, molded pedestal, with his cloak draped over his left shoulder, wearing his characteristic winged hat (*petasos*) and with wings at his ankles. In his right hand he holds a money bag, and in his left a winged staff (*caduceus*) consisting of two intertwined serpents. Probably from a *lararium*.

217
Wall painting: sacro-idyllic landscape with shepherd and goats
Height 50 cm, width 49 cm
Naples Museum, inv. 9418
From Pompeii, exact location unknown

Landscape from the center of a wall panel, probably of the Fourth Style. It portrays an idealized rustic shrine, set within a rocky landscape with trees. In the foreground a man is pushing a goat toward the shrine, as if for sacrifice. On a rock to the right stands a shepherd, and on another rock, to the left, two more figures, one of them a statue.

Rostowzew, "Architekturlandschaft" 87; Peters 148; *Pitture di Ercolano* 2, 151.

217

15

216

VI Trade and Occupations

218

Inscribed marble slab advertising the Baths of M. Crassus Frugi

Length 1.15 m, height 57 cm
Naples Museum, inv. 3829
Found in 1749, reused as a shelf within a shrine just outside the Herculaneum Gate

Thermae M[arci] Crassi Frugi aqua marina et baln[eum] aqua dulci Ianuarius l[ibertus]. "The Baths of Marcus Crassus Frugi. Sea water and fresh water bathing. Januarius, freedman."

These baths must have been located near the sea shore, probably on the promontory that in antiquity marked the west side of the mouth of the river Sarno, and that is known to have contained thermal springs. The owner was presumably the consul of A.D. 64, who died a few years later and who is known to have owned another comparable bathing establishment near Baiae (Pliny, *Nat. Hist.* XXXI. 5). This inscription, the first to be found by the eighteenth-century excavators, is best interpreted as a roadside advertisement for the baths, set up by the freedman who had charge of them.

CIL x. 1063; *ILS* 5724; A. Maiuri, *RAAN* n.s. XXXIV (1959) 73-79; D'Arms 214-215.

219

Inscribed limestone slab recording the modernization of the Stabian Baths

Length 84 cm, height 44 cm
Naples Museum, inv. 3826
Found in 1857 in the Stabian Baths

C[aius] Vulius C[aii] f[ilius] P[ublius] Aninius C[aii] f[ilius] IIv[iri] i[ure] d[icundo] laconicum et destrictarium faciund[a] et porticus et palaestr[am] reficiunda locarunt ex d[ecurionum] d[ecreto] ex ea pequnia quod eos e lege in ludos aut in monumento consumere oportuit faciun[da] coerarunt eidemque probaru[nt.].

"Caius Uulius, son of Caius, and Publius Aninius, son of Caius, chief magistrates, put out to contract the construction of a sweating room *(laconicum)* and a scraping room *(destrictarium)* and the reconstruction of the porticoes and the exercise yard *(palaestra)*. [This they did] in accordance with the decree of the decurions, out of the money that they were by law due to spend on games or public building. They had charge of the work and they approved it."

218

219

The *laconicum* was a room for sweating under conditions of intense dry heat, and it can be identified with certainty as the still-extant circular room with a conical vault, which was later converted into a *frigidarium*. The *destrictarium,* for cleaning off the oil and dirt accumulated during exercise, which one did with a strigil (No. 220), lay to the north of the *laconicum* and was later eliminated. The porticoes were those of the present *palaestra*. The modernization of the Stabian Baths was undertaken quite soon after the foundation of the colony in 80 B.C., and the magistrates in charge of the work were both probably among the original colonists.

CIL x. 829; *ILS* 5706; H. Eschebach, *RM* 80 (1973) 235-242.

220, 221

Strigil and oil flask

Bronze
Length of strigil 23 cm
Naples Museum, inv. 70079 (strigil), 69970, 69927 (oil flask and stopper)
From one of the sites in the Vesuvius area

Before the introduction of fat-based soaps in the late Empire, the cleansing medium used by athletes in the *palaestra* and by bathers of both sexes was a mixture of low-grade olive oil and pumice. This was applied to the body and then scraped off by means of a long, narrow, scoop-like scraper, or strigil. A common form of public benefaction was money for a free distribution of such oil. Sets of strigils, often together with a small oil flask, or *aryballos,* are commonly found attached to a loop that went round the wrist for convenience in carrying.

Daremberg and Saglio, s.v. *Strigilis.*

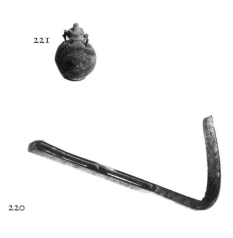

220

221

222

222
Three glass unguentaria (perfume flasks)
Heights 9.5 cm, 8.6 cm, 8.5 cm
Naples Museum, inv. 114890, 12062, 12392
From Pompeii; 114890 from the *tablinum* of IX, 6, 5 with several toilet articles, including No. 59

All free blown, such little flasks were among the first articles mass-produced in blown glass, and were sold with their contents. Their forms are so varied that it seems that the different shapes were the trade marks of specific types of oils, ointments, or perfumes. Later first century A.D.
Isings 40, form 26, and 42, form 28a.

223
Three bone gaming pieces
a. Black; on the reverse the number IIII
b. White; on the reverse the number IIII
c. White; on the reverse the number XI
Lengths 4.5 cm, 5.1 cm, and 5 cm respectively
Naples Museum, inv. 109837, 109848, 109854
From Pompeii

The shape may represent a trussed fowl. Piece *a* was found together with ten others of the same form, bearing the numbers I, II, III, VII, VIII, X, XI, XIII, XIV. Pieces *b* and *c* were found together with eight others, numbered I, II, III, V, VII, VIII, IX, X. This suggests that in one form of the game a

complete set contained fourteen such pieces, numbered serially. But the discovery in Athens in 1886 of a set of nine similar pieces, numbered I, III, VI, VII, VIII (two examples), X, XII, and found together with a silver gaming board of a scalloped circular design with twelve points, may indicate a variant using only twelve pieces.

A set of six comparable pieces, shaped like boars and numbered I, II, VI, VII, VIII, IX, was found in 1937 in a house at Herculaneum, in a wooden box.
M. Laurent, "Tessères en os du Musée d'Athènes," *Le Musée Belge* VII (1903) 83ff.

224
Four knucklebone gaming pieces
Naples Museum, inv. 76972, 76981, 76987, 76990
From Pompeii

Knucklebones, a traditional game already popular in classical Greece, was played with a set of four pieces *(tali)*, either *astragali* of sheep or goats or pieces made from terracotta, glass, bronze, or precious materials to the same conventional shape. The pieces were oblong and rounded at the ends, with two wider and two narrower long sides, each of which presented a recognizably different surface and had a different value (1, 3, 4, and 6) and name. There were many variants of the game, but in its simplest and commonest form each player threw the four *tali*, scoring according to the value of the long sides that fell uppermost, not on a simple numerical basis but, as in poker or poker dice, in accordance with certain combinations of numbers. The top throw, a "Venus" or a "Royal" *(basileus),* consisted of four faces all different, and the lowest throw, "The Dogs" or "Four Vultures," of four plain faces (1); another poor throw was the *senio,* some combination unknown of the twisted face (6) and three other faces. In a version played by the emperor Augustus (Suetonius, *Life of Augustus* 71, 2) any player throwing "The Dogs" or a *senio* put 4 denarii (small coins) into the pool, which was scooped by the first player to throw a "Venus."
J. P. V. D. Balsdon, *Life and Leisure in Ancient Rome* (New York 1969) 155.

225
Four ivory dice
a. Cube 1.2 cm
Naples Museum, old inv. 552
From the Vesuvius area
b. Cube 2.1 cm
Naples Museum, inv. 115530
From Pompeii VIII
c. Cube 1.3 cm
Naples Museum, inv. 116480
From the entrance to IX, 7, 4, one of a pair
d. Cube 1.4 cm
Naples Museum, inv. 119371
From a tavern, VII, 15, 4, one of a pair

Roman dice *(tesserae),* like modern dice, were small cubes with the values 1–6 in groups of dots or letters on the six faces so arranged that two opposing faces always added up to seven. The Greeks usually played with three dice, but by the beginning of the Empire the Romans started to use only two, shaken in a little cup, although they continued to use three for board games such as *duodecim scripta.* There were probably names for all the different combinations, as in knucklebones (see No. 224).
J. P. V. D. Balsdon, *Life and Leisure in Ancient Rome* (New York 1969) 156.

226
Cicada in rock crystal
Length 6 cm
Naples Museum, inv. 109629
From House I, 2, 3, found 12 April 1873

Found together with a small crystal duck, a small crystal amphora, and a faceted lump of crystal, in the *tablinum.* Rock crystal, of which the best quality came from India, was prized for its rarity. Other recurrent subjects were fish, shells, walnuts, and small vases. It is not known whether these were simply collected as *objets d' art,* given as New Year's presents like Nos. 288-291, had a funerary significance (*Gnomon* 1976, 519), or whether some were also used as gaming pieces.
Bull Inst XLVI (1874), 202f.; cf. *BMC Gems* nos. 3971-3985.

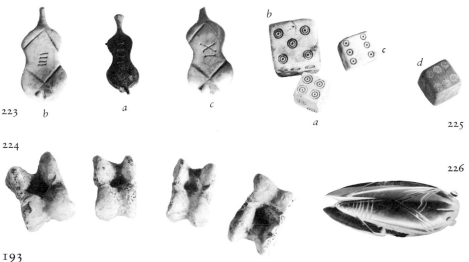

223   *b*   *a*   *c*

224

225

226

227a

Bone tally piece from a board game
Diameter 3.3 cm
Naples Museum, inv. 77104
From Pompeii

On one side is a hand, palm forward, with the thumb and forefinger touching to form a ring and the other three fingers clenched. On the reverse, in Roman numerals, "XIII." There are several other versions, with different arrangements of the fingers, among the Naples Museum collections (e.g., inv. 77127, 109864). Each side appears to have a different significance, as the numbers on the back (none higher than XXV) bear no relation to the numbers indicated by the fingers on the front. Such pieces may have served as score-counters in some board game.

CIL x. 2. 8069. 101; Henzen, *Annali dell' Inst* XX (1848) 282.

227b

Four bone gaming counters
a. Obverse: a female head in profile
Reverse: IIII/ΛIBIA (= Livia)/Δ
Diameter 3.3 cm
Naples Museum, inv. 77129
From the Vesuvius area
CIL x. 2. 8069. 9.

a *b*

b. Obverse: façade of a building with a statue in a large niche
Reverse: II/EYPOΛOXOY (= *Euro-lochou*)/B
There was a village called Eurylochos near Alexandria
Diameter 3.0 cm
Naples Museum, inv. 109586
From Pompeii, 9 April 1863, "Portico del passetto pensile"
CIL x. 2. 8069. 8.

c *d*

c. Obverse: seated figure of a woman, her chin resting on the knuckles of her left hand
Reverse: II/ΦYΛIC (= *Phylis*)/B
Diameter 3.2 cm
Naples Museum, inv. 119383
From Pompeii I, 1, 6, 31 August 1874

d. Obverse: head of a youth in profile with a fillet in his hair
Reverse: XIII/EPMHC (= Hermes)/IΓ
Diameter 3.5 cm
Naples Museum, inv. 120299
From the peristyle of v, 4, 1, 9 October 1890

The Romans were enthusiastic players of board games; we find improvised boards scratched on the pavements of public buildings throughout the Empire. Of the two most popular games, *duodecim scripta* and *latrunculi,* there is enough evidence from ancient authors to reconstruct in broad terms how they were played. But of others we know very little, beyond the gaming pieces (e.g., No. 223). The four counters exhibited here belong to a board game, possibly invented in Alexandria in the early Empire, which involved sets of fifteen counters variously carved on one side with the heads or busts of gods and goddesses *(d)*, the Imperial family *(a)*, famous athletes, caricatured mythological figures *(c)*, views of buildings in Alexandria *(b)*, and victory crowns from ancient games. On the reverse is an inscription in Greek identifying the design on the front. Above the inscription is a number in Roman numerals (from I to XV), and below it, its equivalent in Greek (A to IΓ). The heads and busts greatly outnumber the buildings and crowns, which must have had a special significance. A set from a child's tomb in Kertch comprised 12 heads or busts, 1 building, and 2 crowns.

Rostovzeff, *Rev Arch* IV Ser. V (1905) 113.

228

Wall painting: bakery
Width 52.5 cm, height 61.4 cm
Naples Museum, inv. 9071
From the *tablinum* of House VII, 3, 30

The setting is the front room of a baker's shop, where a baker, dressed with surprising formality and seated in a dignified position, is handing out loaves of bread to three eager-looking customers. Most of the loaves are round and puffy, and scored before baking into wedge-shaped divisions. Loaves of this form have been found at Pompeii. This was the standard variety, but the baker shown here has other kinds as well, rolls in a basket and a pile of sliced or ring-shaped bread at one corner of the shelf behind him. The painter's style is lively and straightforward, interesting because he must have worked from memory rather than using a traditional pattern. The bakery painting comes from a private house. One feels that it glorifies the owner's trade (or at least his business interests), which is made to look as genteel as possible. It has also been suggested that the central figure is an official, seeking popularity by the free distribution of bread.

Bianchi Bandinelli, illus. 50, fig. 50; Grant, *Cities of Vesuvius* 207.

228

229

230

229
Large hexagonal glass flagon
Height 35 cm
Naples Museum, inv. 13181
From Pompeii

The body was blown into a mold, and the rim turned out and polished. The large, flat handle with combed lines was welded on separately. Such bottles were used for storing liquids, and the form is also found in smaller, short versions.

230
Tall square glass bottle
Height 41 cm
Naples Museum, inv. 13009
From Pompeii

A taller version of No. 231, but blown into a mold. The type appears about the middle of the first century A.D. Such bottles were used all over the Empire for containing liquids, their shape making them very easy to pack. A wooden box of them was found in the House of the Menander.

Isings 66, form 50b; Maiuri, *Menandro* 457f.

231

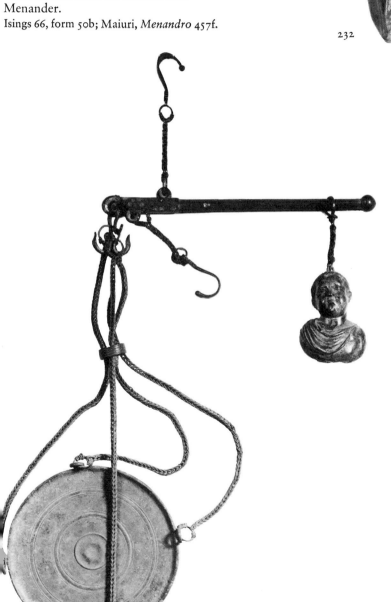

231

232

234

231
Low square glass bottle
Height 21 cm
Naples Museum, inv. 114835
From Pompeii, atrium of IX, 8, 6

An unusually large version of an otherwise common form, free blown and squared off by pressure on a flat marble surface. It was found together with 3 similar bottles, 6 square storage jars, several cylindrical jars, and other flasks in a house that in the final period was used commercially, presumably by a dealer in whatever these receptacles contained.

Isings 63f., form 50a.

232
Triangular glass bottle
Height 16.5 cm
Naples Museum, inv. 13075
From Pompeii

One of a pair. Blown into a mold, the handle, a flattened bar of glass, welded on separately. The shape is unusual, as yet known only at Pompeii.

Isings 66.

233
Two glass bottles in a pottery basket
Height of bottles: 16 cm and 8.6 cm
Basket: height 14.5 cm, length 22.5 cm
Naples Museum, inv. 12845, 12895-6
From Pompeii

The two bottles are small, straight-sided versions of a common cylindrical storage jar, blown into a mold. The handles, made of thick flat bars of glass, are welded on separately.

MB 3 (Rome 1839) 240, pl. II.

234
Bronze steelyard balance
Height (from hook to plate) 73.5 cm, length of arm 31 cm
Naples Museum, inv. 74039
From Pompeii

The balance operates on the familiar principle of the steelyard, with an eccentric fulcrum, the scale pan hanging from the shorter arm and the counterweight hanging from a loop that is free to move along a graduated scale along the longer arm as described by Vitruvius (x, 3, 4). Commonly, as in this example, there are two alternative positions of the fulcrum and two corresponding graduated scales, one of which reads (in Roman numerals) from 1 to 14, the other from 10 to 50. The counterweight is in the form of the bust of a boy, perhaps the portrait of a young member of the Imperial family. The eyes are inlaid in silver.

An inscription punched in dots on the shorter arm gives the consular date A.D. 47 and certifies that the weights are in accordance with the specifications laid down in that year by the Roman aediles Marcus Articuleianus and Gnaeus Turranius and known as "the Articuleiana." Standard weights and measures were an important feature of the Roman commercial system, and in this case it was the official standards established in Rome that were the point of reference.

CIL x. 2, 8067.2; Daremberg and Saglio, s.v. *Libra.*

235
Bronze balance
Length of arm 26 cm, drop of scale-pans 29 cm
Naples Museum, inv. 116438
From the House of the Centenary (IX, 8, 3)

The scales are of the simple equipoise type, hung from a hook in the center of the arm. They were found in the southwest corner of the western atrium, along with various other balances, forceps, and pincers, together constituting what appears to be the equipment of a doctor. The cup-shaped pans would have been very suitable for weighing powders and other loose medical commodities.

236
Bronze stamp
Length 6.8 cm, width 2.3 cm
Pompeii, Antiquarium, inv. 1870-4
From the entrance to the Thermopolium (VI, 16, 33), 27 June 1904

The stamp gives, in abbreviated form, the name of Lucius Aurunculeius Secundio, a member of a family that came originally from Suessa (Sessa Aurunca), a town in northern Campania, 42 miles from Pompeii. Such stamps (*signacula*), bearing the name of the owner of a workshop or of his agent, were widely used as trademarks and for advertisement in the manufacture not only of bricks, pottery, and lamps, but also of more ephemeral products such as loaves of bread. Several carbonized loaves in the Naples Museum are stamped *[C]eleris Q. Grani Veri ser[vi]*, "[Made by] Celer, slave of Quintus Granius Verus."

NSc 1908, 292; Castrén 141; Mau-Kelsey 497f.

235

236

237

238

237
Wall painting: warships
60.5 cm by 61 cm
Naples Museum, inv. 8554
From the Temple of Isis (VIII, 8, 28)

On the upper part of the fresco is an illusionistic seascape with warships. These galleys illustrate the type of fast, light craft that made up the Roman navy following its founding by Augustus and formed a part of the fleet commanded by the elder Pliny at Misenum. A painted cornice separates the seascape from the lower part of the fresco with its arrangement of leaves and flowers painted in exuberant arabesques on a solid black background.

Mon. Pitt. III, fig. 8; cf. L. Casson, *Ships and Seamanship in the Ancient World* (Princeton 1971) 144, note 15.

238
Fish mosaic
Originally about 90 cm square
Naples Museum, inv. 120177
From House VIII, 2, 16

A studio piece made of very fine tesserae, laid within a tray-like frame of terracotta,

for use as the central panel (*emblema*) of a larger, less delicate pavement, the design of which is not known. It probably belonged initially to House VIII, 2, 14 and was reused when this was rebuilt in the early Empire and incorporated in this much larger House VIII, 2, 16.

Against a black background is displayed a gallery of edible sea creatures, portrayed with a lively naturalism that enables most of them to be identified, in almost all cases, with species still found and fished in the Bay of Naples. Among the more familiar are octopus, squid, lobster, prawn, eel, bass, red mullet, dogfish, ray, wrasse, and a murex shell. The inclusion in the left margin of a small stretch of rocky landscape, which is quite out of character, is perhaps to be explained as a fill-in taken from a different source. There are several other mosaics at Pompeii that are so similar in subject and workmanship that they must be derived from the same original and are very possibly by the same hand. About 100 B.C.

O. Keller, *Die antike Tierwelt* (Leipzig 1913) 393; Pernice VI, 151; A. Palombi, "La fauna marina nei mosaici e nei dipinti Pompeiani," *Pompeiana* (1950) 427-429.

239
Still life painting: loaf of bread and two figs
Width 23 cm, height 23 cm
Naples Museum, inv. 8625
From Herculaneum

Still lifes, rare in the Second and Third Styles, were very popular in the last period, when they were commonly used as parts of larger compositions.

The circular loaf, marked out into seven sections, closely resembles the surviving carbonized examples found at Pompeii and at Herculaneum. The figs are displayed on a window ledge, a favorite mannerism of these still lifes. This little panel probably comes from a Fourth Style architectural scheme.

Beyen, *Stilleben* 81, note 1; Croisille 33, no. 24.

240
Four still life panels
Width 1.54 m, height 37 cm
Naples Museum, inv. 8647
From Herculaneum

Each of these panels was originally the centerpiece of a large panel in a Fourth Style wall, as in the peristyle of the House of the Dioscuri. After being cut out, they were framed together to form a frieze. The first two are very different in style from the other two.
a. A plucked chicken, hung by its feet, and a rabbit hung by one forepaw.
b. Left, strung from a ring by its beak, a partridge. Right, a pomegranate and an apple.
c. Upper shelf, three thrushes. Lower shelf, six pink mushrooms.
d. Upper shelf, two birds, probably partridges. Below, two eels.

Beyen, *Stilleben* 59ff.; Croisille 40, no. 46.

241
Two large painted panels with still lifes
Height 74 cm, width 2.34 m
Naples Museum, inv. 8611
From the *triclinium* on the west side of the garden, which lies within the property (*praedia*) of Julia Felix (II, 4, 3)

These two still lifes, which are unusually large, come from the upper part of the Fourth Style walls of a dining room.
a. (damaged). Lower step, part of a vase, with its lid leaning against it, a strip of woolen material, and a two-handled drinking cup (*kylix*). Upper step, a cockerel with its head dangling, dripping blood.
b. A raised block carrying a large glass bowl full of fruit (apples, pomegranates, grapes, figs). At a lower level, a pottery vase containing dried fruit (prunes?) and, leaning against it, a small amphora-shaped jar, its lid tightly sealed by means of cords attached to the handles.

Beyen, *Stilleben* 30, no. 2; Croisille 30, no. 11.

239

240
241

242

242
Three painted still life panels
Width 1.29 m, height 41 cm
Naples Museum, inv. 8644
From Herculaneum

Each of these panels was originally the centerpiece of a large panel in a Fourth Style wall (cf. No. 241). After being cut out they were framed together to form a frieze.
a. Young bird and a light-colored pottery jug, over the mouth of which is placed a glass beaker with rilled decoration of a type frequently found in Campania and possibly manufactured at Puteoli (Pozzuoli.) On the shelf above are indistinct objects: leaves, material, or possibly sheets of tripe.
b. Silver vase, with a small bird perched on its tall handle; a trident; seafood and shellfish (*frutta di mare*), including murex shells; and a large crayfish. On the shelf above, two cuttlefish.
c. A rabbit nibbling at a bunch of grapes and a dead partridge hanging from a ring. In the window, a large red apple.
Beyen, *Stilleben* 72ff.; Croisille 39f., no. 43.

243
Composite picture made up of four separate fragments taken from Fourth Style walls
Width 49 cm, height 43 cm
Naples Museum, inv. 9819
The writing materials and the still life came from Herculaneum, the other two from somewhere in the Vesuvius area.
a. A silver urn, probably from the upper zone of a wall.
b. Left, two book-scrolls of papyrus, one half-unrolled; the titles, on little tags, hang from the wooden baton on which the papyrus is rolled. Right, a diptych, or wooden two-leafed writing tablet (as No. 17).
c. Landscape: a rustic shrine with figures.
d. Half of a still life panel, similar to Nos. 240-242: an apple, a pear, and a pomegranate.
Croisille 52.

244, 245
Wall paintings: scenes of banqueting
Naples Museum, inv. 120029, 120031
From House v, 2, 4

Two of three related panels that consti-

tuted the centers of the Fourth Style compositions in the *triclinium* at the northwest corner of the peristyle. All three portray the three couches appropriate to a *triclinium*, but the actual ⊓-shaped arrangement is opened out to simplify the composition. Though often interpreted as showing the successive stages of a single feast, the fact that the secondary figures of the side panels of the same walls illustrated personifications of the Seasons suggests rather that they are views of separate banquets held on various occasions. The third scene (inv. 120030), which included musicians and nude dancing girls, is unfortunately not well preserved.

244
Width 66 cm, height 68 cm

On the left-hand couch a reclining man places his hand on the shoulder of a second man, perhaps a late arrival, also seated, having his shoes removed while a slave offers him a cup. Faintly legible above the figures are the letters SCIO ("I know"). On the middle couch one man lies back raising a large cup while another is helped into his cloak by a slave; above the first man, BIBO ("I drink"). The right-hand couch is empty, and beside it a man, supported by a youth, leans over, apparently vomiting.

245
Width 60 cm, height 64 cm

Apparently a summer banquet, held in a garden under an awning. In the middle is a table set for food and drink and a young slave brings wine in a pair of *askoi*. On the left-hand couch reclines a couple, nude from the waist up; the woman raises a drinking horn (*rhyton*) to her mouth, while her companion holds a plate (*patera*). A single figure on the central couch, the host, addresses the company with the words: FACITIS. VOBIS. SVAVITER. EGO. CANTO. ("Enjoy yourselves. I'm singing.") Of the couple on the right-hand couch, the man holds a drinking cup (*cantharus*) and replies: EST. ITA. VALEAS. ("OK. Good luck to you.")
Mau, *Bull Inst.* LVII (1885), 254f., nos. 13 and 12; Schefold, WP 71.

246
Wall painting: woman surprising two lovers
Width 52 cm, height 60 cm
Naples Museum, inv. 111209
From a room beside the *fauces* of House VI, 14, 29

The scene, of which several other versions are known, comes from a late Fourth Style wall. Its exact significance is unknown. A man and woman recline on a couch, eating bread and fruit from a table; she holds a silver drinking cup (*cantharus*). They are looking, in apparent surprise, toward another woman who enters from the left followed by a small attendant carrying a casket.
Sogliano 641.

247
Wall painting: entertainment after a meal
Width 46 cm, height 44 cm
Naples Museum, inv. 9016
From House I, 3, 18 at Pompeii

The central panel picture (now rather faded) of a Third Style wall. The diners recline on couches, the empty dishes and cups piled on the table and floor. In the center a girl who has picked up a silver ladle is dancing to the tune of the double pipes, watched by the woman seated on the left. On the right, another seated woman, heavily draped, is perhaps a chaperone, and peeping round the curtain are two small attendants.

Such scenes are frequently found on Pompeian walls (see No. 246); they derive from Hellenistic originals of which the exact meaning is now lost.
Schefold, WP 12 and 334.

248
Large bronze two-handled bowl
Diameter 34.5 cm, height 12.2 cm
Naples Museum, inv. 73599
From Pompeii

The two handles consist of a series of ring moldings grasped in the mouth of a pair of dolphins, which spring outward from a Silenus head escutcheon on the underside of the rim.
Pernice IV, 10ff.

243

248

245

244

247

246

249
250

249
Bronze jug with long spout
Height 16 cm
Naples Museum, inv. 69148
From Pompeii

Globular jug with a long channeled spout. The handle, which is decorated with two swans in low relief, ends in a Medusa head.

250
Bronze jug (oenochoe)
Height 13 cm
Naples Museum, inv. 69018
From Herculaneum

Apart from shallow grooves at the base of the neck, the rounded body is plain. The mouth is pinched in to form a deeply lobed spout. The ornament is concentrated on the elegant, upstanding handle, which was cast separately: at the top, facing forward, a lion's head, and at the junction with the body, in place of the animal's paw that is usually found in combination with the lion's head, a boss in the form of a woman's head in an Egyptian headdress. Similar pieces found in central Europe (e.g., A. Radnoti, *Die römischen Bronzegefässe von Pannonien* [Budapest 1938] pls. XIII, 72, and XLIX, 1) are either actual exports from Campania or are local pieces influenced by such exports.
Cf. *MB* 3 (Rome 1839) pls. XXVII; Pernice, *AA* 1900, 187, no. 14.

251

251
Bronze jug (oenochoe)
Height 20 cm
Naples Museum, inv. 69046
From one of the sites in the Vesuvius area

The elegant vertical channeling was engraved after casting. An escutcheon in the form of a siren perched on a foliated boss marks the point of junction of the ribbed handle with the body.

252
Bronze jar (amphorula)
Height 39.5 cm
Naples Museum, inv. 69629
From one of the sites in the Vesuvius area

There are two identical examples of this type of jar in the Naples Museum. The handles are made in the form of two ribbed plant stems with leaves at the lower ends, joined with volutes to an escutcheon in the form of the figure of a swan with a snake in its mouth.

252

253
Bronze strainer
Length 32 cm, diameter of bowl 11 cm, height 7.5 cm
Naples Museum, inv. 77605
From Pompeii

The simple but decoratively detailed bronze strainer was probably used for straining wine. Perforations form a rosette in the bottom of the bowl, encircled by a wavy band between straight lines, and, on the side, a meander. A long flat handle with a crisply contoured profile extends

253

from the out-turned lip, and on the handle is the inscription *Victor fe[cit]*, "Victor made it." The simple formula suggests that Victor was a slave or freedman, belonging to a generation of enterprising workmen who transplanted workshops from Italy (Campania?) to Gaul.
Spinazzola 300 (upper right); Chiurazzi 180, no. 356; A. Carandini, "Alcune forme bronzee conservate a Pompei e nel Museo Nazionale di Napoli," in *L' instrumentum domesticum di Ercolano e Pompei* (Rome 1977) 167.

254
Bronze handle from a vessel
Length 17.3 cm
Naples Museum, inv. 72663
From one of the sites in the Vesuvius area

One of a pair of cast bronze handles, probably from an amphorula of the same shape as No. 252. Along the handle, in low relief, is a plant design incorporating acanthus leaves, and on the escutcheon, where it was soldered to the body of the vessel, a bearded male head with wild hair and pointed ears, either Pan or a satyr. The eyes are inlaid in silver.
Cf. Pernice, *AA* 1900, 184, nos. 9 and 10; Tassinari, *Gallia* Suppl. 29 (Paris 1975) no. 187.

254

255

255
Curved bronze handle decorated with amorino and sea horses
Length 13 cm
Naples Museum, inv. 72972
From Herculaneum

A little winged amorino is perched on the curling tails of two sea horses; below them are gently rolling waves. The group originally formed a handle, possibly one of a pair, on the edge of a large flat plate.
MB 9 (Rome 1845) 232, pl. L; *Bronzi di Ercolano* I, 25 and 275, note 15.

256, 257
Pair of handles in the form of human hands
Bronze
Overall width 18 cm
Naples Museum, inv. 123300, 76/118
From Pompeii

The hands are linked by a channeled grip, decorated at the midpoint with a ring set with small knobs. Along the base of each hand is a flat strip that ends in two bird's-head volutes. Such handles, sometimes with smooth grips and rosettes on the rings in place of the little knobs, are found on large bowls and, on a much larger scale, on stoves and equipment for heating liquids.

Pernice IV, 31f.; H. Willers, *Neue Untersuchungen über die römische Bronzeindustrie von Capua und von Niedergermanien* (Hannover and Leipzig 1907) 72.

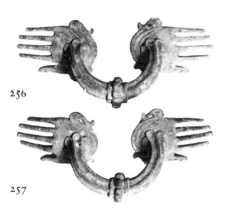

256

257

258

259

258
Red pottery (terra sigillata) plate
Height 4.3 cm, diameter 17.6 cm
Pompeii, Storerooms, inv. 13168

Plates of this kind are found in great quantity at Pompeii and must have been part of the standard, better-quality earthenware table setting. The vertical rim forms a background for a decoration of thunderbolts and rosettes, which were made separately of clay and applied before the plate was given its coating of highly purified clay slip and fired. A footprint-shaped

stamp contains the initials G N. AT. A[.], used by one of the potters trained in Arezzo who set up workshops in Pozzuoli (Puteoli) on the Bay of Naples.

C. Goudineau, *La céramique arétine lisse* (Paris 1968) 306, type 39; A Oxé and H. Comfort, *Corpus vasorum arretinorum* (Bonn 1968) nos. 146, 147 or 149; G. Pucci, "Le sigillate italiche, galliche e orientali" in *L' instrumentum domesticum di Ercolano e Pompei* (Rome 1977) 14.

259
Red pottery (terra sigillata) bowl
Height 6.8 cm, diameter 12.3 cm
Pompeii, Antiquarium, inv. 408-3

The vertical rim has an applied decoration of rabbits and rosettes and helmet-like forms. This kind of appliqué ornament was easily executed and apparently inexpensive since it enjoyed great popularity in the first century. The bowl carries the stamp of L. Rasinius Pisanus, a potter who worked at a still unlocated site in Italy.

C. Goudineau, *La céramique arétine lisse* (Paris 1968) 305, type 38; A. Oxé and H. Comfort, *Corpus vasorum arretinorum* (Bonn 1968) no. 1558, 93, 94; G. Pucci, "Le sigillate italiche, galliche e orientali" in *L' instrumentum domesticum di Ercolano e Pompei* (Rome 1977) 13.

260–262
Three red pottery (terra sigillata) bowls
Found in the *tablinum* of House VIII, 5, 9 on 4 October 1881, together with eighty-seven others of the same forms and thirty-seven pottery lamps, all packed in a wooden crate. The bowls were made by several different Gaulish potters, and the lamps were probably made in northern Italy. This suggests that the Pompeian consignee had dealt through an agent in the north rather than directly with the potteries.

260-262   260   262   261

260
Diameter 20.5 cm
Naples Museum, inv. 112974

Stamped in the center of the inside by the maker Vitalis, who was active about A.D. 60-85. There were five of his bowls in the consignment, all of the same form (Dragendorf 29). The decoration comprises an upper frieze of festoons enclosing large rosettes, and a lower one of trellised zigzag lines with one or two little rosettes in the spaces.

D. Atkinson, *JRS* 4 (1914) 49, no. 28.

261
Diameter 16 cm
Naples Museum, inv. 112984

Stamped as No. 260 but by Mommo, one of the most prolific of South Gaulish potters. Twenty-three of his bowls of this form (Dragendorf 29) and ten more of the same shape as No. 262 (Dragendorf 37) were found in the crate. The two bands of decoration are divided into rectangular panels, the upper containing arrowhead shapes alternating with running dogs, the lower, amorini and stylized flowers.

D. Atkinson, *JRS* 4 (1914) 44, no. 8.

262
Diameter 16.8 cm
Naples Museum, inv. 112997

The letters MOM were incised in the mold in large cursive letters under the decoration, probably by the potter Mommo (see No. 261). The form is Dragendorf 37, one of the commonest of the Gaulish forms. Below a band of ovolo moldings and a wreath of ivy leaves is a broader zone of rectangular panels containing alternately S-shaped patterns above circles and pairs of human figures. Round the bottom runs a chain of V-shaped leaves.

D. Atkinson, *JRS* 4 (1914) 56, no. 54.

263

263

Red-orange pottery amphorula
Height 21.5 cm
Naples Museum, inv. 110388
From Pompeii

The jar copies the form of bronze vessels like No. 252. The glossy surface is created by coating the piece with a highly purified version of the body clay. This jar was made in the area of modern Tunisia, where the foundations of an enormously successful export business were being laid.
J. W. Hayes, *Late Roman Pottery* (London 1972) 190, form 161, 1.

264

Carpenter's plane of iron
Length 19 cm, height 10 cm
Naples Museum, inv. 71964
From Pompeii

The tool bears a close resemblance to the traditional carpenter's plane except that the stock was made of iron, possibly with a wooden handle. The angle of the share, or cutting edge, seems to have been adjustable.

265

Iron hammer
Length 26 cm
Naples Museum, inv. 71883
From Pompeii

As in a modern geologist's hammer, the handle is made in one piece with the head. Ordinary carpenter's hammer-heads, socketed for wooden handles, have also been found at Pompeii, which suggests that this piece may be a specialized tool used by some other type of craftsman.

266

Bronze folding rule
Length 29 cm
Naples Museum, inv. 76696
From Pompeii

The rule is divided into two equal parts, hinged at the center. One half carries a small bar on one side, pivoted so as to slot into two hooks on the other half and hold the fully extended rule rigid. Although the length falls just short of a standard Roman foot (about 29.45 cm), this lies well within the margin of error permissible in a system that for most practical purposes depended more on relative proportions than on absolute dimensions.

267

Bronze plumb-bob
Diameter 5.6 cm, height 4.5 cm
Naples Museum, inv. 76661
From Pompeii

A solid inverted cone of very slightly concave profile, with a small knob in the middle of the top to take the string and another at the point.

268

Broad mason's chisel of iron
Length 19 cm, width of blade 9 cm
Naples Museum, inv. 71771
From Pompeii

Although of little use on hard stone, a chisel of this sort would have been very effective on the softer local volcanic tufa, both for splitting and for squaring off the faces.

269

Bronze compass
Length of arm 20 cm
Naples Museum, inv. 76686

The form is indistinguishable from the simpler types in modern use.

270

Bronze callipers
Length 15 cm
Naples Museum, inv. 76/266
From one of the sites in the Vesuvius area

The form, hinged at the top with two inward-curving arms, is indistinguishable from that in use today.

271

Bronze carpenter's or mason's square
16.1 by 16.1 cm
Naples Museum, inv. 78/321

The tool differs from most modern squares in having a flange on one of the outer edges. This feature was probably intended to render the square more stable. The ends have an ornamental profile.

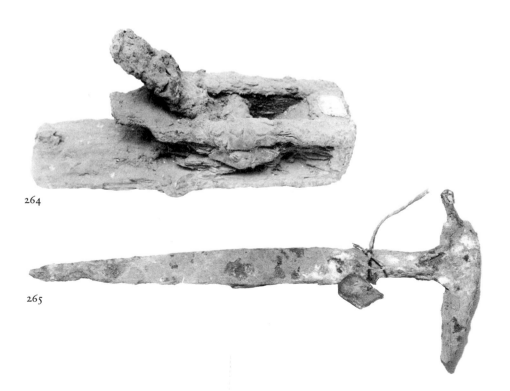

264

265

26

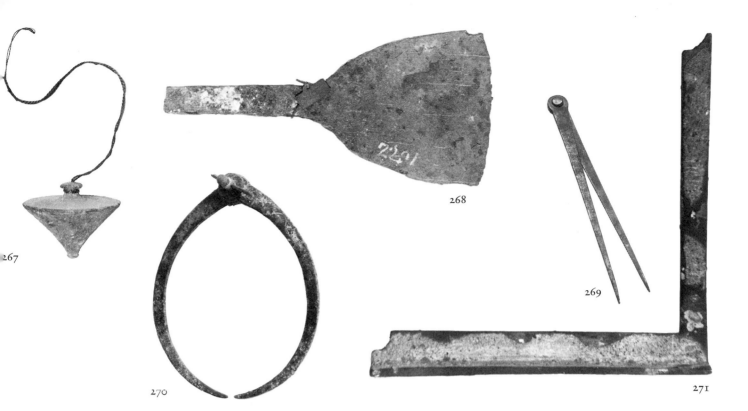

267

268

269

270

271

272
Bronze pen
Length 12.9 cm
Naples Museum, inv. 78/279

Pens were usually fashioned of hollow reeds, with one end sharpened to a point (see No. 274). For a pen of bronze or copper, a thin sheet of metal was rolled to approximate the shape of the hollow reed, with one end of the metal worked into a point.

273
Bronze inkwell
Height 5 cm
Naples Museum, inv. 75083

The inkwell is in the form of a cylinder made from a rolled strip of bronze with discs applied to top and bottom ends. A highly stylized ivy vine is incised around the opening. The lid with its off-center grip turns on a carefully made hinge.

274
Wall painting: writing instruments
Width 41 cm, height 16.8 cm
Naples Museum, inv. 4676
From Pompeii

Wax tablets, a double inkwell and a papyrus or parchment scroll, with a reed pen and a small bag for carrying sharp-pointed pens and *styli,* make up a group of typical Pompeian writing implements (see No. 17).

A wax tablet, *tabula cerata,* was a flat, rectangular wood or metal tablet with raised edges, upon which a thin layer of wax was spread. The writing was scratched into the surface of the wax with a *stylus,* a slender shaft of brass-covered iron or bone, with a sharp point at one end and flattened at the other for smoothing the wax so that it could be reused. Several tablets might be joined by small cords to form a kind of book, with each tablet having a small wooden button at the center to separate the surfaces of adjoining tablets and protect the writing. Such tablets were used for notes and

memoranda, letters, accounts, and children's lessons at school.

More permanent records and works of literary worth were written in ink on a *volumen,* or scroll, using a sharpened quill or reed pen, or, more rarely, a copper or bronze pen (see No. 272). The writer or reader would unroll the scroll to reveal one section at a time. The section of scroll pictured in the fresco is only partially completed, and the writer has rested his pen for a while against the inkwell. The open chamber of the well probably held black ink, made of soot, cuttlefish ink, wine dregs, and water. The other chamber may have held red ink, made from cinnabar.

T. Dyer, *Pompeii* (London 1871) 534; Croisille pls. CIX, 205, CX, 207.

272,273

274

275
Inscribed slab recording the architect of the theater
Marble, restored from 3 pieces
Length 90.5 cm, height 23 cm
Naples Museum, inv. 3834
Found in 1792 in the Large Theater

M[arcus] Artorius M[arci]
l[ibertus] Primus architectus.
"Marcus Artorius Primus, freedman of
Marcus [Artorius, was] the architect."

The inscription relates to the major
reconstruction of the Theater undertaken
during the reign of Augustus. The work
on the seating area and its substructures is
known to have been undertaken by the
Holconius brothers (see pages 39f.) around
the turn of the first centuries B.C. and A.D.
(*CIL* x. 833, 834). The even more radical
reconstruction of the stage building (to
which this inscription may refer) was evidently financed separately but was roughly
contemporary.

The architect was a freedman of the
Artorii, a local Campanian family, and
may well have learned his profession as a
slave, working with another architect. His
name appears also on a fragmentary
marble epistyle (*CIL* x. 807) found, dis-
placed, to the west of the Temple of Venus
and attributed by Fiorelli to the columnar
structure (*tribunal*) at the west end of the
Basilica.
CIL x. 841; *ILS* 5638a; Castrén no. 44, 4.

276
Relief showing a coppersmith's workshop
Italian marble
Height 42 cm, width 54 cm
Naples Museum, inv. 6575
From Pompeii

The relief was probably set into the wall
of a workshop. It illustrates three of the
main processes of the coppersmith's craft.
In the center the smith is seated on a
bench, holding with a pair of tongs a lump
of hot metal on a small anvil, ready to be
struck by an assistant who wields a heavy
hammer; above are the heavy double
doors of the furnace. On the right the
smith is seated at a bench, engraving or
embossing a large circular dish. Above
him crouches an animal (a watch-dog?),
and above that is an assortment of pastry-
molds, dishes, plates, and buckets. On the
left, he is weighing something out in a
large pair of scales. Although there must
have been a special charge for his more
elaborate pieces, it is likely that, as in
many early societies, the simpler pieces
were sold by weight.
O. Jahn, *Berichten der phil.-hist. Classe der
Königl. Sächs. Gesellschaft der Wissenschaf-
ten* 1861, 360ff.; H. Blümner, *Technologie und
Terminologie der Gewerbe und Künste* IV
(Leipzig 1884) 251.

275

277-280
In classical times the normal bulk container was the amphora, a vessel with a
large pointed or rounded body and a very
strong neck with two handles. The great
majority of these were used for wine and
oil, but they could also be put to more
specialized uses, e.g., in Campania for soft
fruits and for the fermented fish-paste,
garum, a delicacy known to have been
produced at Pompeii. There is no direct
relationship between the shapes and their
contents, and they were commonly reused
for products quite different from those for
which they were originally manufactured.
The producing areas normally established
potteries of their own, and the characteristic shapes and fabrics are an invaluable
index of the patterns of commerce.

277
Large wine amphora
Height 1.21 m
Pompeii, Storerooms, inv. 15391

Amphoras of this form (Dressel IB) were
made in Italy during the second and first
centuries B.C., especially in northern Campania, where they were used to contain
Falernian and Caecuban wines. These
wines were highly esteemed in their day
and are known to have been aged in the
amphora. The inside would have been
given a coating of pitch to seal the otherwise porous fabric, and the mouth was
stopped with a cork disc fixed with
pozzolana cement.

278
**Wide-mouthed amphora (Dressel
form 22)**
Height 87 cm
Pompeii, Storerooms, inv. 15450

The painted inscription on the neck reads
MAL[a] CVM[ana] VER[a] ("Real
Cumaean fruits") followed by the weight
of the contents, *LXIIII* (64 pounds) and
the letters *P.C.Z*, presumably the initials
of the owner or consignee. Over the tail
of the *Z* is written the name of the agent
or bailiff who packed the amphora,
Cornelius[?].

279
Small amphora
Height 57 cm
Pompeii, Storerooms, inv. 15390

Small amphoras of this type are hardly
ever found in the commercial cargoes recovered from shipwrecks. It was produced
for local purposes within the Pompeian
area.

280
Cylindrical amphora
Height 88 cm
Pompeii, Storerooms, inv. 15451
From a room in the garden of the House
of the Centenary (IX, 8, 6)

Recent studies have shown that there are
many varieties of cylindrical amphoras of
this general form, classified by Schoene
(*CIL* IV) as form 11. This particular example falls within the range of Ostia form
LIX (Panella 571-572, 632, nos. 48, 49).
They were probably made in North Africa
and contained olive oil (cf. Beltram Lloris
522-523). The mouth would have been
sealed with a terracotta disc fixed in position with wax.

On the neck is painted the name *L[uci]
Helvi Zos[imi]*, possibly that of the agent
or shipper.
CIL IV, Supp. 5847.

281
Wall painting of a potter at his wheel
Height 75 cm, width 54 cm
Pompeii, Antiquarium, inv. 2193-4
From a potter's workshop (II, 3, 7) on the
outside of the southwest corner of the
shop

The potter is shown seated on a low
wooden stool, dressed in the customary
short workman's tunic and working at a
tall jug mounted on a simple kick wheel.
Beside him on the ground are several
small jugs and vases. To the left stands the
figure of Vulcan, Roman god of fire,
protector of furnaces and kilns.

Most of the ordinary pottery in domestic use at Pompeii (see Nos. 282-287)
was made locally. Several potters' workshops are attested, including a large one
outside the Herculaneum Gate (Mau-
Kelsey 378) and one, which also made
amphoras, in I, 20, 2-3.
NSc 1939, 198ff.

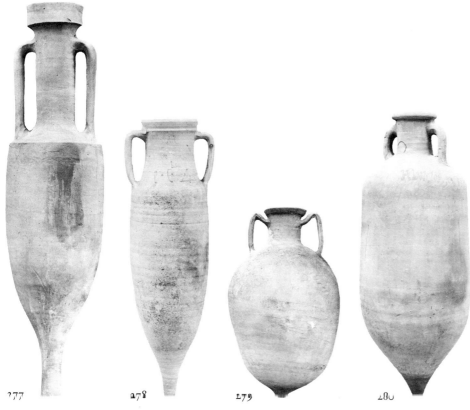

277　278　279　280

282
Large, squat one-handled jug
Height 14 cm, diameter 26 cm
Pompeii, Storerooms, inv. 15397

Made in thick, coarse pottery, the jug was probably used for water, the thick walls and small mouth helping to keep it cool in hot weather.

283
Pottery jug with trefoil lip
Height 23 cm
Pompeii, Storerooms, inv. 15396

Rather finer ware than the other local domestic pottery exhibited, it was probably used for serving wine or water in a bar or tavern, or in one of the poorer private houses. The form is derived from the Greek *oenochoe*.

284
Cooking pot on a pottery stand
Height of pot 28 cm, height of stand 16 cm
Pompeii, Storerooms, inv. 15398, 15399, 15395

A slightly larger version of No. 286. Because the underside was rounded, such pots needed a stand for serving or for storage.

285
Pottery strainer
Height 23.5 cm, diameter 26 cm
Pompeii, Storerooms, inv. 15393

The rounded bottom of the vessel is perforated by a series of holes, of the size of knitting needles; the handles are designed for suspension, and the grooved neck would have been suitable for tying a cloth over the mouth. A number of vessels of this specialized form have been found. They may well have been used for straining curd cheese to make ricotta, which was a major component of Roman cookery, just as today it is still very widely used in the preparation of typical south Italian dishes.

276

281

282　283　284　285　286　287

286
Cooking pot on an iron stand
Height of pot 26 cm, greatest diameter
24 cm
Pompeii, Storerooms, inv. 15394, 15394b

Jars of this distinctive form, with or
without handles and found in varying
sizes (see No. 284), were regularly used
for cooking, placed directly on an open
charcoal fire or else, as in this instance, on
an iron support.

287
Pottery bowl
Height 13.5 cm, diameter 27 cm
Pompeii, Storerooms, inv. 15392

Hundreds of these general-purpose
kitchen bowls, of varying sizes, have been
found in Pompeian houses. They were
used for the storage, preparation, and
serving of food.

287a
Terracotta cooking pan with lid
Pan: height 5.9 cm, diameter 21.6 cm
Lid: height 5.7 cm, diameter 21.8 cm
Pompeii, Storerooms, inv. 665

This kind of pan could be used either for
cooking or for serving. The gray bands on
the exterior are the result of uneven firing
conditions. Imported pans were in use in
many Roman cities, but in Pompeii local
potters managed to hold off the out-of-
town competition.

287a

VII Leisure

288, 289
Two terracotta figurines of gladiators
Height 13 cm
Naples Museum, inv. 20340, 20259
From Pompeii

Probably from the same mold, one of
them (20340) preserving traces of coloring. The figure wears greaves (*ocreae*; see
No. 295) on both legs, an unvisored helmet with a crest and a breech cloth, and
his exposed right arm is bound with
leather thongs; he carries a strongly convex shield (*parma*) and is armed with a
short sword. His costume and armor are
those of a "Thracian" (*Thrax*) except
that Thracian armor normally included a
very distinctive, sickle-shaped scimitar.
The *Thrax* was usually matched against
a heavily armed *Hoplomachus*, or "Samnite," or the lighter *Myrmillo*. It seems
likely that such figurines of gladiators
(see also Nos. 290, 291) served as small
gifts presented on the occasion of the New
Year feast of the Saturnalia.
Von Rohden 52 and pl. 41, 1; Levi nos. 851,
852; Winter II, 387, 2b and 2c.

290
Terracotta figurine of a gladiator
Height 12 cm
Naples Museum, inv. 20260

The figure wears a single greave on the
left leg and a visored helmet with a tall,
angular crest. He carries a large, rectangular, curved shield and is armed with a
short sword. His armor and weapon indicate that he is one of a rather ill-defined
group of heavily armed gladiators, all of
whom seem to be variants of the original
Hoplomachus, or "Samnite" type.
Von Rohden pl. 41, 1; Levi no. 851; Winter II,
387, 2d.

291
Terracotta figurine of a gladiator
Height 14 cm
Naples Museum, inv. 20341
From the House of Marcus Lucretius
(IX, 3, 5)

Like Nos. 288, 289, he wears two greaves
and a crested helmet; but the helmet is
visored, his shield, though small, is rectangular, and he wears a tunic. His weapon is missing. Perhaps a variant of the
Thrax.
Von Rohden 52; Levi no. 852; Winter II,
387, 2c.

292
Bronze gladiator's helmet
Height 40 cm, width across neck guard
33 cm
Naples Museum, inv. 5643
From Herculaneum

A heavily armored gladiator's fighting
helmet, without decoration. The visor,
which includes a broad flange pierced with
two holes to fasten it down, is made in
four parts, riveted together and strengthened by a strip of bronze running from the
brow to the chin. It is hinged to the helmet
behind the ears. A broader flange around
the base of the helmet itself protected the
back of the neck and part of the shoulders.
Fiorelli, *Armi antiche* no. 273.

293
Bronze gladiator's helmet
Height 45.5 cm, length 41 cm
Naples Museum, inv. 5650
From Pompeii

This type of bronze gladiatorial helmet
was a part of the full-dress armor of a
"Samnite" gladiator. The casque is decorated with the head of a sea-nymph rising from the waves at the center, flanked
on either side by a snail shell (*turritella*)
and a leaping dolphin. The high crest
ends in a griffin's head. To protect the
face, the helmet is fitted with two half-
visors, each formed of a network of bronze
rings with a solid flanged section below.
A strip of bronze as reinforcement runs
from top to bottom between the two sections. The initials *M C P* are incised in
the brim.

294
Gladiator's bronze shoulder armor
Length 30.5 cm, height 30.5 cm
Naples Museum, inv. 5639
From Pompeii

Shoulder armor was part of the equipment of a *retiarius*, whose weapons were
a net, trident, and dagger. Appropriately,
this "net-man" chose to have his armor
decorated with marine emblems such as
a crab, an anchor, a rudder, and a dolphin
twisting around a trident.

295
Pair of gladiator's bronze greaves
Length 53 cm, width 19.5 cm (both pieces)
Naples Museum, inv. 5666, 5667
From Pompeii

The rich relief decoration of this pair of
greaves, or leg protectors, is divided into
four zones containing Dionysiac symbols.

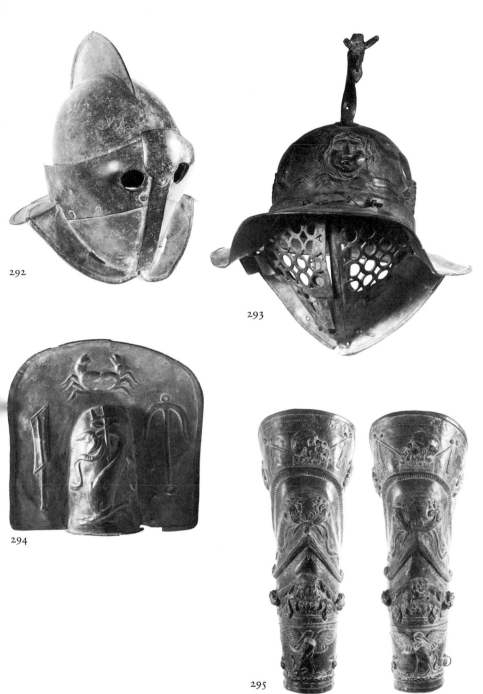

292

293

294

295

At the center of the top zone is the head of a Silenus between two *thyrsi*, with Bacchic masks on the sides, all resting in baskets. The zone covering the knee shows two horns of plenty, filled with fruit and spikes of grain tied with long fillets. Below this, on a lion's skin are three more Dionysiac masks, while, at the bottom, a stork with outspread wings attacks a serpent, which she will feed to her two little ones standing on the sides. Near the upper edge of both greaves are inscribed the letters *M C P*.

Chiurazzi 253, no. 582.

296
Gladiator's bronze shield
Diameter 37 cm
Naples Museum, inv. 5669
From Pompeii

The central silver boss, with a Medusa head in high relief, is surrounded by two concentric olive garlands in low relief and an outer border of olives and single olive leaves. This would have been a dress parade piece, although in shape and size it resembles the actual shields carried by some of the "Thracian" gladiators *(Thraeces)* and also by the mounted gladiators shown in the stucco reliefs on the Tomb of Umbricius Scaurus at Pompeii, now destroyed but known from drawings.

Fiorelli, *Armi antiche* no. 288.

297
Dagger
Iron, bone, and ivory
Length 30.5 cm, length of blade 19.4 cm
Naples Museum, inv. 5682
From Pompeii

A fighting weapon, with an iron blade of which the tang runs the full length of the grip, which is of bone with a pommel and guard of ivory. Such weapons were carried by the more lightly armed types of gladiator, including the *retiarii* (net-men), and by the *myrmillones*.

Fiorelli, *Armi antiche* no. 313.

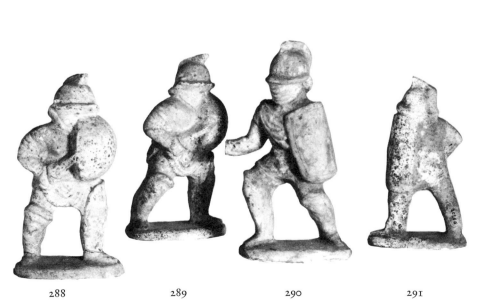

288

289

290

291

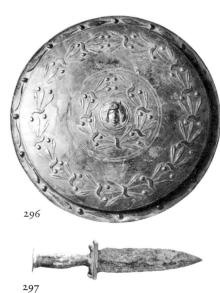

296

297

298

299

organized into teams, or factions, the support for which was Empire-wide. At first there were only two factions, the Reds and the Whites, but early in the first century A.D. two more were added, the Greens and the Blues. In the long run this proved to be too much for the Romans, who at heart were as clearly two-faction in racing as the Americans and the British are two-party in politics, and by the end of the second century A.D. the Blues had absorbed the Reds, and the Greens the Whites, a situation that greatly facilitated the expression of rival enthusiasms. It was a clash between the Blues and the Greens that in January 512 reduced the center of Constantinople to ashes, leaving at least thirty thousand dead behind it—an all-time record for active spectator participation.
B. Maiuri, "Ludi ginnico-atletici a Pompei," in *Pompeiana* 184-185; Helbig no. 1511.

300
Bronze head of a horse, with traces of gilding
Height 51 cm
Naples Museum, inv. 115390
Found in the Theater at Herculaneum, January 1739

At least six equestrian statues in gilded bronze decorated the seating area *(cavea)* of the Theater at Herculaneum and were brought to the surface piecemeal in the course of the first tunneled excavations. This head belonged to a statue that was probably set up in the last ten years before the eruption. Many fragments of the same statue and of the others still exist in the Naples Museum, but some of the larger pieces were judged to be "good for nothing," and, since the heads of the riders were missing, it was agreed "to make two great medallions with the mouldings of Brass, about 2 yards high, with the Pourtraits of the King and Queen of Naples" (Venuti, *Heraclea* 54).

The horse was probably shown rearing slightly on its hind legs, tightly reined in by its rider. The arrangement of the straps of the bridle is unusual, paralleled only in a much later bronze horse's head from Augsburg, and the decoration on them, with cup-like bosses between small studs, is found elsewhere only on a fragment of another bronze horse, now in Baltimore.

Technically the work is of very high quality, of a thinness at least twice as fine as most bronze-casters would attempt today—a factor that must have contributed to the crushing and dismemberment of these pieces to which the accounts of their discovery bear witness. The metal, as in most bronzework of this period, has a high lead content. This greatly helped the application of a layer of fine gold leaf over the entire surface. The gold was beaten on over a thin layer of mercury that had been fused with the bronze after casting, thereby securing a molecular amalgamation of the two, and the layer was further compacted by burnishing it with a smooth,

298
Wall painting: palaestra scene
Width 208 cm, height 67 cm
Naples Museum, inv. 78/7
From one of the sites in the Vesuvius area

The athletes at the left of this scene have been identified as jumpers carrying weights *(halteres)* in their hands, but their confronted, squaring-off poses and the thick lacings around their forearms show that they are boxers. A nearby herm and a palm of victory give the scene a vaguely classical flavor. The athlete at the right, oiling himself with drops shaken from a bottle held high, is based on a familiar statuary type. Boxing was a Greek sport, but the use of heavily strapped gloves introduced in the second half of the fourth century gave it a brutality hardly surpassed by that of Roman gladiatorial games. Compositions similar to this fresco had already appeared on black-figure prize amphoras of the fourth century and in wall paintings of the second century B.C. on Delos. At Pompeii athletic scenes like this normally decorated the walls of *palaestrae* (exercise courtyards) in bathing establishments.
B. Maiuri, "Ludi ginnico-atletici a Pompei" in *Pompeiana,* 177f.; cf. M. Borda, *La pittura romana* (Milan 1958) 153, 155-156; J. Frel, *Panathenaic Prize Amphoras* (Athens 1973) 26, fig. 25.

299
Wall painting of a chariot race
Height 57 cm, length 92 cm
Naples Museum, inv. 9055
Probably from the House of the Quadrigae (VII, 2, 25), although the inventory books say from Herculaneum.

The picture, which is bordered below by a red line but is certainly incomplete above and to the left, shows four four-horsed racing chariots *(quadrigae)* and, top left, the legs of the horses of a fifth. The drivers *(aurigae)* stand, as was customary, on a very light two-wheeled frame, dressed in short tunics. The driver on the right wears a red tunic, those in the center and on the far left both appear to be in green, and the driver at the very top is in white. For protection in the event of a crash (and these were common) they wear tight-fitting leather helmets and a harness of leather thongs on body and legs. On the white ground below the picture there are faint traces of an inscription painted in large letters, which suggests that it comes from a street-front, perhaps of a shop or tavern.

There was no provision for chariot-racing at Pompeii itself, but many cities both in Italy and in the provinces did possess a *circus* or *hippodrome,* and as a spectator sport it rivaled and eventually superseded gladiatorial contests. It was

300

302
Terracotta statue of an actress
Height 1.11 m
Naples Museum, inv. 22248
Found with No. 301

The mask, shown fastened on with a band decorated with little flowers, is that proper to a courtesan in tragedy. The figure, whose left hand was already damaged in antiquity, was colored. There are extensive remains of the white underlay and traces of brown paint on the hair and of blue and red on the drapery.

PAH I, 23 Jan. 1762; Von Rohden 46, pl. xxxv, 2; Deonna, *Les statues de terre cuite* (Paris 1908) 203.

semi-precious stone, such as an agate or a chalcedony. The head and neck were cast separately from the body of the horse, the joint being hidden and strengthened by means of a bronze collar. The figure of the rider would also have been cast separately.

Venuti, *Heraclea* 54; Kluge-Hartleben II, 78 and 80f.; H. von Roques de Maumont, *Antike Reiterstandbilder* (Berlin 1958) 84f. For technical details see *BdA* series 4, xlv (1960) 42ff.

301
Terracotta statue of an actor
Height 1.15 m
Naples Museum, inv. 22249
From the entrance to a garden in one of the houses in VIII, 2 or 3, near the Theater (VIII, 3, 14?)

Found with No. 302 and from the same house as No. 82. The actor, dressed in tunic and mantle, is wearing the mask of a youth in tragedy. In its finished form the statue was brightly painted. The discovery of this pair of statues, the first terracotta statues to be found at Pompeii, made a deep impression on the great German art historian Winckelmann. Considered to be the work of the same hand, they have been variously dated between the last years of the first century B.C. and the years immediately before the eruption.

PAH I, 23 Jan. 1762; Von Rohden 46, pl. xxxv, 2; Deonna, *Les statues de terre cuite* (Paris 1908) 203.

301

302

303

303
Terracotta mask
Height 14 cm
Naples Museum, inv. 116712
Found in the atrium of House no. 24 on
the Via Stabiana, 7 August 1867

Replica of a theatrical mask, provided
with two small holes at the top for suspension. It is suggested that the furrowed
brow, hooked nose, and enormous open
mouth portray Maccus, the stock figure in
Atellan farce (see page 91), whose leading
characteristic seems to have been excess
of every sort.
Levi no. 874.

304
Amber statuette of an actor
Height 8.4 cm
Naples Museum, inv. 25813
From Pompeii

Probably a character from Roman mime,
wearing an ample cloak, the figure belongs
to a series of amber carvings on the same
theme of which Naples Museum has two
others and the British Museum five, said
to be from Nola. They were produced in
Aquileia, in northern Italy, about the
middle of the first century A.D. Amber was
highly prized by the Romans from the
early first century A.D. (when the trade
routes to the source of supplies in the Baltic
began to operate) as an amulet and for its
alleged medicinal qualities as well as for
carving. Roman women often carried a
piece in their hands in summer, and amber
carvings of animals, fruit, and ears of
wheat were given as New Year's presents.
Fiorelli, *Scavi* 157, no. 56 (20 Feb. 1863);
Siviero no. 568; D. E. Strong, *Catalogue of
the Carved Amber in the Department of
Greek and Roman Antiquities* (British Museum 1966) 5, 35, 91 and nos. 109-113.

304

305
Mosaic panel: rehearsing for a Satyr Play
Width 55 cm, height 54 cm
Naples Museum, inv. 9986
From the *tablinum* of the House of the
Tragic Poet (VI, 8, 5)

The rehearsal for a Greek Satyr Play, the
characteristic postlude for a Greek dramatic trilogy. The action takes place in
front of an Ionic portico hung with *oscilla*
(see No. 69) and draped with wreaths and
fillets, above which is an attic façade
decorated with pilasters, four large golden
wine vessels, and a pair of herm-like musicians. The bald and bearded figure wearing a Greek mantle (*himation*) and sandals
is the chorus master, possibly the dramatist himself. He watches two actors wearing goatskin loincloths, who appear to be
rehearsing dance steps to the notes of the
double pipes played by a richly robed and
garlanded musician (who would himself
have appeared on the stage). On the right
an attendant is helping another actor into
a shaggy Silenus costume. Behind the
seated figure, on a pedestal, is a male
tragic mask, and at his feet a female tragic
mask and a Silenus mask.

305

The mosaic, which was the centerpiece
of a black and white mosaic pavement
decorated with a meander pattern, is a
studio piece (*emblema*) derived from a
Hellenistic panel painting, perhaps one
painted to commemorate a victory in a
theatrical contest. In the course of adaptation to its present form the perspective of
the architectural setting has become hope-
lessly confused, with the two flanking
pilasters brought forward to consitute a
frame. It dates from the years between
A.D. 62 and 79.
E. Pfuhl, *Malerei und Zeichnung der Griechen*
(Munich 1923) 841f.; Pernice VI, 99f., 171;
Bieber, *Theater* 11f., 20, 130; Kraus and von
Matt no. 49.

306-309
Wall paintings: four theatrical masks

From the House of the Stags at Herculaneum, where they constituted the lower
parts of four of the vertical members that
divided the middle zone of the Fourth
Style scheme into panels. Each is shown
placed at the head of the steps leading up
onto a stage, within a frame of garlands
with Dionysiac attributes.

306
Mask of a father, in New Comedy
Length 97 cm, height 65 cm
Naples Museum, inv. 9838

The rolled arrangement of the hair, the
speira, was characteristic of New Comedy.
The white hair and beard indicate the role
of an old father.

307
Tragic mask of Andromeda
Length 93 cm, height 64 cm
Naples Museum, inv. 9850

Andromeda's mother, Cassiope, claimed
that her daughter was more beautiful than
the Nereids, and in expiation of this rash
boast Andromeda herself was exposed,
chained to a rock, to be devoured by a sea
monster sent by Poseidon. Perseus, using
the Gorgon's head to turn the monster
to stone, rescued and subsequently married her. See also the picture of this scene
in the House of the Priest Amandus (page
103).

308
Mask of a youth, in New Comedy
Length 66 cm, height 42 cm
Naples Museum, inv. 9804

The same hairstyle as No. 306. Beside the
mask is a book basket (*capsa*) and, on the
step, a short, curved staff (*pedum*).

309 (color plate, vol. I, p. 78)
Tragic mask of a youth
Length 62 cm, height 62 cm
Naples Museum, inv. 9805

His hair is piled high on his head and
crowned with a ribbon and a wreath of ivy
leaves. Against the steps leans a *thyrsus*.
Bieber, *Theater* 228; Agnes Allroggen-Bedel,
*Maskendarstellungen in der römisch-
kampanischen Wandmalerei* (Munich 1974)
126-127, nos. 2 (318), 6 (316), 4 (315), and
3 (317).

310

310

Wall painting of a scene from New Comedy

Height 29 cm, width 38 cm
Naples Museum, inv. 9034
From Stabiae

The panel, which was set into a larger wall scheme, is almost certainly a *pinax*, or painted replica of a late classical or early Hellenistic Greek panel picture. It portrays the dance group that in New Comedy took the place of the chorus in Old Comedy, consisting in this instance of a dwarf, a woman playing a double flute, and two men dancing, one of whom holds cymbals while the other beats a tambourine. The same Greek original is copied in a fine mosaic panel, signed by Dioscurides of Samos and datable to the end of the second century B.C., found in the so-called Villa of Cicero at Pompeii (Naples Museum, inv. 9985).

Bieber, *Theater* 95f.; Webster, *New Comedy* 92, NP 54.

311

Wall painting: erotic scene

Height 54 cm, width 51 cm
Naples Museum, inv. 27696
From Pompeii

311

The encounter takes place on a richly draped couch against a curtained background. The gestures come as much from the pornographic theater as from the world of sensuous pleasure. The painter was an inferior mannerist, relying on awkward rhetoric rather than suave anatomical understanding.

Grant, De Simone, and Merella 154, illus.

312

Wall painting: erotic scene

Height 37 cm, width 37 cm
Naples Museum, inv. 27697
From Pompeii

As is usual in Pompeian paintings with erotic subjects, the richness of the couch and draperies matches or, indeed, overshadows the action represented. The wreaths on the heads of the participants suggest these amorous frolics occurred after a symposium or banquet. Although erotic subjects played a small, private part in the art and life of Pompeii, scenes such as this have done much to influence the modern image of Roman decadence in the Julio-Claudian period of the Empire.

Grant, De Simone, and Merella 153, illus.

312

306

307

308

309

313
Little silver dish on a silver stand
Height together 5.5 cm, diameter of dish
8.6 cm, diameter of stand 7.9 cm
Naples Museum, inv. 25324 (dish) and
25547 (stand)
From Pompeii

The little tripod stand has animal's-paw
feet, and the edge is decorated with an
ovolo molding with traces of gilding. The
dish has thin crescent-shaped handles
decorated with elongated birds' heads and
rosettes (as on Nos. 320, 323).
Strong 153; cf. Maiuri, *Menandro* 364,
nos. 44-55.

314
Little silver dish on a silver stand
Height together 5.8 cm, diameter of dish
6.9 cm, diameter of stand 8.1 cm
Naples Museum, inv. 110853 (dish) and
25549 (stand)
From Pompeii, found separately; 110853
was found 24 November 1875.

Little dishes of this sort were probably
used for serving hot sauces or (since the
form is found also in glass) small sweet-
meats.

315
Small fluted silver bowl
Height 5.1 cm, diameter 11.7 cm
Naples Museum, inv. 25553
From one of the sites in the Vesuvius area

Inverted conical bowls of this form, with
concave sides decorated with vertical
fluting and a scalloped rim, were common
in the first century A.D.
Strong 160.

316
Small fluted silver bowl
Height 5 cm, diameter 7.9 cm
Naples Museum, inv. 25557
From one of the sites in the Vesuvius area

A smaller version of No. 315. It lacks the
small rounded projections at the ends of
the flutes.

317
Silver spoon
Length 7.8 cm
Naples Museum, inv. 25413
From Herculaneum

The form of the handle is typical of
Roman spoons. This example has a simple
knop finial, and it is fastened to the bowl
by a "rat's tail" attachment. Spoons were
the only form of flatware normally used in
classical antiquity; forks were unknown,
and food was brought tò the table in
ready-prepared portions, which did not
call for the use of a knife. Silver spoons
are common and are found in quite modest households.
Strong 155-156.

318
Silver spoon
Length 14 cm
Naples Museum, inv. 25416
From one of the sites in the Vesuvius area

A larger version of No. 317, with a more
elaborately molded baluster knop.
Strong 155-156.

319
Silver egg cup
Height 8.4 cm
Naples Museum, inv. 116349
From House VIII, 2, 23

The little shallow cup on a short stem,
mounted on a large, lozenge-shaped base,
formed part of a service comprising four
ornate drinking cups, four smaller cups,
several little dishes like Nos. 313, 314,
four plates, four egg cups, and various
serving bowls.
Strong 154.

313

315

316

314

317 318

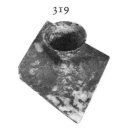
319

[3]20
[T]wo-handled silver drinking cup
[c]antharus)
[H]eight 8.5 cm, diameter of bowl 12.5 cm
[N]aples Museum, inv. 25294
[f]rom one of the sites in the Vesuvius area

[T]he bowl and the elaborately turned foot
[a]re plain except for a beaded border
[b]elow the rim and a simple stamped motif
[o]n the foot. The handle mount terminates
[i]n a pair of birds' heads (see No. 323).
[F]or similar cups, see Strong 133-134.

[3]21
[Si]lver plate
[D]iameter 17.7 cm, across the handles
[2]2 cm
[N]aples Museum, inv. 25297
[f]rom one of the sites in the Vesuvius area

[T]he plate is in the form of a shallow
[c]oncave dish without a foot ring. The
[se]gmental handles, cast separately and
[so]ldered on, are decorated with a central
[p]almette motif, flanked by foliage, ivy
[le]aves, and the usual elongated birds'
[h]eads.
[St]rong 148f.

[3]22
[Si]lver jug
[H]eight 12.5 cm, diameter of mouth 5.3 cm
[N]aples Museum, inv. 25692
[f]rom Pompeii

[Sm]all, rounded shape with a plain, solid
[ca]st handle.
[Fo]r the form, see Strong 140.

323
One-handled silver dipper, or skillet
Height 5.7 cm, diameter of lip 11.1 cm,
length of handle 9 cm
Naples Museum, inv. 25344
From Pompeii

The bowl is plain. The handle, which was
cast separately and attached to the bowl
by means of two curving arms in the form
of elongated birds' heads, is decorated in
relief with a symmetrical foliate design
terminating in a Dionysiac head with large
ears, flanked by two ducks' heads (see
No. 320). Vessels of this shape, usually
found in pairs, had a long history, first
appearing in the first century A.D. They
are commonly found also in bronze, and
they were most probably used for serving
liquids, though not for the actual heating
of them.
Strong 147-148.

324
**Silver cup (calathus) decorated with sprigs
of ivy and grape vines**
Height 11.5 cm
Naples Museum, inv. 25300
From Pompeii

The foliage is rendered with a brilliantly
varied use of the repoussé technique. In
places the forms are merely sketched on the
background, and in other areas they break
into a high relief that seems almost completely free of the surface. The ivy and
the grape vine, both plants sacred to
Bacchus, god of wine and revelry, are
observed with an extraordinary naturalism. The thinness of the leaf surface, the
delicate veining, and even the growth
rings where the stems have been cut
through are all convincingly shown. The
foliage densely covers the background and
enriches the basic form of the cup. At
Pompeii the *calathus* form appears frequently in glassware, like No. 95, as well
as in silver. The foliage is worked in an
outer case, while the moldings at the top
are soldered onto a plain inner liner.
Ernst Künzl, "Der augusteische Silbercalathus
im Rheinischen Landesmuseum Bonn" *DJb*
169 (1969) 329-331, note 15d; cf. A. Oliver,
Jr., *Silver for the Gods* (Toledo 1977) 103,
no. 60.

324

322

321

323

325

325
Silver cup (skyphos)
Height 8 cm
Naples Museum, inv. 145506
From the House of the Menander

This two-handled cup (*skyphos*), one of a
pair, consists of a repoussé outer shell, a
liner, and soldered-on base and handles.
The decoration shows six deeds of Hercules in a vigorous, eclectic style. Details
were originally picked out with gilding.
The hero is alternately the beardless
youth and the older man, bearded and
muscle-bound. He brings in the Eryman-
thian Boar struggling on his shoulder, in
the scheme known since Archaic times. He
clubs at the head of a centaur, either his
inebriated host Pholos or Nessus, ravisher
of his wife, Deianira. He shoots down the
vicious, buzzard-like Stymphalian Birds.
On the other side Hercules makes an
incongruously Parthenonic, horse-taming
gesture at the tree with the golden apples
of the Hesperides. The apples are guarded
by a snake twining round the tree trunk,
artistic prototype of the serpent in the
Garden of Eden. The next adventure does
involve horses, the man-eating mares of
Diomedes, which trample a prostrate
victim very like a fallen Lapith on one of
the Parthenon metopes. Hercules subdues
them in another, rarer horse-taming pose,
early classical in origin. Finally, a rather
sober, conventional, bearded Hercules
leads in Cerberus, the three-headed watch-
dog of the underworld.

We know that Lysippos made a series
of the Labors of Hercules for Alyzia, and
that these were later brought to Rome.
Attempts have been made to trace many
Hellenistic or Roman versions back to
these prototypes. The silversmith of the
Hercules cups may have drawn on these
as he certainly did on a variety of other
sources.
Maiuri, *Menandro* 310-311, 314ff., no. 4,
figs. 122-124, pls. XXVIII-XXX.

326
Silver cup (modiolus)
Height 8 cm
Naples Museum, inv. 145510
From the House of the Menander

This is one of a pair of mug-shaped silver
cups, made up, as was customary for such
vessels, of an outer shell worked in
repoussé, a smooth inner cup, a cast,
soldered-on handle. Winged Cupids and
Victories, destined, obviously, to beat
them, drive paired horses in the dangerous
ancient sport of chariot racing. Navigation was even more crucial than speed,
and maneuvers to make one's opponents
crash on the tight curves of the elongated
oval track were an important part of the
charioteer's skill. One of the Cupids has
already come to grief. He sprawls on the
ground, his horses rearing and shying in
their tangled harness. In the background
are the monuments of the *spina,* the central island of the racecourse. Two columns
support a row of eggs and dolphins; these
were moved to indicate which lap of the
race was being run. Cupids earnestly engaged in adult activities are familiar from
Pompeian painting; the conceit is Hellenistic in origin. Their mock-serious
chariot race appears on Roman sarco-
phagi, for which the House of the Menander cups are an interesting antecedent.
Maiuri, *Menandro* 343ff., no. 11, fig. 134 and
pls. XLI-XLIV.

326

327 (not illus.)
**Reproduction of one of the painted Sec-
ond Style walls from the newly excavated
villa at Oplontis**
Length 8.80 m, height 5.60 m
Lent by Imperial Tobacco Limited
Reproduced by courtesy of the excavator,
Professor Alfonso De Franciscis

The building to which this painting belongs was part of an opulent seaside villa
(*villa marittima*) about three miles west of
Pompeii, in the modern Torre Annunziata. The eruption buried it beneath
nearly two meters of ash and pumice, then
five meters of volcanic mud, and although
the site has been known for a long time
and was the subject of desultory exploration in 1839-40, it was not until 1964 that
systematic excavations were put in hand
by Professor De Franciscis.

The remains at present exposed comprise the greater part of the main residential block, together with its domestic
service quarters, and to the east of it (not
shown on the plan) part of an extensive
villa rustica annex. On the north side the
main block backed onto a garden. The
south façade opened onto a terraced platform, which in antiquity probably fronted
directly onto the sea. Viewed from the sea
or from the garden behind, the residential
block would have been roughly symmetrical about a line of large rooms
running north and south, comprising a
projecting atrium complex at the south
end and, at the north end, beyond a small
internal garden courtyard (Room 20), a
large *oecus* (Room 21) opening onto the
garden between the columns of a gabled
porch. These rooms and those to the west
of them constituted the main residence.
To the east, screened from the main façade
by a row of smaller rooms, were more
utilitarian rooms grouped around an inner
peristyle. These included the quarters of
the domestic staff. Along the south frontage, following the outline of the plan, ran
a continuous portico, such as one sees in
the wall paintings of *villae marittimae*
(e.g., No. 1).

At the time of the eruption only the
servants' wing was occupied. The main
residence, stripped of its furnishings, was
awaiting modernization and redecoration.
Another few years, perhaps months, and
the magnificent series of Second Style
paintings that are its especial glory would
probably have gone the way of the paintings in the large garden *oecus* (Room 21),
the walls of which were found already
stripped bare. As it is, five rooms retain
their original Second Style decoration: the
atrium (5); a bed-chamber (11) and a day-
room (23) on either side of it; a *triclinium*
dining room (14), which adjoins the unusually large and well-appointed kitchen
(7); and the large hall (15), which occupied the middle of the south front of the
west wing.

No. 327, which covered the whole of the east wall in Room 15, still retains the formal simplicity of the early Second Style schemes, viewed as if through a simple colonnade of lofty Corinthian columns set on a low plinth projecting from the wall behind. But above eye-level the solid wall has been almost entirely eliminated, surviving only as an iconostasis-like screen, with two horizontal architraves and a central arch, which partition up the receding architectural vistas portrayed beyond them. In the two lateral bays a pair of monumental double colonnades frame the central motif, a Delphic tripod, shown upraised on a tall, slender, circular pedestal and viewed as if through an open gateway leading into a garden. One notes the theatrical masks displayed on brackets; the *pinakes* in their wooden frames perched above the outer ends of the screen; the clever contrast of color between the upper and the lower colonnades; and in the two narrow outer bays the friezes of shields, a motif repeated both in the atrium and in Room 23. The perspective is not the strict, single-viewpoint perspective of Renaissance and modern practice, but it is a remarkably sophisticated piece of visual illusionism. Painted around 40 B.C. it is one of the surviving masterpieces of the fully developed Second Style.

Parts of the building were subsequently modernized a generation or so later. To this time belong the fine early Third Style paintings in the bath suite, perhaps also those of the *cubiculum* in the west wing (Room 38), which still retains its exquisitely painted red ceiling. The north façade in its present form may also be of this period. To the final phase before A.D. 79 belongs the highly simplified decoration of the inner peristyle of the east wing.

To whom did this villa belong, and can we give it a name? As regards ownership, there is some evidence that its last occupant was the wife of Nero, Poppaea Sabina, who died in A.D. 65. The Poppaei were a well-known Pompeian family, and it is an established fact that Poppaea Sabina, while empress, owned property within the territory of the city. Her death, followed in 68 by that of Nero, would help to explain why the property, though in good condition and destined for restoration, was still unoccupied in A.D. 79.

As for the name, Oplontis (or Eplontis), this is found only in two late itineraries and on the Roman map known as the Peutinger Table, where it is marked as a road station between Herculaneum and Pompeii. This may be a survival from pre-eruption times (such documents are notoriously conservative) or denote a later settlement. There are many records of classical finds in Torre Annunziata, in at least one instance coming from what was evidently another luxury villa. The "Oplontis" villa is a vivid reminder of how much may still await discovery.